The House Is (Not) a Prison

The House Is (Not) a Prison: On the Queerness of Architecture

Colin Ripley

Concordia University Press
Montreal

Cover: Allen's Cruz
Design and typesetting: Allen's Cruz
Copy editing: Joanne Muzak
Proofreading: Saelan Twerdy
Index: Natalie Greenberg

Typeface: JJannon by Optimo
Printed and bound in Canada by Friesens, Altona, Manitoba

This book is printed on Forest Stewardship Council certified paper and meets the permanence ofpaper requirements of ANSI/NISO Z39.48-1992.

Concordia University Press's books are available for free on several digital platforms. Visit www.concordia.ca/press

First English edition published in 2025
10 9 8 7 6 5 4 3 2 1
978-1-988111-61-2 | Paper
978-1-988111-62-9 | E-book
978-1-988111-91-9 | PDF

Library and Archives Canada Cataloguing in Publication
Title: The house is (not) a prison : on the queerness of architecture / Colin Ripley.
Names: Ripley, Colin, author
Description: First English edition. | Includes bibliographical references and index.
Identifiers: Canadiana (print) 20250231913 | Canadiana (ebook) 20250231921 | ISBN 9781988111612
(softcover) | ISBN 9781988111919 (PDF) | ISBN 9781988111629 (EPUB)
Subjects: LCSH: Homosexuality and architecture. | LCSH: Architecture, Domestic. | LCSH: Prisons—
Design and construction. | LCSH: Queer theory.
Classification: LCC NA2543.H65 R57 2025 | DDC 720.86/64—dc23

Concordia University Press
1455 de Maisonneuve Blvd. W.
Montreal, Quebec H3G 1M8
Canada

Funded by the Government of Canada
Financé par le gouvernement du Canada
Canada

Concordia University Press gratefully acknowledges the generous support of the Birks Family Foundation and the Government of Canada.

This book has been published with the help of a grant from the Federation of the Humanities and Social Sciences through the Awards to Scholarly Publications Program (ASPP), using funds provided by the Social Sciences and Humanities Research Council of Canada.

Contents

Acknowledgements

Not surprisingly perhaps, given how long this project has taken to get to this stage, there are many people and organizations whose efforts and support need to be acknowledged.

I will start with several faculty at the European Graduate School. I would particularly like to thank my dissertation supervisor, Slavoj Žižek. I also thank Avital Ronell and Mladen Dolar, both of whom provided ongoing support and insightful comments, as well as Catherine Malabou, Benjamin Bratton, Judith Butler, and Dean Chrisopher Fynsk, all of whom provided support and meaningful discussions of the work at various stages.

I would like to acknowledge the role played at the beginning of this project by several faculty at the Princeton University School of Architecture in the early 1990s, when this work first started to appear as a possibility: Georges Teyssot, Alessandra Ponte, Mark Wigley, Beatriz Colomina, Elizabeth Diller, and Joel Sanders.

Annmarie Adams, Scott Sørli, John Ricco, Martino Tattara, and Albert Dichy all provided important insights during various conversations; M. Dichy also facilitated access to the Genet archives at IMEC in Caen, France. Elgin Cleckley, Sascha Hastings, Martino Tattara, Olivier Vallerand, and Scott Sørli also provided important input. I also thank my colleagues at Toronto Metropolitan University, especially Marco Polo, John Cirka, Mark Gorgolewski, and Dean Tom Duever, while my partners in RVTR, Kathy Velikov and Geoffrey Thün, encouraged me to carry out this work and offered the space in which to do it.

The contribution of a few M.Arch. students at Toronto Metropolitan University on work related to this book also needs to be acknowledged: Parandis Abdi, Caleb Culmone, Michael Evola, Gabriel Garofalo, Daniel Bedoya Gomez, Andres Guzman-Romero, Adam Hollings, Ruslan Ivanytskyy, Arpy Katrjian, Tejal Lad, Tess MacPherson, Konner Mitchener, Maya Orzechowska, Freedom Stone, Paul Szywacz, and Abhishek Wagle.

Additional input was provided by journal editors who helped to develop particular pieces of the work, including Dirk van den Heuvel, Robert Alexander Gorny, Anna Richter, Regner Ramos, and Michael Abrahamson; the organizers of the Queer Modernisms II conference at Oxford University (Jesse McLaughin, Lloyd Houston, and Rio Matchett); of the Modernism in the Home conference at the University of Birmingham (Matilda Blackwell, Rachel Eames, and Brittany Moster); and of Modernist Structures at the University of Caen (Amy Wells, Jennifer Kilgore-Caradec, and Hélène Aji).

Funding support has been provided by the Social Sciences and Humanities Research Council of Canada, ECO Canada, Ryerson Creative Fund, RIOS, the Faculty of Engineering and Architectural Science Office of the Dean, the Office of the Dean at The Creative School, and the School of Interior Design at Toronto Metropolitan University.

Finally, I would like to thank my friend the late Scott Jowett for giving me a copy of *The Thief's Journal* in 1983; Anna MacLachlan, for accompanying me on a visit to St. Genet in 2005; and my husband, Jason van Eyk, for his encouragement, rigorous reading, and ongoing insight.

Foreword: Ripley's Game

Slavoj Žižek

Patricia Highsmith's *Ripley's Game* is a candidate for the best crime novel of all times—and if there ever was a queer author of crime novels, it is definitely her. My claim is simply that what Highsmith achieved in her domain, Colin Ripley did for queer studies.

The reason I find Colin Ripley's *The House Is (Not) a Prison: On the Queerness of Architecture* irresistible is that it is a sublime book in the Lacanian sense of the term: Ripley elevated writing about being queer to the level of Thing, which, in this case, means universal *formal* theory. The book systematically ascends from the singularity of its topic (queer sexuality, i.e., sexuality that deviates from the heterosexual norm) through the particular social meaning (behaviour that is strange, unusual, not expected, or even destined to fail—see the British colloquial expression "queer the pitch," which means "ruin the chance of success") up to the level of what one cannot but designate as general formal ontology—queerness in the sense of imbalance, deviation, broken symmetry, out-of-jointness of the reality itself, as if reality itself arises out of a kind of ruined balance or symmetry of the cosmos. The usual view is that of a balanced universe which is temporarily derailed by some excess, but then balance is reestablished when the excess is brought back to measure. From a queer viewpoint, the excess is constitutive of reality, so that the abolition of the excess entails the abolition of the very balanced state with regard to which excess is excess. In sociopolitical domain of class relations, the balanced approach is exemplified by fascism: for a fascist, class struggle emerges only when one of the classes disturbs class co-operation with its excessive behaviour (workers demand too much from capitalists; capitalists exploit workers too much)—in both cases, the figure which introduces discord is a Jew (financially exploiting productive capitalists, instigating workers to rebel), so one should liquidate the Jew and in this way reestablished the just class balance. For a Marxist, on the contrary, the relationship between classes is by definition that of a discord and imbalance, so that the only way to abolish class antagonism is to abolish classes as such.

And the central claim of Ripley is, of course, that the same goes for sexuality. His view is well-founded in Freudian orthodoxy: the basic premise of Freud's *Three Essays on Sexuality* ([1905] 1926) is that perversions exist in normal people also, in multiple deviations of sexual aims, as well as in the tendency to linger over preparatory sexual aspects such as looking and touching. Freud formalized the distinction between the "fore-pleasures" of infantile sexuality and the "end-pleasure" of sexual intercourse; children have sexual urges, from which adult sexuality only gradually emerges via psychosexual development. So "a disposition to perversions is an original and universal disposition of the human sexual instinct and that...this postulated constitution, containing the germs of all the perversions, will only be demonstrable in *children*" (Freud [1905] 1962, 155).

Here a step further is needed: we (some of us) arrive at the heterosexual norm only through deviations, and this path through deviations is not an organic "natural" process but a process of brutal symbolic cuts, prohibitions, and impositions. This is the basic paradox of human sexuality: what appears as a "natural" sexual orientation, the way in which reproduction (the biological function of copulation) happens, is the final outcome of a complex socio-symbolic process. The "progress" from infantile sexuality to the heterosexual norm is not the process which follows a pattern of natural development. What, then, is so scandalous about infantile sexuality? It is not the sole fact that even children, presumed innocent, are already sexualized. The scandal resides in two features (which are, of course, the two sides of the same coin). First, infantile sexuality is a weird entity which is neither biological(ly grounded) nor part of symbolic/cultural norms. However, this excess is not sublated by adult "normal" sexuality—this latter also is always distorted, displaced: "When it comes to sexuality, man is subject to the greatest of paradoxes: what is acquired through the drives precedes what is innate and instinctual, in such a way that, at the time it emerges, instinctual sexuality, which is adaptive, finds the seat already taken, as it were, by infantile drives, already and always present in the unconscious" (Laplanche 2002, 49).

The "natural" form is the outcome of a complex symbolic process: the starting point (infantile sexuality) is not yet fully "cultural," but it is also not "natural," so that perversions (whose model is infantile sexuality) do not simply disappear, they are not simply left behind in normal adult heterosexuality. They remain in the form of kissing, touching, and the eroticization of non-sexual parts of the body: "Normal" sexuality erotically works only through the shadows and remainders of these elements, otherwise it is just raw coupling, like the insemination in *Handmaid's Tale*. Perverse "deviations" are thus necessary, we arrive at the norm only through them, so that (to put it in Hegelian terms) what appears as "norm" is the ultimate self-sublated perversion. We encounter here what Hegel called "absolute recoil": as deviations from the Norm, perversions presuppose the norm, the pleasure they generate resides in the transgression of the Norm; however, this Norm itself arises through deviations, as the ultimate deviation. In other words, the very process of deviation retroactively constructs what it deviates from, or, as Hegel would have put it, perversion is an act which posits its own presupposition, it is an effect which retroactively posits its cause. In the domain of cinema, recall *Gilda* (1946, Charles Vidor): the convoluted plot full of "queer" sadist and homoerotic sexual undertones ends up in an unconvincing happy end in which all the perversity magically disappears—what is truly queer is this libidinally unconvincing ending.

Ripley's book is not about queer sexuality, as if there are two species of two species, straight and queer; it is about how *sexuality as such is queer*. Queerness changes its status from predicate to subject which is a universal ontological feature. That's why Ripley deals in his book with queerness of architecture, with special focus on the work of Jean Genet: not to discover in architecture traces of queer sexuality but to discover in architecture at a more general level traces of the same queerness which "distorts" sexuality. His reading of architecture analyzes queer distortions in purely formal terms: while "normal" architecture deals with clear division between outside and inside, with straight walls separating spaces, "queerness" articulates itself in everything that deviates from such straight space—curved walls, elliptic structures which blur clear divisions, a false outside which exists only as looked upon from the inside, an inside which, once we are within it, miraculously looks larger than seen from the outside, double walls with interstitial space in which entities like electric cables, mice, cockroaches, and fantasized trolls dwell, space of canalization in which excrements disappear from our reality after we flush water, etc. Plato described apropos beauty the gradual ascent from the beauty of an individual's body through bodily beauty as such up to the Idea of Beauty as such, and Ripley provides a materialist version of such ascent: from queer sexuality through more formalized architectural queerness up to Queerness as a universal ontological category. That's why his book is more than just worth reading: If seriously read, it is destined to change radically our basic experience of who we are.

The House Is (Not) a Prison

The thief walks silently up to the door and sets his bag on the ground. He has been watching the house, getting to know it as one knows a lover: its moods, its fears, its whiteness, its emptiness. I see his hand caress the white pilotis as he walks past them, I feel his heart beating in the ecstasy of the act.

He opens his bag and takes out his pick. Gently, but insistently, he penetrates the keyhole. The house starts to moan, silently to itself, but I can hear it, and he can too. With expert fingers, he caresses the pick in the lock until the door comes open, and the first penetration is echoed by a second, as the thief enters the house: the house of architecture.

Prologue: The House of the Thief

"Just wait here for a moment please. I'll be right back."

The impossibly tall and handsome young man with the questioning eyes pushed a button and began to walk away. As the gate began to close, Anna and I looked at each other, wondering what had just happened. It all seemed a bit, well, surreal, and I was astonished by my nerve—this was so unlike me. And who was this young man? Certainly not the image I had expected to greet me at the gate to Saint Genet. We stood there, silently, in the Mediterranean sun, looking at each other nervously, anxiously.

A week earlier, I found myself in the Paris office of Albert Dichy, literary director at Institut Mémoires de l'Édition Contemporaine and noted scholar on the life and work of Jean Genet. At the beginning of my academic career, I had come to France to do some preparatory research about Genet, and in particular to visit the Colonie Agricole et Pénitentiare de Mettray, where Genet spent several years as a teenager, and took advantage of a few days in Paris to meet with Monsieur Dichy. We had a long, rambling and exciting interview about mirrors, hotels, stairways, houses, and how all of those figured in the life and the myth of Genet, about Genet's mistrust of mirrors (according to Dichy, Genet would not visit a café with mirrored walls, for fear that his reflection would be seen), about his habit of keeping a packed suitcase under his bed, about the various hotels he frequented in Paris—fascinating material for a designer and researcher to work with. At some point I asked him about the house Genet had built for Lucien Sénémaud, which is mentioned in Edmund White's biography of Genet. I was intrigued by this house, by the way it fit into my theory of the house in Genet's work, and particularly by the idea that Genet gave the house to his younger lover on the occasion of his marriage to a woman.

The discussion with Albert Dichy quickly both confirmed my intuition about the house—with some caveats, of course—and expanded (maybe even exploded) the scope of the question. Not only had Genet had the house built, Dichy informed me, but he was in large part the designer of the house. Not only did architecture play a crucial role in the work of Genet (well, at least this was my hypothesis), here we have the moment when Genet becomes architect. And beyond that, it seems that the house for Sénémaud was not the only example of Genet as architect (even excepting his design work for the theatre). Dichy described three houses or parts of houses designed by Genet: one somewhere in the Pyrenees, in a town with a Basque name; one in Morocco, a house where Genet worked while he was in Morocco, although he lived in a hotel; and the house for Sénémaud, in Le Cannet, near Cannes.

Dichy had little to tell me about Sénémaud's house (there is nothing descriptive in my notes) but gave me the address of the house, or at least the partial address, from memory. He said that if I was really interested I should contact Jacky Maglia, Sénémaud's stepson, who grew up in the house and still owned it. As the interview was coming to a close, Dichy dug through some files to find Maglia's address in Greece.

And so here I found myself, with my friend and travelling companion Anna, standing outside the gate to the house on the Montée des Oliviers in Le Cannet. It had taken us most of the day to locate it. This was before the time of Google Maps, and the Montée des Oliviers was almost impossible to locate either by consulting local maps or by asking local residents. After a few hours of searching, we found the street (someone tipped us off that there was a garage on the corner), parked the car, and walked up the hill. Even then the situation was not clear. We walked to the top of the hill, where there was a locked gate and a pathway beyond. We were sure we had come to the end of the search, that Lucien Sénémaud's house was somewhere beyond that gate, somewhere out of sight. A bit dejected, we started to walk back down the hill, when Anna called my attention to a brass plaque mounted low down in a wall on the side of the road, a brass plaque that read "St Genet PRIVÉ." This must be the house—but the house itself was behind a fence and another locked gate; we could see only glimpses of it. We weren't quite sure what to do, to just leave, or climb the fence... to break and enter like Genet might have, or maybe to come back in the middle of the night...but in the end I decided to play intrepid researcher, and I rang the buzzer.

After a few minutes wait the gate slid open, just a couple of feet, and a young man, the aforementioned impossibly tall young man, looked out at us. "Can I help you?" he asked.

For a moment he seemed as surprised as I was, and I guess that's fully understandable. In absolutely clear English he then said we should wait there, and he would be right back.

Another few minutes passed, then the gate opened again, and the impossibly tall young man—now the impossibly tall young man with a smile like the Mediterranean sun—stood in front of us again. "Come in, please. My grandfather would like to speak with you." We went in through the gate and up a set of stairs built out of stones. The house seemed like a well-designed but traditional villa—certainly not a great work of modern architecture (not that that is what I would have expected), but well considered and with charming if rustic details. At the top of the stairs, up on a terrace, was an older gentleman, relatively small, grey haired, and with a friendly enough face. Behind him was a lovely Asian woman, roughly his age, smiling broadly. He held out his hand and welcomed us: "Bonjour et bienvenue. My name is Jacky Maglia and this is my wife Inako. Would you like some tea?"

Scene One

On an upper platform is a small garden table and four chairs. On the table is a bowl of fruit and a teapot—the Japanese type, cast iron, heavy. Three cups, old-fashioned, and three plates, laden with crumbs and orange rinds. The cups and plates do not match. On the scrim behind is an image of the Mediterranean, seen as though from a hill in the distance. There is a pirate ship on the water, with young pirates, naked from the waist up, climbing the rigging, cutlasses held aloft. The image lasts only a minute before fading to a view of a work shed, and of the hill that continues up: the sea is not actually visible from this site, but the image of the water comes back periodically during the scene that follows. Other images may be added in as appropriate. Throughout the scene, Olivier (the impossibly tall) will come in and out of the shed—he is doing some gardening.

Inako, who is not dressed in a kimono but rather in jeans and a slightly oversized orange t-shirt, leaves the stage with the teapot. Anna is generally silent throughout this scene, as is Inako. Anna pays close attention to the discussion, pours tea, peels oranges. Occasionally, Anna will help out by suggesting translations. The audience should understand from Anna's interjections that there may be some inaccuracies in this transcript.

Jacky Maglia: So—what brings you to my house on this beautiful morning? What can I do for you?

Researcher: Well, I'm a professor of architecture based in Toronto, Canada. I've been doing research about the position of architecture in the work of Jean Genet—maybe we could say architectural tropes in his work. I was given your address by Albert Dichy in Paris, and since I was on my way here to meet Anna for a little vacation, we thought we should just stop by and see if we could find the house.

Jacky Maglia: Interesting! There has been some interest in the house over the years but really I think you are the first architect to come. Philosophers, yes, and radicals, thieves, and maybe the odd terrorist (depending on who you ask), but no architects.

Researcher: But we are surprised to find you here—Monsieur Dichy gave me an address in Greece and suggested that I should contact you there. (*He takes out his notebook and a pen.*) By the way, would it be alright if I were to take some notes while we talk?

Anna: Just for an aide-memoir...

Jacky Maglia: Oh I'd rather you did not take notes...I'm happy to talk to you, but you know we don't really cherish being in the news...I think part of the reason for this house, secluded as it is, was to avoid all the people who wanted to write stories about Him.

Anna: About Genet...?

A pause. The researcher and Anna look at each other for a moment. The audience should understand from this that neither can recall, after all this time, and without a notebook or recording of the conversation, how Jacky Maglia referred to Genet. In this text, he will be, simply, Him. The capital H is meant, or not meant, to invoke or not invoke the divine, or the regal—the Saintly. There are of course many other details that, as a result of not having any recording devices, have been lost in the years since this scene took place. And, in a similar vein, there has been some embellishment—some of which is conjecture, some rhetorical content, even some blatant theorizing. The audience should understand from this, and from the attitudes and reactions of the characters, to take what is said around this table with a large grain of sea salt.

Inako enters with a replenished teapot. She notices the camera on the table, and gestures to Jacky Maglia. Anna pours the tea.

Jacky Maglia: Oh—and please, no photographs. (*A pause while he puts sugar in his tea.*)
Inako, are there any biscuits?
Greece...well, yes, we have spent time in Greece and I guess Dichy would have an address for us there. Mostly, though, we live in Japan now. Have you been to Japan?

Researcher: No, I never have. Someday.

Jacky Maglia: It's a fascinating culture. You must know the work of Tanizaki, *In Praise of Shadows*. No? You really have to read it. It's about presence and absence, about the thinness of the modern world.

Researcher (*addressing the audience directly*): Genet wrote some interesting things about Japan—maybe these will figure later in this piece. I'm remembering the section in *Prisoner of Love*, for example, in which he compares the perfectionism of the amphorae makers of Tunis with the Japanese ceramicists' fascination with the imperfect. I wonder what that might have to do with thinking about architecture. Or his writing about light and shadow—in an interview with Antoine Bourseiller—is that what Maglia is trying to tell me about here? There are too many shadows at play to decode this...the shadow of Chartres Cathedral flying over the pole on its way to visit the Nara shrine... Some of these shadows will come into play, some will not.

To Maglia: Genet's first trip to Japan was to visit you, am I right? After you moved there with Inako?

Jacky Maglia (*not responding to this last question*): Well, in any case it's quite a coincidence that you caught us here. We just got in yesterday evening, and we leave to go back to Japan tomorrow morning. We're just here today actually to finalize the sale of the house.

Researcher: Amazing. What incredible luck. I'm not sure what to say.

(*Pause*)

Well, we should make the most of this opportunity. What can you tell me about the house? Do you remember when Genet had it built?

Jacky Maglia: Oh, yes. I think I was about thirteen at the time.

Researcher: So that would have been around 1947? And I understand from Edmund White's account that Genet actually designed the house?

Jacky Maglia: That sounds a little early—I think maybe that was when the process started, although it took some time, five or six years. I guess I would have been around thirteen when it was completed. I know I was seven when my parents got married, which was around the time the house was started.

Researcher: Yes, that was 1947 for sure. The house was a wedding present, I think.

Jacky Maglia: He was in control of everything of course, from the purchase and laying out of the land all the way down to the colours of the flowers and the sizes and patterns of the bricks. The piece of land was quite large to begin with, and He had the road enlarged to get up here. I don't remember there being a lot of other houses around here at the time.

Researcher: Do you know if there are any drawings of the house—any plans or sketches?

Jacky Maglia: I don't think so, at least none that I remember. The house was built by an Italian mason, I don't remember his name, who worked in long discussions with Him. No, I don't think there were any real plans, just a lot of on-site and in-progress changes. The house, as you can see, is very much "in style."

Inako returns with a plate of Japanese biscuits.

Researcher: What do you mean by that? By "in style?"

Jacky Maglia (*ignoring that question*): I remember the process being very physical—a lot of decisions made by doing things, trying them, and then redoing them. Things got moved around, altered, remixed, if you like. There was a lot of hard work, and we all chipped in. I remember carrying sack after sack of concrete up the hill and then going back down with boulders. I remember for sure I was about thirteen at this time, so I guess the house was pretty much done.

Researcher: That's still quite young.

Anna: I'm sorry for interrupting, but maybe you could explain things a bit for me? This is all very interesting but I'm not really sure what's going on.

Researcher: What do you mean?

Anna: Well, what does this house have to do with Jean Genet? (*To Maglia*) And how did you come to live here?

Researcher: Ah. Yes. I'm sorry, I should have explained a little more before we got here, but of course I thought we would just drive by, take a few photos, and be on our way. The basic story runs something like this—correct me if I get anything wrong, at least this is how Edmund White tells the story (1993, 313–16).

Basically, in about 1947, Genet's lover, Lucien Sénémaud, married a woman, Ginette Chaix. Sénémaud, among other things, was an auto mechanic—Genet later set him up in a garage—and played the part of one of the two prisoners in Genet's film *Un chant d'amour*. Genet approved of the marriage (maybe even arranged it, or pushed Sénémaud into it) and in fact the relationship between him and Sénémaud continued for some time. Anyway, at some point Genet decided to build a house for Lucien and Ginette—for the first time, he had some serious money, as a result of the success of *The Maids*. White, and for that matter Sartre, think that the house was Genet's attempt (and not his only attempt) to create a family life for himself, but I think there are other ways to read the situation, or at least some significant nuance to add. In any case, it's unique, intriguing, suggestive.

Jacky Maglia: Yes, as I understand it, that's pretty much right. Well, as far as the facts go. As for His intentions, that was always hard to tell. I spent a lot of time with Him, you know, and even up to the end it could be hard to know what He was thinking. But yes, I think He was searching for family, for a kind of familial life. The house was a kind of physical manifestation of that life.

Researcher: I think one could trace that search in many aspects in his work and in his life.

Jacky Maglia: Yes, I think so.

Anna: Oh, I see—so Lucien Sénémaud was your father?

Jacky Maglia (*After a pause*): Well. (*Another pause*) I had many fathers.

Researcher:	You were with Genet when he died, if I remember correctly. And you were his principal heir as well, according to White.
Jacky Maglia:	Yes, I was in Paris with Him, and I found the body in the morning. Like I said, I had many fathers. But no, to answer your question directly, (*to Anna*) Lucien Sénémaud was not my father, at least not my biological father. Ginette Chaix was my mother and, as I mentioned earlier, I was about seven when the two of them married. Olivier, who you met at the gate, is Lucien's grandson.
Anna:	Ah! I see!
Researcher:	But he called you his grandfather!
Jacky Maglia:	Did he?
	(*Pause*)
Researcher:	Well, back to the house. Edmund White says that everyone slept in a downstairs room, except Genet, who stayed in a hotel (1993, 315). Stephen Barber, on the other hand, said that a room was reserved for Genet in the house—although he seldom used it (2004, 67). Maybe you can clarify this for me?
Jacky Maglia:	Sure. In a way they are both right. But—would you like to see the inside?
Researcher:	That would be wonderful!
Jacky Maglia:	Okay, let's go.

The characters stand up and face the screen, on which images reminiscent of a typical mid-century French domestic interior are shown. They are blurry and inconsistent—after all, these are not images of the house itself. Or perhaps they are images of another house, maybe the Villa Savoye or Philip Johnson's Glass House. The house itself must remain absent throughout this discussion. This is like the repeating card game with no cards in Prisoner of Love. *The images are superimposed with sketch drawings of the plan of the house (poorly drawn), photos of Genet and Sénémaud, and so on.*

Jacky Maglia: I suppose you would be disappointed to not take any photographs now, but you should know that in any case the interior has been renovated, after His time here—I don't remember exactly when. But maybe I can answer your questions anyway.

This large space that we use now as a living room used to be all open. These two toilets as well as these two bedrooms were added on in the renovation. This stair leads down to a kind of work room, I guess we may have slept there at some point, that seems to make sense to me, but I don't quite remember the circumstances, whether that was a normal thing or something we did during the construction. On the other hand, I do remember the kitchen was downstairs to start, we moved it up here to this corner of the house when we renovated. This spot where the kitchen is was originally His room, although He never used it—well, I shouldn't say never, He would stay here sometimes, for a few weeks or a day at a time, but He always went back to the hotel in the end.

Researcher: (*To the audience*): In general, the house is a two-storey structure on a roughly square plan. At the time of my visit, the upper floor was made up of a living area, with the lower floor a single open space designated as a work area.

After we left the house I did a sketch of the plan from my memory. It's very rough (far too rough to show here). I hope someday to be able to develop a more precise version, although I expect that it will by now have been renovated once again. It's important to note that this plan represents the house as renovated at some time after the death of Genet;

Maglia was not able to provide dates for the renovation. In the absence of documentary evidence such as drawings, photos, or even a good description of the house, it is difficult to make any real commentary—and as far as I can tell Genet never himself wrote anything about the house except a few words here and there in some letters, mostly requesting funds. However, at least some preliminary inferences can be made. First, it seems likely that the organization of the house was much simpler in its original form, possibly in the form of two large rooms, one above and one below. As I have already mentioned, Edmund White claims that everyone slept in a single downstairs room (1993, 315), except for Genet, who would stay in a hotel, but this reference was taken from a letter requesting funds from his publisher to continue construction and so is likely to represent a temporary situation. It's more tempting, although without any documentary proof, to suggest that the original sleeping and living quarters were on the upper floor, with work areas below, as such an arrangement would mirror the arrangement of the *maisons* at Mettray. Such, at least, is my historian's fantasy of the house. My theoretician's fantasy is somewhat less plausible, locating the downstairs room as the world of the male, of Lucien and the boys, leaving Ginette Chaix alone in the upstairs realm, reconstituting the form of a Bachelor Machine. (*Turning to Maglia*): Interesting. And this is interesting—Genet's room, I mean the kitchen, has a pretty incredible view, out over the gate and then all the way down the hill.

Jacky Maglia: Yes, he could see anyone who was coming up the street.

Researcher: So he could make a quick getaway if he had to? Did he keep a packed suitcase under the bed? I guess this is why Genet and Sénémaud at first considered calling the house The House of the Thief?

Jacky Maglia: Did they? I wasn't aware of that. Funny. But maybe, yes. I'm not sure. I don't remember the suitcase, although of course it's true there were always packed suitcases. Where did you hear that from?

Researcher: I'm not sure, someone must have told me about it—that Genet always kept a packed suitcase under the bed wherever he slept. It's an interesting story even if it's not true. I wonder what he kept in it.

Jacky Maglia: That's really all there is to show, I'm afraid.

Researcher: Well, thanks for this tour, it's very much appreciated. The house is interesting. I certainly would have liked to see it before it was renovated.

The characters sit back down at the table. Inako takes the teapot and exits the stage. The view down the lane from the kitchen window expands until it fills the entire backdrop, then keeps expanding, becoming more and more blurry, until it is just a blur of colour.

Researcher: I have a couple more questions for you, if you don't mind.

Jacky Maglia: We have to get to the lawyer's office soon, but we have a few minutes still.

Researcher: Alright, I will try to be quick. Albert Dichy said that I should ask you about the other houses Genet designed. He thought you might have some drawings for one of them—I think he was referring to a house in Morocco.

Jacky Maglia: Well, there were two houses in Morocco as far as I can remember. And also one house in the Pyrenees, about thirty kilometres from Pau. I don't remember much about that one—it was an abbey originally, maybe eighty years old, two storeys. He did designs for a new stair and a new attic level plan. I'm not actually sure it was built in the end—he wound up selling the property to a friend. A notary, I think.

Researcher: Not Laurent Boyer? M. Dichy said that he arranged the sale, all the legal stuff.

Jacky Maglia: (*Pause*) That's probably what I'm thinking of.

Researcher: I'd really like to know more about the stair—after all the images of stairs in his work. I'm thinking about the stair at Fontevraud in *Miracle of the Rose*, the stair in Barcelona in *The Thief's Journal*. I guess it's interesting too that he would renovate an abbey, after what he writes about the afterlife of abbeys in *Miracle of the Rose*.

On the screen appears an image of the stair from the Villa Savoye as well as the quote from Miracle of the Rose *(Genet 1988, 64–65):*

> There are things one could say about destinies, but note the strangeness of that of monasteries and abbeys (which prisoners call the bee): jails and preferably state prisons! Fontevrault, Clairvaux, Poissy!

Jacky Maglia: I seem to remember though that Laurent Boyer maybe drew the plans for the house in Morocco, the one in Larache...maybe...But in any case, no, I don't have them. Maybe a call to M. Boyer. In any case, it was an interesting plan, it went against the typical form of a house in that part of Morocco. You understand how a house works in Morocco? Have you ever been there?

Researcher: No, I have to say this is all new to me.

Jacky Maglia: Well, you could think of a site divided up into four lots with four houses that together make up a hidden garden in the middle...like this (*he shows the plan with his hands*). Do you understand?

Researcher: I think so, yes. (*An image of the hands appears on the backdrop.*)

Jacky Maglia: But what made this house unusual was that it was turned inside out, like this (*he turns one hand outwards*) so that in just this corner the garden was in the front of the house.

The other house in Morocco was definitely not built, and Genet had help in the design by an architect, I think he was from Rabat, with a name like du Meziers or something like that. It was a more complicated design. On the street there was to be just a wall, a white wall as you see in Morocco, but with a blue door in the middle of it. The doorway was cut into the wall at an angle, so that when you would open the door you would not see into the courtyard. The courtyard was to be planted with orange trees. On the left when you came in was Inako's atelier...

Researcher: So you were to live there with him?

Jacky Maglia: Well, yes, this was the family home, so to speak. But He never stayed in any of these houses, or at least He rarely slept in them—like here, He would usually go to a hotel at night.

On the right side when you came in from the street was the men's area—the men and women were to be separated here. There were to be two bedrooms, each with a mezzanine above, and a kitchen located between them, with a large area for sitting and working facing the garden. And a terrace covering all of this.

Olivier reappears on the terrace.

Olivier:	I'm sorry but it really is time for us to be going.
Jacky Maglia:	Ah, yes, as I mentioned we need to go see the lawyer. I will be a bit sad to no longer have this house, but you know how these things go. It is time.
Anna:	This was wonderful and very enlightening for me. Thank you so much for your hospitality, and for the tea and oranges.
Jacky Maglia:	You're welcome, of course! I only hope I was able to answer some of your questions. I'm afraid, though, that I may have just raised more.

Stage lights dim. All exit.

Introduction

Leonardo Da Vinci's drawing of the Vitruvian Man, drawn in about 1490, is certainly one of the most immediately recognizable and influential images in Western culture—and beyond. The image can be found on posters, on medallions, produced as an action figure, used as tattoos, alluded to on television shows (think of the android-in-a-circle from *Westworld*) and, of course, on t-shirts—and on postage stamps issued by Italy, Monaco, Romania, Togo, Guinea, Japan, Thailand, Argentina, and Mexico, and those are just the ones I found with a Google search. In addition to the Vitruvian Man, one can find images of a Vitruvian Woman (Getty Images offers twenty-six different versions), Vitruvian Skeleton (this is the image on the Mexican postage stamp), Vitruvian Heavy Metal Guitarist, Vitruvian Cat, Vitruvian Homer Simpson, Vitruvian Pikachu, Vitruvian Barbie, Vitruvian Robot, Vitruvian Leonardo Di Caprio.

Over the course of the long life of this image, the precise ideography that underlies it has become, not exactly lost, but certainly muddled; understandings of the significance of the image are often less than precise. At some point in my training as an architect, I learned that the image represented a turning point from a god-centred universe to one that is human centred, with the universe represented by the geometrical figures of circle and square literally centred on the human figure (with the circle centred on the navel and the square centred on the genitals). The image made a claim in this reading for the perfection of man, whose figure connected the heavenly form of the circle and the earthly form of the square. Indeed, in this reading man becomes a microcosm of the universe; geometry, which organizes and represents the structure of the universe, derives in the first instance from the human figure. In the early modern world, this idea of geometry replaces a focus on materiality as the primary driver of architectural thought. Da Vinci thus prefigures investigations into human form as diverse as those of Jean-Jacques Lequeu (1757–1826), Eadweard Muybridge (1830–1904), Étienne-Jules Marey (1830–1904), Frederick Winslow Taylor (1856–1915), Le Corbusier (Charles-Édouard Jeanneret, 1887–1965), and Henry Dreyfuss (1904–1972) and, through a strange set of shifts, the fields of anthropometrics and ergonomics, those sciences that transform the human body, quite literally, into geometry. I also became aware, if dimly, that the image constituted a reaching back

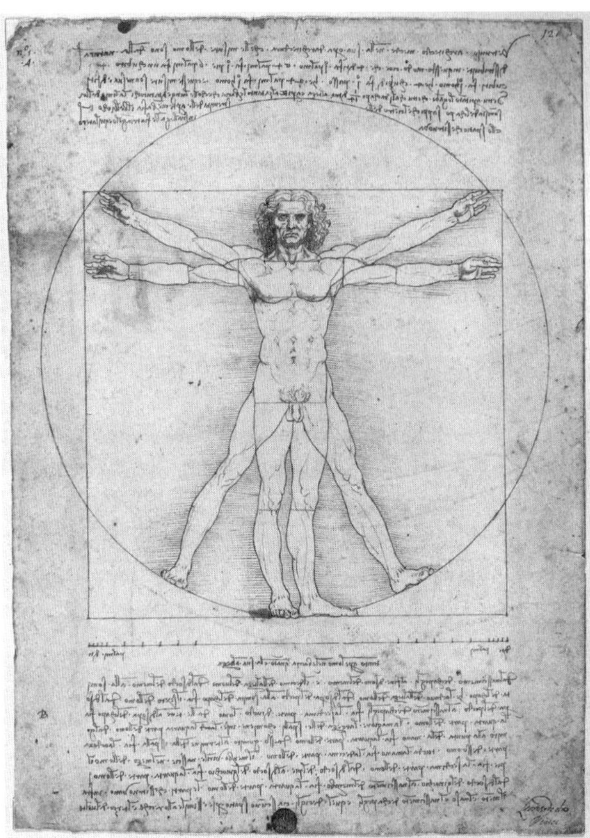

0.1 Leonardo da Vinci, *Vitruvian Man*, 1492. Pen, ink, watercolour, and metalpoint on paper, 343 x 245 mm. (Gallerie dell'Accademia, Venice)

into the ancient past in at least two ways: first, as a direct illustration of a passage of Vitruvius's *De Architectura*, an ancient Roman treatise on architecture often thought of as the starting point of architectural thought (for the sole reason, it seems, that it survived), and second, for the image's supposed connection to Protagoras's famous thesis, from the fifth century BCE, that "man is the measure of all things." The image seemed to be suggesting that we could begin to remake the world in our own image and that by doing so we would make the world more perfect, more ideal. With this reading, I came to understand Da Vinci's image as foundational not just for humanism but for modern society in toto.

In short, this image serves symbolically as an origin statement for the modern discipline of architecture. A fundamentally flawed origin statement, mind you: it is easy to point out that the proportions of the body depicted by Da Vinci do not mirror the proportions of real people, for example, and the circle and the square, it turns out, are not representative of the actual geometries of the cosmos or the earth (indeed, we might say today that circle and square only exist as human concepts). What's more, it's easy to point out that the Vitruvian Man is, to begin with, a man, and in fact a Caucasian man, neither old nor young, fit and strong and healthy. The image seems to radiate a sense of not only physical but also emotional and even ethical health; the rendering of the face suggests a seriousness of purpose, and the glorious mane of hair suggests a leonine vitality. We obviously can't say that Da Vinci is representing a straight man—that concept would not arrive for another four centuries—but we can say that he is representing an overtly masculine figure.

These niggling concerns have been easy to set aside in service to what comes to be seen as an aspirational drawing: after all, Da Vinci had a depiction of perfection as his goal. Recently, though, we seem to have awoken as a culture, and these concerns are no longer niggling—rather, they become core. Can we any longer accept that the female, the racialized, the old, the fat, the sickly, the disabled, the *queer*, are somehow excluded not only from perfection but from a relationship with both the universe and the divine? Da Vinci doubtless did not have this in mind; nonetheless, it is a lesson embedded in the image, and a lesson that we have absorbed over the generations since.

At some point while I was working on this book, I found myself teaching a graduate seminar in architectural theory on the topic of *other bodies*—that is, a seminar in which we asked what architectural theory has to say about all the bodies not represented in Da Vinci's drawing. During this semester of living in intimacy with the image, I came to realize that there is another way of understanding it. While this founding document of Renaissance and hence modern architecture is commonly understood to describe geometry as rooted in the human body ("man is the measure of all things"), giving man a privileged position in the universe, I came to see it instead as man caught in the geometrical figure, imprisoned, tortured, distorted, and domesticated. I came to see this image as emblematic of Western culture's subjugation of the human body and the human being to a set of conceptual constructions. Architecture, then, could not really be understood as a tool made in service of humankind, but rather must be seen as a means of containing, defining, and producing the modern subject.

This book flows, in a way, from this perverse reading of Da Vinci's drawing. It is indeed a *queer* reading that has the potential to lead us to a *queer* theory of architecture, as it invokes architecture's role in producing norms and subjects—in other words, in our self-domestication. In the chapters that follow, I offer a provocation: that this argument is in fact a queer theory of architecture in the sense of sexuality, since sex, through its corollaries of gender, property, family, and inheritance are central to this notion of domestication.

How can architecture be queer? How does queerness—especially my queerness—show up in architecture? These are questions that have nagged me for the past quarter-century, since I was a student of architecture and a hesitantly emerging gay man at Princeton University in the early 1990s. Queer studies was emerging in American academia at that moment, and discourse about how these ideas might relate to architecture were pervasive among Princeton faculty and students, at dinner parties and reading groups, in coming-out projects and queer theses (e.g., Colomina 1992; Colomina et al. 1994; Ricco 1993, 1994; Ripley 1993, 1994; Sanders 1999; Urbach 1993, 1996). Answers to the questions proved evasive, however; after a few years of projects and writing focusing mainly on obvious tropes such as the closet (Urbach

1996), the gay bar (Ricco 1994; Urbach 1993), and the locker room (Sanders 1996), interest seemed to fade away, signposted perhaps by the 1997 publication of Aaron Betsky's *Queer Space*.

For me, though, this question of architectural queerness never went away, staying with me through my career, first as an architect and then as an academic, a career during which I was struggling (and I understand that there is nothing unique about this) to understand who I am, what it means to be a gay man living in this world, and how it is that my own difference comes to play in the work I do. *The House Is (Not) a Prison* is therefore an intensely personal project, but also, I think, a project that is on point with the current situation. Queer issues in architecture have, in recent years, again reached a certain level of interest among architects, scholars, and students of architecture, as we can see by the publication of a small but growing cluster of books, journal issues, and artistic production dedicated to the question (see Bonnevier 2007; Crawford 2015; Furman and Mardell 2022; Gorman-Murray and Cook 2020; Gorny and Van den Heuvel 2018; Jobst and Stead 2023; Kolb 2017; Plasse-Taylor 2022; Preciado 2014; Ramos and Mowlabocus 2021; Vallerand 2020) as well as a growing number of queer architects and spatial artists working towards a queering of the field (such as MYCKET, Andy Summers, Atelier ANF, Pablo Bronstein, Aaron McIntosh, Andrés Jaques, TheQueerArchitect). This new scholarship takes a somewhat different position from that of the 1990s, one that is rooted less in identity and more in process. *The House Is (Not) a Prison* pushes this shift one step further: instead of looking for characteristics of queer architecture, or looking at how we could make things queerly, *The House Is (Not) a Prison* asks how architecture and its making are always-already queer. Instead of looking for a theory of queer architecture, this book seeks to develop a queer theory of architecture.

While that earlier work came out of a community struggling for rights and recognition, bound up in the effects of a deadly plague, struggling for the right simply to exist and as a result working hard to find answers to questions around its place and role in the world and in architecture, today's queer scholars, activists, and practitioners are more concerned with the ways in which a queer view can effect change in the broader world. The relative destigmatization of LGBTQ youth, at least in the developed world, has allowed a new generation of young thinkers to reimagine the world with queerness as an integral part of its constitution. Meanwhile, the expansion of the idea of queer beyond *gay* to include, at its broadest, all forms of opposition to white male capitalist heteronormativity has allowed the development of broad unexpected alliances and moved issues of sexual difference into a central role of resistance. Furthermore, the growth of *trans* into a major and significant experience for ever-larger numbers of people has forced us to confront some of the deepest assumptions that lay at the root of our culture, ultimately bringing into question even the role of our bodies and the future of our species, our relations to other species and to the non-human and the technologically generated. In short, if the architectural thinkers of a quarter-century ago were interested in queer space as a slightly strange, curious but minor phenomenon—as a minor architecture—the current interest is rather in understanding how a consideration of *queer* can allow us to imagine and design different—and better—futures (Bloomer 1992b; Kolb 2017; Ricco 1994). What new worlds can result from rethinking the assumptions of straightness under which the world, and in particular the discipline of architecture, has claimed to, or perhaps more appropriately, claimed not to, operate? How can we not only imagine these new (queer) worlds, but possibly, just possibly, help to bring them to realization? To make use of a bit of hyperbole, the questions, concerns, and potentials brought to the front by a consideration of queerness have moved into a position of criticality not just for those individuals in our culture who identify (or have been identified) as queer, but for all of us.

To develop a queer view of architecture that can produce new worlds, we will need to understand deeply the ways in which sex, sexuality, straightness, and queerness enter the construction of architecture. This is not a simple task. Indeed, it is not easy at first glance to see how such questions are even able to be posed. My contention is that the institution of architecture presents itself as neutral on questions of sexuality, as independent of sex, positioning concepts such as sex, sexuality, the erotic, and the queer as external to architecture—and certainly the idea that there is an erotic or sexual component to architecture can be a difficult one for people, even architects, to accept. The problem that I see here—and this is possibly the core argument in this book—is that this externalization of the queer is already an architectural effect, one without which architecture does not exist. Indeed, we start to see architecture as something like a machine that constructs an interior (and hence an exterior), or a normal and a queer, while simultaneously mobilizing further mechanisms that serve to obfuscate, hide, and veil that construction. As a result, the queerness of architecture is invisible from within architecture.

In *The House Is (Not) a Prison*, my goal is to interrogate the workings of this architecture-machine. This requires an unusual method of looking at architecture, of seeing buildings, one that does not look straight on, so to speak, from the point of view of architectural thought and through the procedures and methods of architectural analysis: to do so would only reify and reconfirm the veils and hidings of architecture. Rather, it is necessary to look from the sides of the eyes, to look awry, to peer around the corners and under layers. As Sara Ahmed says in her discussion of queer phenomenology, "by bringing what is 'behind' to the front, we might queer phenomenology by creating a new angle, in part by reading for the angle of the writing, in the 'what' that appears" (2006, 4). To put it a slightly different way, this ambition requires looking at architecture from the position of its outside—that is, from the position of the queer—and then finding ways to penetrate through its defences, its screens, its veils, its axiomatic locks.[1]

Positions

There have been several theoretical positions posited in relation to the primary theme of the book. These positions can be categorized according to the degree of relation between queer and non-queer: binary positions (positions of the other); exclusionary positions (positions of non-relation); and inclusionary positions (positions of the void). Finally, I will discuss a fourth possible characterization, that of positions of uncertainty or relationality.[2]

Probably the simplest and most intuitive way to understand the place of queerness within modern architecture is through frameworks that consider queer architecture as *other* than simply architecture, or in opposition to what we might call mainstream or even straight architecture. From this position, queer architecture might be considered as a minor architecture, following Gilles Deleuze and Felix Guattari's (1986) characterization of a minor literature: an architecture that makes use of the methods and forms of the dominant architecture, but deterritoriazizes and then reterritorializes these forms, reorganizing them as lines of flight (Bloomer 1992b; Ricco 1994). These minor architectures may be discerned through program—buildings that are designed for use by queer inhabitants—such as in John Paul Ricco's (1994) discussion of gay sex clubs (Urbach 1993) or Betsky's (1997) analysis of Philip Johnson's Glass House. Queer architecture might then be seen as a subversion or overturning of key aspects, especially foundational aspects, of mainstream architectural design, aspects derived from the specific apparent sexualities of queer subjects, such as the need for (or avoidance of) privacy, the specific construction of invasive scopic regimes and the role of the body, especially the naked body, such as Mark Robbins's (1992) *Angles of Incidence* project. Alternatively, the queerness might be seen in a refusal of a clarity of organization, a confusion of functional value, an indeterminacy of spatial characteristics: this is an architecture of queerness that finds its roots in the perceived fluidity of queer sexualities and queer gender roles. Such an architecture is founded in program and use and rejects or at least challenges the clear gender-based organization of mainstream building planning. Such ideas are most often worked through in the realm of the single-family house, as in, for example, the 1994 *House Rules* exhibition at the Wexner Center (Hays et al. 1994).[3]

As well, there are minor architectures that act in the realm of materiality or form, such as architectures that give precedence to ornament over structure, or that problematize that relation, or that make use of bent forms in opposition to the straight elements of orthodox mainstream architectural composition (Bloomer 1992a). More recent work, such as that of Lucas Crawford (2015), has sought to uncover aspects of avant-garde architecture—particularly, in the case of Crawford, in the work of Diller Scofidio + Renfro—that problematize the idea of a fixed gender profile, raising theoretical issues in relation to trans identities. Minor architectures, like minor literatures, have been understood as political forms, mechanisms by which members of groups that have been othered or excluded from discourse or society, that have been made invisible as a group in the typical world of architecture, can lay claim to a place for themselves while establishing difference and visibility.

These binary positions can be problematic, however, in that they do not consider the mechanisms by which queerness is already present in mainstream architectural thinking. Further, these positions posit architecture per se as straight architecture, providing a place for queerness as a thin added veneer, reifying and reproducing a consideration of straightness as normal or natural. Furthermore, these positions of otherness fail to recognize the critical role that architecture plays in the production of that otherness in the first place.[4]

Slightly less problematic in this respect are positions around queer architecture that seek to locate elements of queerness within otherwise non-queer architecture. Examples of this work includes various discussions of single-sex places and rooms within buildings and especially within houses, such as kitchens and drawing rooms. The attention in this work is to the homosocial as latent queer space; Paul B. Preciado's (2014) work on the architecture of *Playboy* is exemplary in this regard. Other work refers to the inherent queerness of building components such as windows and doors (Latour 1988; Teyssot 2013), the question of the public washroom (Sanders 2018), or most famously, the question of the closet (Sedgwick 1990; Urbach 1996). In all these instances, elements of perceived queerness are understood as infections or as stains, as interruptions of *other* into the otherwise disciplined and normative architectures of these buildings, as places of refuge for the queer protagonists of the (hi)stories being told, stains and infections that are dangerous, that might spread, that in the end call into question the straightness of the buildings within which they sit. On a larger scale, these discourses draw from Michel Foucault's (1986) concept of the heterotopia: the bounded, often monosexual spatial institution that can stand for and illustrate otherwise repressed aspects of the society that surrounds it.

The binary position of otherness is a short step away from positions of exclusion, positions that point to ways in which architecture as a disciplinary practice excludes minority voices—women, queers, racialized people. Such positions recognize the presence of minor architectures—

queer architectures, feminine architectures, etc.—but point out the ways in which these are kept outside of architecture per se, focusing the critique on the normative apparatus of architecture. Drawing loosely on Foucault's discussion of the construction of sexuality as a discourse in the nineteenth century, exclusionary positions would point out the ways in which mainstream architecture, and particularly mainstream modern architecture, is constructed along lines of "official" or approved gender roles including the development of the modern family, citing, for example, the ways in which the construction of the house and of housing in the nineteenth and early twentieth centuries followed a contemporaneous reorganization and strengthening of the heterosexual family unit (what would become known, in the mid-twentieth century, as the nuclear family; Foucault [1976] 1990). In this history, the reformation of the family is understood as a vital part of the construction of the modern liberal state and its cousin, the modern capitalist economy. The emergence of housing, the architectural corollary of the family, as an architectural issue during exactly this same period points to the role architecture played in this story. The house in this view is understood as a machine in which reproduction (of the worker and consumer, of the family unit itself, and of the state) takes place. Sara Ahmed (2006), for example, points out the mechanisms by which the house, formed around the requirements of the heterosexual family, serves to reproduce those expectations, producing a self-regulated mandatory sexuality. Sexualities that are not direct participants in this economy of reproduction and succession are thus excluded from direct participation in architectural discourse. To paraphrase Jack Halberstam (2011), such sexualities are identified as failures, an identification that Halberstam and others seek to recuperate as tactical resistance. Indeed, part of the role of architecture in this view is to constitute the relations between sexualities of reproduction and architecture as simply *natural*: to insist that any other sexualities exist, if they exist at all, in a non-relation to architecture. As I wrote with ironic intent in a 2018 publication, "the problem of queer housing remains persistent and recalcitrant because the house—the single-family house and by extension apartments, condominiums and the like—is a central structure of heterosexual hegemony, the primary architectural expression of hetero-normativity" (Ripley 2018, 95). The non-relation of architecture and queerness can be taken beyond this intentional exclusion, however, if we recognize the ways in which architecture and building do not simply happen, but emerge from a lengthy trajectory of conceptual, material, economic, professional, and constructive practices. The quotation just cited continues as follows:

> All housing, at least in the developed world, is designed and constructed from within that hegemonic tradition, using models that assume hetero-normativity in its users: even if the client for a new house is, for example, a gay couple, all decisions made in the design are made from within a straight tradition, all construction is produced by a construction industry formed around non-queer hegemonic industrial and business practices, all materials sourced and processed from within an exploitative colonizing regime of resource extraction. And what would be different anyway? Wouldn't our hypothetical gay couple want the same things as everyone else: a master bedroom with ensuite bath, a guest bedroom or maybe a room for the kid, a yard where they can sit out and a patio for barbecuing, a living room with a huge TV… (95)

This article consciously takes a radical position in relation to queer architecture, a claim that a truly queer architecture would require the dismantling of all structures—built and otherwise—of the straight world to be able to rethink queerness not in a binary mode, not simply in its *difference from* heteronormativity, but in relation to its own being. In other words, the article takes the position that a queer architecture is impossible in a straight world.

In contrast, or perhaps as a complement to these positions of exclusivity, are theoretical positions that see exclusion as a ruse or a fiction (and to be fair, this was my ironic intent in the previous quotation). Rather, these positions see queerness, or at the least a queer potentiality, in all buildings or at the core of all architectures. One example of such a position would further Judith Butler's (1990) concept of performative identity into the realm of architecture, conceptualizing buildings as stages on which these performances take place. Other writers, such as Andrew Holder (2017), might suggest that there is an essential queerness at the heart of all architectures—in essence, that architecture is always-already queer, and that the act of designing requires a queering of the world. These positions hold that the insistent heteronormative stance of modern architecture is an attempt to cover up, or hide, this inherent and always-present queerness. Indeed, such positions may go further to suggest that queerness is a core concept in modernity, that queer is needed for straight to be recognized and institutionalized. This is of course just the idea that theory needs an *other*: It is not just queer that is needed to produce straight, but also the *exclusion* of queer in order to recognize the interiority of straight.[5]

These positions of inclusion might be extended to suggest that what is central to architecture, what exists at its core, is neither heteronormativity or queer sexualities, neither straight nor queer, but simply sex. This argument would suggest that sitting at the core of architecture, as a fundamental and fundamentally inaccessible void, an unknowable knowledge, is simply sex itself. The separation into straight and queer is nothing other than the artifact of the primary violence of architecture, the violence of separation into us and them, the creation of outside and inside. The violence of architecture is thus revealed as a violence of literal outing and a violence of queering, of the production, naming, expulsion and effacing of the queer.

Ironically, as I mentioned above, this mechanism—the construction of (at least the appearance of) an interior and an exterior, the separation of us and them—is itself a fundamental and fundamentally architectural mechanism, among the primary core purposes of architecture as discussed by Elizabeth Grosz (2001) and others, following Derrida's ([1976] 2016) work on the outside of language. In other words, positions of inclusion would suggest that not only is architecture unable to acknowledge the queerness at its core, or rather at the core of the modern world, but that one purpose of (modern) architecture is to produce the apparent absence of queerness, to construct the conditions of its apparent expulsion. Beyond this expulsion of queerness, architecture plays a second role of hiding and veiling this expulsion, of producing a disciplining of its own materials, of buildings, that acts to naturalize the effects of the mechanism while simultaneously effacing the traces of the mechanism itself. Indeed, one of the byproducts of this position on queer architecture is the recognition of this double or coupled mechanism of architecture, by which it produces effects and then removes the traces of its own actions. This double mechanism is nothing more that the maintenance of the architecturally proper—and of course the relationship between architecture and the proper, between architecture and property, is both tight and clear. Architecture establishes both property and the proper. Queer architecture cannot, by definition, be proper: It is established in advance as improper, and without any proper relationship to property.

One way to understand, perhaps, the conflicted relation between queerness and architecture in the modern world is through a brief consideration not so much of space but of time. Architecture's role in relation to property is not just to establish and define the latter spatially, not simply to establish ownership over land, but also to ensure and protect the continuity of this ownership, of property, through time. This concern, for the temporal extension of property, is perhaps what gives rise to the dominant position of permanence and durability within architecture. It is interesting that Mohsen Mostafavi and David Leatherbarrow's (1993) work on weathering in architecture, which brought in the question of time and decay, was understood as a radical departure for architectural thinking. Architecture is seen as both a mode of resistance to the ravages of time and assurance of the continuity of property in transmission from generation to generation. Queerness, because of its distancing from the economies of (re)production and success(ion), is therefore troubling to an architecture concerned with the proper and with property (Edelman 2004; Halberstam 2011; Muñoz 2009). Indeed, one mode of response to this economy as queer individuals is, as Halberstam suggests, to take up failure—failure to engage in reproduction, failure to ensure succession—as modes of resistance (although Halberstam is not particularly clear about resistance to what).

To complicate matters, this view of the proper within architecture, of architecture's relation to property and therefore to succession, is already at odds with the utopian impulse within modernism; we would do well to bear in mind Pierre-Joseph Proudhon's famous dictum, "property is theft," written in 1840 at the beginning of architectural utopianism (1876, 12). This relation of property to succession is no doubt the reason for the common separation of children from parents in dystopian novels (consider Aldous Huxley's *Brave New World* or Lois Lowry's *The Giver*) and utopian architectural proposals (such as Charles Fourier's phalansteries). Modern architecture therefore sits in a conflicted relationship to temporal questions of property, aiming simultaneously to support and disrupt.

Finally, there are theoretical positions that are somewhat less fixed, that take a more relational or situational view of the question(s) at hand. These positions start from a declaration that sexuality is not, or at least not always, a stable entity, but rather changeable, situational. Ahmed (2006) uses the concept of orientation to suggest a sexuality that is not dogmatic or fixed; orientations are not universal, but depend on relations to other entities, acting as lines of force, and these lines of force can be altered when new points of attraction appear. So it is, I would argue, with architecture. The orientation of a building is not a given, fixed and unchanging, but situational, depending on context, on weather, on use, on the characters that inhabit it. The relationship between architecture and queer is likewise an active relationship, always shifting, deviating from any straight line, falling back on the line, deviating again. Architecture, from this point of view, is never simply straight or queer, but fluctuates between those two states, like an electron fluctuates between particle and wave, only falling into one state or the other as a result of a reading: that is, because of our human interactions with buildings.

Ahmed (2006) also points out, in her extended discussion of tables, that the meaning of a table is always situational: it depends, for example, on what I intend to do at that table, and who else sits at the table with me. Further, the orientations available for a table are limited to the orientations I have available for my interactions with the table. Similarly, it will be my position in this work that sexuality, that queerness, is a relational question, emerging in part from the interaction, from the relationship, of the human (queer) self and architecture. It will be my position that the reading mentioned in the previous paragraph is not a one-way or fixed event, not a unidirectional arrow, but a bidirectional interaction. Buildings are seen as active participants in their own readings, assisting in the production of both reading and reader; in the process, buildings open themselves to us.

Like Ahmed's table, though, we can only collaborate with buildings on producing the readings we are able to produce: our own orientations, our own predilections and characteristics constrain and limit how we can read a building. And of course, architecture, as disciplining mechanism for any building, gets in the way, presenting mandatory readings and denying or veiling others. Sometimes, more devious, violent, or hallucinatory methods are needed to break through the veils of architecture, to come, in our relationships with buildings, to queer meanings that change how we see both the buildings and our selves.

Organization of the Book

The book's title, *The House Is (Not) a Prison*, is taken from a comment Le Corbusier made about the Villa Savoye in the 1930 film *Architecture d'aujourd'hui*. This book argues, though, that the house *is* a prison—that is, that the carceral qualities of modernism (notably, isolation, surveillance, and cellular composition) are clear conceptual components of the modern house within a structure that is inextricably linked to sexual norms around the family. The cell is understood as the primary architectural innovation of the early modern world, the model not only for the suburban house and the condominium unit but also for the modern unified self. If, as has been made clear in literature and film—see, for example, Todd Haynes's *Poison* (1991) and *Far from Heaven* (2003); Gregg Araki's *Mysterious Skin* (2005); or Gus Van Sant's *My Own Private Idaho* (1991)—the suburban house feels like a prison for queer people, I would equally suggest that a queer analysis of the house would focus on the carceral roots of the domestic. The prison, in other words, is the *behind* of the modern domestic scene.

Through a series of formal and spatial interrogations of well-known houses of the modernist era (Le Corbusier's Villa Savoye, Ludwig Mies van der Rohe's Farnsworth House, Philip Johnson's Glass House) in parallel to a discussion of the cell and the prison as exemplary modern forms, a series of fundamental architectural concepts is identified and explored: the violence of the line, the Law of Enclosure, the formative absence of the void, the disciplinary production of the house-machine, the modern dissolution of the wall, the veiling constructive presence of the screen.[6] An understanding is developed of architecture as a machine that produces an illusive but powerful interiority (both literal, in the sense of a room, and figural, through the biopolitics of exclusion) through the construction of a folded and continuous front. The impossible task, then, is to see past this universal front, to find secrets that architecture doesn't want us to see, secrets around gender, sexuality, property, and the origin of the modern self—to see the *behind* of architecture. In the end, the book posits that we must learn to take architecture from behind.[12]

Chapter 1: The Kleptogenetics of Architecture looks to establish the basis of a generative queer theory of architecture, with the aim of locating queerness. The chapter begins with the most fundamental of architectural acts: the drawing of a line, symbolic of the construction of a wall. Using frameworks for understanding violence developed by Walter Benjamin (1978), Benjamin Bratton (2015), and Slavoj Žižek (2009), the chapter discusses the violence inherent in this act, especially the violence that is specific to the binary division: A|B, right|wrong, male|female. Within this framework, queerness is understood as that which problematizes the binary.

It is important at this point to recognize the relationship of architecture to queerness. It is not my contention that architecture represents the normal or that queerness is somehow opposed to architecture in a reinforcement of an established binary. Rather, it is my contention that we should understand architecture as neither queer nor not queer, but instead as the mechanism that enables, constructs, and enforces this distinction. Normal and queer only come into being because of the architectural mechanisms of binary division and enclosure.

The special case in which the line loops back on itself, forming an enclosure (or a noose), produces a particular form of the binary, that of interior|exterior, which leads immediately to me|other, mine|theirs. These concepts (me, mine, the idea of the self) are thus understood as architectural concepts. The Law of Architecture (the production of interior and exterior) produces three specific forms of violence: the violence of domestication, of those on the inside; the violence of exile, of those left on the outside; and the violence of removal of part of the world from the common, that is, the violence of theft. Architecture, and not only architecture, is thus *kleptogenetic*, that is, born through theft, but this is a theft that is hidden and made to be forgotten precisely by the material solidity and permanence of the building, a theft that can only be revealed through a second act of theft. Finally, the chapter discusses the gendered relationships of property and inheritance inherent in this Law and the role of the homosexual in relation to it.

Chapter 2: The Cellular Self investigates how the theoretical constructions from the first chapter manifest as formative elements in the construction of modernism. The chapter starts with a discussion of the first modern prisons, especially Bentham's Panopticon (1791, Figure 2.2), Auburn Prison (1818), and the Maison Centrale de Fontevraud (Fontevraud Prison, 1804), and more particularly of the cell. The cell, an important innovation in penal architecture dating from the early nineteenth century, is here understood as the basic elemental representation of the modern unified self, the space in which we are required to exist as independent individuals, and which we cannot escape. We can read this movement clearly, for example, in the two key architectural prison projects of the eighteenth century, in the contrast between the unfathomable disorder of Giovanni Battista Piranesi's *Carceri* drawings and the ultimate order based on the surveillance of the individual cell in Bentham's Panopticon project. The cell as the locus for the reform of the self was taken perhaps to its extreme at Auburn Prison, in New York State, opened in 1818 (Figure 2.4); here prisoners were not allowed to have any communication with each other.[7]

The development of the cell as the fundamental building block of modern architecture is then discussed. Building on the work of Pierre Vittorio Aureli and Maria Shéhérazade Giudici (2016), I show that modern architecture entailed a shift in primary organizational strategy from *composition*, as exemplified by the work of Jean-Nicholas-Louis Durand at the beginning of the nineteenth century, to *cellular repetition* as seen in the urban projects of Le Corbusier a hundred years later (Figure 3.1)—or in the suburban projects of Levittown a few decades after that (Figure 4.3). My argument here is that the cellular form brings with it, from its origins in prison architecture, both its insistence on the disciplining of interchangeable unitary subjects *and* the inherent queerness of the cell.

The chapter goes on to discuss other varieties of architectural void. We should recognize here that almost any type of architectural space, any room, is at heart a void. My interest, though, is in what I call primary voids, that is, spaces in which the characteristics specific to a void, particularly its absolute separation from the remainder of the universe, are especially strong. There is clearly a certain *queerness* to any such space, and it should come as no surprise that many voids or near-voids bear a strong connection to queer lives and thought: the closet, the bath, the back room at a sex club.[8] My point here is not, however, to say that some voids are normal, or normalizing, and others are queer, or queering. Instead, such spaces are of interest because of their relationship to that other idea developing at the same time, that of the modern unified self, and for the ways in which the presence of the self became important in the development of modern architecture, as a quality to be both nurtured and disciplined, surveyed and hidden.

Chapter 3: La maison, ce n'est pas une prison discusses the best-known of modern architectural machines, Le Corbusier's Villa Savoye, the famous *machine for living in* (Figure 3.1). The analysis is prompted by a title slide in some copies of Pierre Chenal and Le Corbusier's 1930 film *Architecture d'aujourd'hui*, in which an intertitle says of the Villa Savoye "La maison, ce n'est pas une prison. L'aspect change a chaque pas." (The house is not a prison. The view changes at every step. Figure 3.3.) The chapter asks, then, in what ways could the Villa be a prison, or what commonalities might we find in them?[9] Through this analysis, the concepts "house" and "prison" are understood to function as distorted images or transforms of each other, and each type is understood as a modern disciplinary machine. [10]

The chapter starts by asking what it would mean if we were to take Le Corbusier at his word: how can we consider the Villa Savoye, the most famous of all modernist houses, to be not simply *like* a machine for living in, or a *metaphoric* machine, but a literal machine? After all, the machine is probably the dominant image of modernity, starting with the thermodynamic machine of the Carnot cycle, the steam engine, the nineteenth-century city, and Freud's Oedipus; the internal combustion machine of the twentieth century; the Bachelor Machine of Michel Carrouges, which becomes the desiring-machine of Deleuze and Guattari; and the internalized machine of the Deleuzian society of control (Carrouges 1975; Deleuze 1992). If we are to think of the Villa Savoye as a machine, we could then ask a few basic questions: what is the energy source that runs the machine? What is its expected output? How can we describe the cycle of flows on which it operates, and, if this is a classical or thermodynamic machine, what is the difference that drives it? The analysis therefore starts with circulation, focusing on the redundant circulatory mechanism of stair and ramp in the Villa Savoye in conjunction with its clearly gendered sectional relationship in the scheme. From this viewpoint, the Villa Savoye's section becomes the schema of a sexual Carnot cycle, the incessant circulation up the ramp and down the stair between the masculine world of the chauffeur on the ground floor and the feminine realm of Mme Savoye on the roof. The energy that drives this system is nothing less than raw sexual energy, here contained and put to work by society (or, more literally, by the legal systems of modern France) to produce modern subjects—that is, to reproduce. The house is thus both participant in and constructor of an economics of sexual desire which is, because of its necessary connection to the role of the family, explicitly a heterosexual economics.

How could we account for queerness in this analysis? How does the machine of the prison interface with the sexual Carnot cycle of the house? The analysis here brings into play the two remaining characteristics of the classical machine: friction and waste. The homosexual is not seen to participate in this domestic economy of sexual production. Worse still, the homosexual, the queer, operates as friction: queerness diverts sexual energy, steals energy, away from the family, in other words, away from work useful to society. *Queerness, therefore, is theft.* The house is always a prison.

Finally, waste, and the generation of waste, is a necessary and unavoidable component of any thermodynamic machine (arguably of any machine, even abstract machines). The role of the prison is thus clear: *The prison is the primary site of containment for the waste products of bourgeois society.* Such a site of containment, though, is not static, but rather must be also thought of as a machine, with its own inputs and outputs, energy sources and circulation.

Chapter 4: On Stained Sheets goes into a deeper investigation of the relationship between architecture and sex. After an initial section that positions architecture not as an erotically neutral enclosure but rather as an active participant in human sexualities, the chapter moves on to discuss in some depth what I call architecture's masturbation problem. Following closely the work of Thomas Laqueur, in his 2004 study of masturbation, *Solitary Sex: A Cultural History of Masturbation*, the chapter presents the ways in which was masturbation came to be understood as antithetical to the developing profession of architecture.

Laqueur's positioning of masturbation as imaginary, solitary/secret, and excess provides a suitable framework to construct an understanding of this non-relationship. As a product of the imagination, a practice grounded in fantasy, masturbation runs in direct opposition to an architecture establishing itself as the producer of the real. While the secrecy of masturbation depends, to a large part, on architecture, architecture's primary concern in this period is for the construction of the social. Finally, part and parcel of architecture's new role as the constructor of the physical apparatus of society was a concern for the *disciplined* construction of that modern world, for the elimination of excess. To be clear, though, the issue was not with excess as such, but particularly with non-productive, undisciplined excess. And masturbation, I argue, was understood at the end of the nineteenth century as the epitome of such undisciplined activity.

This chapter concludes with a discussion of the present day, following Alain Badiou's *Pornographie du temps present (The Pornographic Age*, 2020) and Paul B. Preciado's (2017) discussion of the pharmacopornographic era. In this phase of late capital, sex has been repositioned from an activity of reproduction to one of production. In this world, pornography—that is, the image of desire—takes precedence over the real, and masturbation, literal or figurative, becomes our most important activity (and the most important form of work), structured precisely by Laqueur's three characteristics: it is imaginary, spurred on by the images of advertising; solitary/secret, most often carried out today through internet scrolling; and obsessive, excessive, and addictive.

And what is architecture in this world? It is no longer able to take on the role of construction of the real, although of course this cannot be admitted, least of all to architects; today, all architecture can do is play the role of producer (in the sense of the producer of a play or film) of the desire-image. Architecture today, even in its constructed three-dimensional form, cannot be more than image. Architecture in this world is no longer the arbiter or producer of the private, the secret, or the solitary as such, when architecture can be and is penetrated at any moment by technological incursions through its walls. And architecture, far from being the apparatus of discipline, the model of restraint, has become the very figure of excess, of stuff, as any view of a contemporary city or walk through a biennale will make clear: the sheer proliferation of more and more formal and material diversity, much without reason or sense, and none of it speaking to its neighbours. This is the atomized and atomizing architecture of pure excess, the architecture of ejaculation.

In short, architecture's place in the world, architecture's mandate, has been completely overturned. Any calls for a more socially or environmentally responsible architecture are the pure call of nostalgia, looking to regain an image of a lost world. *In the world of masturbation, architecture can only be pornography.*

Chapter 5: Living in Glass Houses moves from an investigation of the mechanics of the modern house to a concern with the information technology of its enclosure. The chapter begins by tracing the disappearance of the wall over the course of the modern era, one of the primary tectonic and formal developments of modern thinking and practice in architecture. This development arose from the invention in the nineteenth and early twentieth centuries of new construction systems, notably the steel and later concrete frame, both of which had the effect of dissociating structure from enclosure. We can see this clearly in the early domestic buildings of Le Corbusier, particularly in his Dom-Ino project of 1913 and in the Villa Savoye, as well as in one of the most influential architectural manifestos of the era, Le Corbusier's *Five Points for a New Architecture.* We can trace its further development through a series of *un-houses*: Mies van der Rohe's Barcelona Pavilion of 1929; the two great glass houses of the post-war era, Mies's Farnsworth House (Figures 5.3, 5.4) and Philip Johnson's Glass House; and two radical projects of the 1960s that take the idea even further, Yves Klein's Air Architecture projects produced between 1957 and 1962 (Klein and Ruhngau 2004) and Reyner Banham and François Dallegret's Environment-Bubble of 1965 (Banham 1965).

How are we to understand, in terms of this discussion around queerness, the drive to dissolution of the building envelope in the modern world? We will have to acknowledge first that any removal of the separation of the enclosure is only, at best, apparent; the separation of inside and outside remains absolute, and indeed Savoye, Farnsworth, and the Glass House all, like Mettray, relied on extensive landscape holdings to provide privacy. Second, we can note that the dematerialization of the building envelope has the corollary effect of both emphasizing and disciplining the enclosure. Third, the unified, dematerialized enclosure—the glass wall, for example—places strict demands on the organization of the interior. While the plan may be *free*, unfettered by the demands of structure, it is required *by the very fact of the transparency of the façade* to be highly organized. In sum, the unified enclosure represents and constructs, is a necessary component of, the production of a unified, consistent self, including a unified and consistent sexual identity; multiple selves, multiple or conflicting desires, are not allowed.

The chapter then moves on to a discussion of another iconic modern house, Philip Johnson's Glass House, to uncover the disciplinary role of glass. What, exactly, is being hidden by the glass walls of the modern house? The discussion opens with an analysis of a series of iconic photographs of Johnson in or at his Glass House, carefully staged images in which Johnson is presented as an attractive, even sexy, bachelor in his pad, master of his surroundings, the essential modern man (Figures 5.6 to 5.10). The glass screen wall of the house (as well as the opaque screens carefully used to hide any sense of disarray) acts to delimit the scene, dividing the world, in effect, into *in front* and *behind*. The system is perfectly symmetrical: in front is always where we are, and while behind is visible to us it is not physically accessible (as soon as we access the behind, we turn it into in front); what is more, this behind is itself perfectly composed and organized to create the desired image of the front. It is important to recognize that in this sense, the behind is never really behind: it is instead relegated to the surface of the glass screen, a projected image of an inaccessible world.

The chapter moves on to discuss what is not seen in these images. In the case of Johnson's house, this means a discussion of the Guest House, on the same property in New Canaan—a brick box, approximately the same proportions as the Glass House, but which simply contains Johnson's bedroom. This hidden component, necessary for the construction of the images we started with but necessarily outside of the view acts, so to speak, as an invisible-but-present offstage, an *ob-scene*, that interferes with, contradicts, and complements the construction of the scene.[11] The architectural machine of the enclosure thus has a three-part structure:

the front, the scene of action; the image, which sets the stage; and the behind, the ob-scene, the inaccessible real that must remain hidden. Architecture, rather than the manifestation of the interior|exterior relationship, is now understood as the art of the eternal front. Architecture in this sense is not the production of the real but, rather, the production of an image that stands in for the real.

A return to the image we started the chapter with, of Johnson lounging on the lawn in front of his house, serves to conclude the chapter. We might, loosely, say that this image is pornographic in nature: it is a constructed image of a non-reality, an image that relies on the erotic appearance of both Johnson and the house, an image that is meant to both arouse and derive from desire (in this case, desire for the modern lifestyle), and an image that is intended to extract financial gain from this desire (through, in the first instance, selling magazines, but also, of course, selling Johnson as architect). While I say I use the term *pornographic* loosely, Preciado (2014) makes this pornographic structure rigorous and explicit with his analysis of the architecture of *Playboy*, from the same period. Preciado goes further, to see the era of the Playboy Mansion and the Glass House as an early phase of what has become the pharmacopornographic era, an era in which sex is valuable not for the reproduction of new bodies (as in Foucault's disciplinary society) but rather for the production of capital. In the pharmacopornographic era, the machine that drives the production of capital is no longer a thermodynamic engine, a steam engine, or an internal combustion engine, or even a nuclear reactor, but simply a pharmaco-biological engine: a sex drive fueled by the Pill and Viagra on the one hand, and Tinder and Grindr on the other. Sex itself, and most particularly non-reproductive sex, and of that most particularly masturbation, becomes the ultimate form of work. The house is now reduced to a machine for masturbating in.

What is the role of architecture's screens and architecture's images in this scenario? Architecture, including (but not only) domestic architecture, functions largely through its image, an image designed to produce desire and through desire to generate capital. We can see this in the form of marketing campaigns for new condominium developments, the clearest evidence of the city as machine for generating capital. We can also see it in recent institutional projects—museums and others—in which the image of the new building is more important than the building itself, important primarily for *the ability of that image to attract visitors*. Architecture has become its image, the image it projects on its screens. Architecture, in short, has become pornography.

Finally, this book claims that if architecture, as I will demonstrate, is the art of the front, and if queerness somehow sits in an invisible and inaccessible behind to that front, then to counter the modern domestic architecture-machine means precisely to uncover and make visible this on-scene behind. Following Deleuze's conception of his own methodology as one of "taking an author from behind" (1995, 6)—that is, of using the ideas of an author to produce something that, so to speak, combines the DNA of the original author with that of Deleuze in order to produce some monstrous, new, unexpected idea—I ask how we can do the same for architecture, what tactics we might consider to take architecture from behind. Žižek picks up on this notion for his own critique of Deleuze, which he labels "Taking Deleuze from Behind" (2015, 41).

Both Deleuze and Žižek, of course, are using this idea of "taking from behind" to somehow bring a bit of dirt, of sex, into their arguments. For Deleuze, we cannot help but think this is an explicit allusion to the queerness of his work and perhaps of philosophy in general—after all, taking from behind is a fundamental tradition in queer communities. Leo Bersani (1996), in his discussion of Jean Genet's *Funeral Rites*, finds a perverse futurity in anal sex, as the two participants are looking not in each other's eyes but rather are looking together towards the horizon.[13] Taking from behind also has resonances of cowardice (shooting in the back) and of betrayal, and we will need to take both of these into account.

Following Preciado, we could say that *queer* has morphed today into all the forms of resistance to the pharmacopornographic regime. Queer, precisely, is sex mobilized as resistance to the sex-driven machine of capital, and hence to the structures of late capitalism itself. Could we then conceive of an architecture mobilized as resistance to architecture? How might we take architecture from behind, how might we make use of its techniques and methods but produce something that is architecture and yet is not, to produce beautiful monsters that recognize and help us to recognize the queerness that is imbedded in architecture?

Finally, before moving on into the main part of the text, I need to address what many readers will doubtless see as a major gap in the work: all of the major works of architecture discussed in this book are credited as the work of white men and, with one major exception (and perhaps others of which I am not aware), straight white men.

The intention here is not to deny, minimize, or ignore the contributions that women made to the development of modern architecture and the modern domestic scene. A few of these women are well known, such as Lilly Reich, who collaborated as a furniture and interior designer with Mies van der Rohe from 1925 through to Mies's emigration to the United States in 1938 (McQuaid and Droste 1996), or Charlotte Perriand, who held a similar position with Le Corbusier, including significant work on the furnishings for the Villa Savoye such as the famous LC4 Chaise Longue, and who was a significant modern architect in her own right (Perriand and Jousset 2005). Marion Mahony Griffin, Frank Lloyd Wright's first employee, was instrumental in the design of some of Wright's early groundbreaking Prairie-style houses (which do not appear in this book) and an important contributor to the design of Canberra in Australia (Griffin and Wood 2005).

Possibly the best-known house of the modern era designed by a (queer) female architect is Eileen Gray's E-1027, designed and built between 1926 and 1929 (the house was therefore tightly contemporary with the Villa Savoye) as a vacation house for Gray and her romantic partner, Jean Badovici. This house has been widely published, including important studies by Beatriz Colomina (1993) and Katarina Bonnevier (2005). Like the Villa Savoye, E-1027 has had a somewhat queer afterlife, filled with both gender- and sexuality-based aggression and outright tragedy, first from Badovici claiming the house as his own work (he was technically client and owner of the house), to Le Corbusier, on a visit, and against Gray's wishes, painting a mural of three intertwined women on a wall on the terrace, as well as seven other murals. Colomina has this to say about this mural and the seven others that Le Corbusier provided "free of charge":

0.2 Le Corbusier painting mural at E-1027 Villa, Roquebrune-Cap-Martin, France, 1939. (Image FLC)

> Like all colonists, Le Corbusier does not think of it as an invasion but as a gift. When recapitulating his life's work five years before his death, he symptomatically writes about Algiers and Cap Martin in the same terms: "1930. Algiers... seven great schemes (seven enormous studies), free of charge." And later, "1938–39. Eight mural paintings (free of charge) in the Badovici and Helen Grey house at Cap Martin." No charge for the discharge. Gray was outraged, now even her name had been defaced. And renaming is, after all, the first act of colonization. Such gifts cannot be returned. (1993, 29)

In the end, perhaps, the house got its revenge, as it was here that Le Corbusier died in 1965, from a heart attack, after going swimming against his doctor's orders.

The story of E-1027 is an important one to tell, as it lays bare the misogyny, heterocentrism, and colonial attitude at the centre of (modern) architecture. I place *modern* in parentheses here because I would argue—indeed, this is the central argument in this book—that these characteristics, boiled down into the construction of an interior and exterior, are fundamental to architectural thinking and action. Perhaps this explains why I do not make an effort, in this book, to uncover works of architecture by queer men and women, to identify spaces that are somehow *for* queer men or queer women (I think I have been clear that such spaces are impossible), or to explore forms of modernism from outside of the European canon or produced by racialized people. Instead, I have chosen to look again at the "heroes" of modern architecture, or some of them at least, and to look at their work in a different light, from a position that sees these works not as emblematic of progress but as fortresses, or prisons, as stories that stand in the way of the lives we humans want to lead. This book, put bluntly, is against architecture, not championing one form of architecture against another, or looking for a new way of thinking or practicing architecture that could redeem the practice, but against architecture as a whole.[14]

This is exactly the question that is at issue here, in this discussion of subversion in architecture, of the queering of architecture: we cannot queer architecture by changing architecture, because that after all amounts just to the (re)production of the proper. To queer architecture, we need to be always against architecture, even while using architecture against itself. It is this *against* that is most critical here, an against that can never transform itself or become a *for* by simply changing its object, an against whose teleology can only ever be negative. We need architecture not to change, so that we can be against architecture. If we are sincere about our desire for the queer, we will need to embrace anti-architectures, ways of thinking and building that desperately resist the utopic in all its aspects—including the utopia of the non-utopias—embracing the slithering line of the migrant, the transient and immaterial, blood and sperm and concrete and feathers, meaning and non-meaning, life and life, but also death and death, frantically drawing and building our dream worlds until our right arms are exhausted.

This is the story of the first house.

The people were Wanderers, always in search of food. They travelled in groups, family groups.

They slept around the fire in skins or tents. Maybe they had stable sexual partnerships, maybe not. Probably not. Paternity was probably a loose concept.

After a time, the people settled down. They started to grow crops, to domesticate animals. But the goats kept running away, so they kept them tied up. Then the goats ate through the rope, so the people built a big box of stone, or dried mud, or wood, to keep the goats safe. Anyway, they needed somewhere to keep the crops safe, especially over the winter, safe from rain and wild animals and maybe other people.

When some of the women tried to run away from the men (why they wanted to leave does not matter, maybe one of them wanted to run off with a young lover and start a new group), they were locked in the goatshed, for a few hours at first, but they just tried to run away again. In any case, the men soon found this was convenient and started to keep them and other unruly women locked up all the time, except for work and sex.

But the goatshed soon became too small, and the men soon realized they needed to keep the children locked up with the women, so they built a new house just for the women, a house they could visit whenever they wanted sex. Maybe this was communal at first, but soon each man who was a MAN built his own house to keep his own women and his own children and his own goats available for his use.

So the first house was a brothel,
And the first brothel was a prison,
And the first prison was a goatshed.

Chapter 1

The Kleptogenetics of Architecture

Derrida describes map-making, the first writing, as the wounding of the forest, rather than the scarring of the soil. 'Writing as the possibility of the road, and of difference. The history of writing and the history of the road, of the rupture, the *via rupta*, broken, of the path that is broken, beaten, *fracta*, of the space of reversibility and of repetition traced by the opening of the map. The divergence and violent spacing from nature, of the forest that is natural, savage, selvage, place of safety, break it into map-making, the first writing. The silva, the forest, is savage, the *via rupta* is written, discerned, and inscribed violently as difference, as form imposed on the earth as matter as such.' I insert the feminine transcendental here, in the broken earth of agriculture rather than map-making, the furrow, *boustrophedon*, just what map-making is not.

—Gayatri Spivak, Keynote address, Creative Time Summit, Toronto, 2017

There is hardly a more fundamental action for an architect than the drawing of a line, which is, after all, a representation of the construction of a wall. Drawing a line on a piece of paper, like constructing a wall in a field, changes that paper from pure surface into a project. What's more, when I draw a line, I project myself into the project: by drawing the line I split myself in two (this is what lines do), I extend myself. The line I draw is also a promise, first of all a promise of more lines, a promise of a fully worked-out concept, of a construction of stone and concrete and wood and glass, of a place in which one can live, of a new world in the process of becoming, a new world in which I am already present by means of the projection and splitting of self already mentioned. The line is also a hypothesis—unlike the wall, hopefully, we might erase it and redraw it a few times, until we know we have the right line, the line that makes the right promises, produces the right future. In addition to promises, the line also makes claims: the claim, first of all, to the right to draw the line (to build the wall). It makes a claim of ability, a claim of technique, a claim that I have the knowledge and power needed to draw that line, and the ability to understand it not just as a random mark, but as a line, that is, as a mark with meaning.

My action makes the claim that this is my mark to make, my wall to build; this is a claim of power, of standing. And it makes a claim of ownership, that I can make that mark, on that paper (that wall, in that field). The line, the first line on a piece of paper, also has other effects, does other things: it claims the paper, stains it, marks it; if the line is drawn too hard, without finesse, it can tear it; and it divides the paper, stratifies the paper, organizes the paper. The wall turns the ground into a site.[1]

None of these promises, claims, and effects come without violence. Indeed, violence is at the heart of the matter. As Gayatri Spivak and Jacques Derrida point out, the drawing of a line on a map and the digging of a furrow in the ground are primordial acts of violence. The same is true of the construction of a wall, or indeed of the drawing of a line that represents, that promises, that construction. Architecture starts with a core of inevitable violence.

One of the prime (if always unstated) goals of architecture, at least in the modern world, is to cover up, hide, or dissimulate the violence that always exists at its core. As a result, thinking the violence of architecture is not a simple process. Nor is it an issue that is discussed, for the most part, in schools of architecture. Architecture is understood, (still) following ideologies carried forward since the 1920s, as either a neutral form-making process (especially in terms of computer-generated form) or a positive utopia-building exercise (particularly in the guise of sustainable architecture, community-based architecture, disaster relief, etc.). Still, aspects of violence in architecture do occasionally peek through the cracks: take, for example, the media uproar over working conditions on the site of Zaha Hadid's Al Wakrah stadium in Qatar, Forensic Architecture's analysis of Saydnaya, the notorious Syrian torture prison, or analyses of architecture's complicity with regimes of capital (Forensic Architecture 2016; Graaf 2015; Riach 2014). In virtually all cases, however, the resulting violence is placed elsewhere, outside of architecture, blamed on repressive regimes or institutions or abusive individuals. The violence that is inherent to architecture, the multiple forms of violence that are necessary for its existence, are seldom if ever acknowledged.

In an article[2] in which he discusses, in his words, "the transvestitism of power," Benjamin H. Bratton asks the question, "Why does exceptional violence so often act upon architecture, and how is exceptional violence already architectural in its conception?" (2015, 60). To address this question, Bratton returns to Walter Benjamin's 1920 essay "Critique of Violence." In this essay, Benjamin differentiates between "law-preserving" and "lawmaking" violence, in the Jephcott translation, or in Bratton's terms, "constituted" and "constitutive" violence. For Bratton, architecture, in its tracings of power, makes use of "an exceptional violence that is at once constituent and constituted; it both makes use of extant built form to inscribe itself and, at the same time, is a projective affirmation of an alternate political geometry yet to come" (2015, 61). Further, Bratton goes on to argue that architecture does not simply participate in an economy of violence that comes initially from outside itself. Rather, architecture is, in itself, the fundamental root of such an economy. Bratton writes, "Put simply, architecture—as projection and composition, and simulation and dissimulation—is not only the image of the law (of its means and its constitution) but is the very substance of the field of forces that compose enforcement at all. Both substance and medium, architecture is the fundamental metaphor from which violence is derived, and as concrete body, the medium by which the postures of such forms are repeated, and by their repetition they arrange and position the 'force of law'" (Bratton 2015, 62).[3]

How, though, does architecture occupy this place of "fundamental metaphor"?[4] In the following paragraphs I will attempt to trace, at least provisionally, a plan of these mechanisms. A further question then appears, which I will attempt to address towards the end of this section: how is it that architecture can be at once both metaphor and concrete expression?[5]

In *Violence: Six Sideways Reflections* (2009), Slavoj Žižek, also starting from Benjamin's essay, presents a somewhat different (and useful) way of considering different shades of violence, which takes the form of an SOS call: Subjective, Objective, and Symbolic violence. Subjective violence is obvious enough: it is those acts of violence carried out by subjects—by individuals, groups, corporations, institutions, governments, and so on. These are, precisely, acts of violence for which perpetrators can be named: a bombing of a mosque, a death threat on social media, a punch thrown in the schoolyard. While these acts of violence are egregious, Žižek is more concerned with the second category of violence, Objective violence, violence for which no perpetrator can be named. Objective, or systemic violence, is the violence that simply seems to happen, not as the result of particular actions on the part of any actor. Systemic violence, such as the violence wrought by the inequality that arises from capital, is not consciously intended; it is rather the unfortunate byproduct of otherwise smoothly running and (apparently) positive mechanisms. Objective violence does not take the form of discrete acts; unlike the schoolyard punch, Objective violence is always in operation in the form of ongoing processes. As a result, Objective violence is normally invisible, except for moments when it erupts into acts: the pressures of capital on the garment industry in Bangladesh are not noticed until workers are killed in the collapse of a factory. Such acts are immediately labelled Subjective violence, a perpetrator is found, and the always-present systemic violence again hidden. It is my contention that this is exactly the situation in regard to architecture. Violence in architecture only becomes visible with the eruption of discrete violent acts, understood as exceptional acts and attributable to specific perpetrators; architecture itself comes away unscathed, its mantra of world-building for the common good maintained. The Objective violence of architecture, the violence on which architecture is founded and which it founds, remains obscured.

This founding violence of architecture, though, is not limited to the types of violence that could be described as systemic, as unfortunate (for some) by-products of a system; rather, there is always already a certain violence explicitly present in any architecture, a violence that is present precisely in the drawing of a line. Žižek identifies this form of violence as Symbolic violence, as violence that is part and parcel of the symbolic order, violence that arises from language itself (and, one suspects, to complete the SOS schema). As Žižek points out, following Hegel, the act of symbolization is in itself violent, in that it reduces the full being of a thing. For Lacan, it is the violent imposition of a Master-Signifier, beyond reason, that grounds any discourse; for Heidegger, it is the essencing power of language to produce a worldview. So, in Žižek's words, when Heidegger "deploys the notion of 'ontological violence' that pertains to every founding gesture of the new communal world of a people, accomplished by poets, thinkers, and statesmen, one should always bear in mind that this 'uncanny/demonic' dimension is ultimately that of language itself" (2009, 68). Poets, thinkers, and statesmen—and of course architects, whose very disciplinary role is to construct, in solid reality, the essence of a world, and by so doing, to reduce that world to that essence. And so we should not be too surprised to find that Žižek, at the conclusion of this chapter about the Symbolic violence of language, has to fall back into architecture in order to make his point: "The 'wall of language' which forever separates me from the abyss of another subject is simultaneously that which opens up and sustains this abyss—the very obstacle that separates me from the Beyond is what creates its mirage" (73).

Violence of the Line

As mentioned above, and as reinforced by Spivak, the drawing of a line, cutting of a furrow, or construction of a wall contains an essential violence. This violence can be seen on a number of levels. First of all, as anyone who has spent time on a construction site is aware, the construction of a wall requires undertaking significant violence to the earth and to its inhabitants. This is along the lines of what Žižek would call Subjective violence. I'm thinking here of the small creatures (plants, earthworms, etc.) that are killed, maimed, or displaced by the process, or whose habitats are disrupted, burrows destroyed, food sources eliminated, water flows diverted, habitats flooded or dried up, soils compacted by heavy machinery or churned and piled. Although the architectural and construction process at the end of the day seeks to eliminate all traces of this violence—the term used in the industry is to *make good*—such violence, to those who are affected by it, remains traumatic. Architecture, in this very specific sense, always comes into being through violence. Architecture, as a result, carries within itself a latent or potential violence, a memory or trace of the violence of its founding.

But this is just the most obvious violence in architecture. What really matters is its Symbolic violence—the violence of the line.

The latent violence of architecture is related to the concept of essencing, Heidegger's ontological violence. It is the violence of the claim, not only to the physical property of the land (although this is already violence enough), but also to its meaning. Architecture in this sense is a process of reification of ideologies, a reification of ground, a production of site. And this pure Symbolic violence, to make use of Žižek's term, is neither avoidable nor episodic: it is an unavoidable, unending, although (as Benjamin reminds us) normally unnoticed component of architecture, perhaps the most fundamental aspect of architecture. This essencing power of architecture, and our tendency to accept its essences in a state of distraction, is perhaps the most powerful and most dangerous aspect of architecture.[6]

In addition to these Subjective and Symbolic aspects of violence, the line, the wall, also participates in a form of Objective (systemic) violence. The systemic violence that I have in mind is the violence of the cut, of separation, of the division of a smooth plane of connectivity into A and B. This is of course exactly the point. The reason to build a wall is to separate two areas: the house from the wilderness, my bedroom from yours, the reading room from the gymnasium; in most cases this separation is both evidently good and desired. However, despite the results of the process, the apparent benefits of this mechanism of separation, there is always, coming along with it, a structuring violence. This is the violence first of all of the cut, of the wound in the earth, but also the *coup*: the cut, the trick, the coup d'état, the coup de grâce. The cut is already that which overturns. It is also the cut that separates, the machine, the guillotine, the *coup* that separates at the *cou*, the blade that castr—[7]

In *Countersexual Manifesto*, originally written in 1998, Paul B. Preciado, who later completed a PhD in architecture, recognizes the architectural structure of the binary, the function of the wall. Preciado wants to eliminate the wall entirely—or at least to render it ineffective, to neuter it. As Jack Halberstam puts it on the first page of his foreword to the English translation, "Assume the position, man the barricades—or is that non-binary the barricades, trans* the barricades—oh hell, just pull them all down" (2018, ix). Preciado's countersexuality looks to accomplish this neutralization of architecture first by demolishing naturalized practices of gender and sexuality, a process which amounts to a critical practice of revealing their naturalized status, of revealing them as architecture: "This 'history of technologies' shows that 'human nature' is an effect of the constant border negotiation not only between human and animal, body and machine, but also between organ and prosthesis, organic and plastic, alive and dead" (Preciado 2018, 22). Preciado continues, "Western human nature is a product of social technology that reproduces the equation 'nature=heterosexuality' on our bodies, architectures and discourses" (24). For Preciado, "the sex organs, as such, do not exist" (29). Those parts of our bodies that we recognize as sexual parts are named as such through a complex set of cultural practices and technologies. In this sense, penis, vagina, and clitoris are all already prosthetics, technological add-ons (strap-ons) or supplements to bodies that become bodies (become men and women) through this process. Preciado develops a set of countersexual practices, practices that counter the naturalization of penis and vagina through use of the anus (chosen for its ubiquity—everyone has one) and the dildo, chosen for its independence from any system of naturalization: "the dildo has no natural use. There is no orifice that is naturally reserved for it" (69). For Preciado, the dildo can be used to penetrate into and pry open the cracks and holes in the architecture of sexuality (to fuck architecture). The dildo shows up the falseness of phallogocentrism: "the dildo says, the penis is a fake phallus" (70). Preciado goes further though, claiming that the dildo-anus conjunction calls into question the very basis of the naturalized sexual contract: "First, it calls into question the idea that the male body is the natural context for the prosthesis/penis. Then, drastically, it threatens the supposition that the organic body is sexuality's proper context" (72).

Article 11 of Preciado's "Principles of Countersexual Society" states that "countersexual society shall establish the principles of a countersexual architecture. The conception and creation of countersexual spaces shall be based on the deconstruction and renegotiation of the border between the public and private spheres. This task implies the deconstruction of the house as a private space of heterocentric production and reproduction" (38). This is an intriguing provocation for architecture, but at the same time a bit disappointing. Preciado here does not carry the argument through to its projective conclusions. After all, why would we only consider "countersexual spaces"? Wouldn't it be more profitable to think of the prosthetic character of architecture within the economies of sexuality and countersexuality, to think of buildings not just as places in which sex happens, but as active participants in sex? Maybe we can sum up the program for a countersexual house like this: The Countersexual House consists of a dildo and an anus, and nothing more.

We shouldn't forget that the family scene takes place in Oedipus's palace, that is, the family scene takes place in the family scene, in the family home, in architecture. The cut of subjectification, the alienation of the Name-of-the-Father is the cut of architecture.

The first classificatory violence, according to Derrida, is the imposition of the violence of gender in the act of naming. But isn't this division, this splitting and bifurcation, the real fundamental violence of the line? The essential property of the line, of the wall, is this characteristic of classification through division, of dividing A from B, left from right, us from them, gay from straight, male from female. Walls both represent and create binary divisions of the world—this is, I would argue, their basic function. Walls, these same things that, as we have seen, are fundamental acts of violence, are also the things that structure our world into binaries. In other words, the fundamental binaries of which our conceptual world is fabricated, with which we ceaselessly work to ground ourselves in our groundless void, binaries as primary as me|you, in|out, false|true, good|evil, left|right, male|female, nature|artifice, human|inhuman are all architectural operations, derived from the violence of the drawing of the line.[8]

In *Transgender Architectonics: The Shape of Change in Modernist Space* (2015), Lucas Crawford constructs a critique of ways in which architectural discourse has considered questions of gender and of queerness, from the position of transgender thinking. Crawford notes that such discourse remains grounded in, and indeed serves to reify and bolster, the perceived binary divisions of male|female, masculine|feminine. For example, Crawford points out that the recurrent metaphor in trans discourse of the body as house—in the sense of not feeling at home in one's own skin—is itself based in a construction that is bound up in the heterosexual binary. Although I am hopeful that by this point in this discussion the role of the family, of heterosexuality, of the binary in the modern construction of the house will be obvious, Crawford quotes Mark Wigley to make his point: "Marriage is already spatial. It cannot be thought about outside the house that is its condition of possibility before its space" (2015, 27). Crawford goes on to show how discussions about gender within architectural discourse have tended to be caught up in received notions about the character of masculine or feminine; the masculine might be understood as transcendent, connected with structure, erect and rigorous, while the feminine is identified as transient, connected with notions of surface and decoration, curvilinear and fanciful. Crawford suggests, for example, that a more useful discussion of transience in architecture might be to relate it not to one specific gender, to one side of the wall that separates the binary terms, but rather to the instability of gender itself, to the unstable foundations of the dividing wall. Indeed, Crawford must suggest that all three elements of the binary system are in a constant state of trembling, shaking, questioning. Trans people therefore can't really be understood as crossing from one position of stable gender to another—indeed their crossing itself serves to destabilize these notions of gender—nor can they be seen to occupy some third, in-between or boundary state. *Trans* does not occupy the boundary, the wall, the barricades. *Trans* is a move towards tearing it down.[9]

Crawford presents a "blueprint" for a discussion of transing in architecture, which provocatively enough takes once again the form of five points. Although Crawford does not use this phrase, I'm tempted to call this list "Five Points for a Transed Architecture."

> 1. Transing is [*sic*] an aesthetic operation does not entail a move from one gender or materiality to another (or one gender to ambiguity) but instead to the very ubiquity of constant transformation for all.

2. Transing will be relocated from the life of the sovereign subject to the acts and collaborations that happen across bodies, buildings and milieus.
3. As such, transing will not inhere inside the private psychic life of the subject. It is not only outward-facing, but also traverses and undoes the demarcation of a body's inside and its outside. Transing is, then, an act of folding and refolding rather than containing.
4. Acts of transing, therefore, cannot be owned or claimed like identities. They are happenings or movements rather than objects or presences.
5. Transing reveals an aesthetics of the surface. (2015, 14)

Crawford applies his blueprint to a discussion of the work of Diller Scofidio + Renfro (DS+R)—indeed, this list is taken in part from Crawford's analysis of DS+R's Blur Building. I'm more interested, in the context of this book, to think about how it might apply to the Villa Savoye and its sisters, how transing is already embedded in the design of these very queer buildings. An aesthetics of constant transformation, of collaborations between buildings and bodies...a troubling of inside and outside, a breaking-down of the private, their afterlives as events rather than (or as well as) objects, and above all the aesthetics of the surface.

The wandering line of the vagabond is the vector line of movement that opposes the static line of structure. It is the rhizomatic line of Deleuze and Guattari (1987), the line of escape, moving against the architectural line of striation. For Le Corbusier ([1923] 2009), it is the line of the donkey trail, taking always the path of least resistance, which lies against the straight line and the right angle, the line of man. The vector line, of course, is always in opposition to the static line of architecture, which figures as a resistance to flow: the wall that stops the cavalry charge, the shell that looks to break down the wall. Le Corbusier's Villa Savoye, of course, incorporates the vector flow into the building, in the form of the circular drive of the car, the architectural promenade on the ramp. In this way, too, we might imagine Savoye is a queer building, upending the architectural concentration on the static, permanence, in favour of the movement of the vector. In fact, though, the reverse is true: the role of Savoye is not to break down the static line of architecture, but rather to incorporate into architecture the modern vector of the automobile, to imprison it. The young women on the ramp in Pierre Chenal and Le Corbusier's film *Architecture d'aujourd'hui* are not subverting the architecture of the building—rather, they are caught in it, spinning in place. Modern architecture sets out to domesticate the vector; Savoye's vectors—the curve of the entry, the spiral of the stair, the switchback of the ramp—are always suppressed, enclosed, contained by the static square of the floating box (Chenal and Le Corbusier 1930).[10]

The Kleptogenetic Law of Architecture

If the primary mechanism of the line in architecture is the cut, the division, the imposition of the architectural binary, the second mechanism is that of the noose, the surround, the enclosure, the line that turns back on itself, the deadly line of the garotte and also of the snare.[11] This is no less important a mechanism for being second topologically; in fact, it is probably the most consequential of all architectural operations. It is the wall of the medieval city, of the fortress, of the prison, but also the exterior wall of every house and, as such, it creates a particular and very special form of the architectural binary: inside|outside.[12] The enclosure marks not simply a division, but also more radically a separation, marking out and nominating groups, objects, people, land: us|them, mine|yours, in|out. This is the line of demarcation, the line of limits that produces, as an effect, individual entities, both objects and subjects. The line of enclosure brings with it all of the promises, claims, and effects of the simple line, but in addition turns the world into discrete pieces, into property, with all of the effects of that move that we have already discussed—and marks, as we have already seen, an initiating theft, the theft of property. The line of enclosure is fundamental to the idea of utopia, which needs to be separated radically from any contamination by the quotidian, by time, and also to Foucault's concept of heterotopias, which "always presuppose a system of opening and closing that both isolates them and makes them penetrable" (Foucault 1986, 7). This precise boundary of the heterotopia, perhaps like the event horizon of a black hole, protects the space inside the boundary, constituting a protected zone. The boundary allows for an abstraction, a suspension of rules, a simplification of the world; this simplification is what all forms of Foucault's heterotopia have in common, a simplification that allows for a distillation of meaning, an experimentation and proposition on limited terms. Heterotopias are not so much other spaces, other than normal reality, but rather at root are simplified, abstracted spaces. Perhaps the term *heterotopia* is not as useful as something like the admittedly less catchy *aplotopia*, which I take to signify simplified spaces. Indeed, I would claim that all enclosed spaces are in this sense heterotopic (or aplotopic) to a greater or lesser degree, in that they exclude, almost by definition, certain aspects of the world. The line of enclosure, then, is also and always a line of exclusion.

These two aspects of the line of enclosure, containment on the one hand and exclusion on the other, are also fundamental to the creation of the self and especially to the concept of the self-contained, autonomous, and unitary self. Timothy Morton (2018) has linked the creation of the self as an individual and stable entity to the emergence of property, and certainly the idea of family can be linked to the need to transmit property from one generation to the next. The wall of the house is the fundamental fiction of the self, and the fiction of the family is the noose we happily place around our necks. From the viewpoint of queer thinking, I would suggest that the formation of identity, including sexual identity, relies on and is a process of containment and exclusion, of the line of enclosure, of the wall. Sexual identity, hence, is always an architectural concept. As such it is both represented by and fabricated in the architectural scene in which, for most of us, our sexual lives first develop: the house.

It should be clear from my language in the last paragraph that my position is that this seemingly straightforward and clean distinction between interior and exterior is in fact anything but. Rather, I would argue that the role of architecture is to designate precisely what can be allowed to be inside and what must be considered outside, to deny any ambiguity, to stake a precise claim about order and then to reify that order. A brief diagrammatic analysis will help to explain my position.

As with our earlier discussion of the line-that-divides, we can start with a simple diagram of enclosure, say, a circle on a sheet of white paper. We can then apply the labels *Interior* and *Exterior*. This diagram is easy to read: on a pre-existing exterior, we have constructed an interior that is separate, protected, and defined. This interior might be of many types: a farm, a village, a fort, a city, a utopian project, a Foucauldian heterotopia. Whatever the structure of the constructed interior, several comments or observations can be made about the diagram at this stage. First, it will be recognized that the diagram has a third element, the line-that-encloses. The line, in this explicitly architectural diagram, must be recognized as an entity: as a thing, a boundary, a barrier. In simple architectural terms, this is a wall. We recognize that this wall is not in fact a perfect line, but rather a material object, stone, wood, or glass, with its own thickness and internal composition. A location in the middle of the wall itself, embedded in the material of its construction, is an uncertain position, neither inside nor outside. The materiality matters: is this a fence that one can see through, can people and animals climb it, can air and insects pass through its openings? Is this boundary a vast expanse of sea like that surrounding Thomas More's Utopia, or is it a totalizing dome, as in Peter Weir's 1998 film *The Truman Show*? Even that dome had a door through which Truman, in the end, managed to exit. What means of communication between exterior and interior exist in our diagram? Can tradespeople, farmers, and migrants enter? Can arrows and cannons, or information bulletins, find their way out? In other words, what transactions, what negotiations, are allowed between interior and exterior?[13]

Second, it will be objected that our reading of the pre-existing exterior is naïve. Of course, the exterior cannot exist as such prior to the construction of the interior. Both territories come into being simultaneously, with the construction of the boundary. Despite the appearance in this diagram (this is really just a question of scale of representation), interior and exterior are directly symmetric and interchangeable states. It may be a matter of situation: one subject's interior is another's exterior; the interior of a prison is removed from, that is, outside of, society. These two objections, first to the nature of the barrier and second to the assumed asymmetry, call into question the concepts of interior and exterior, suggesting that these categories are at best provisional, unstable, oscillatory.[14]

Architecture's role in this drama is first to constrain the choices, to set the scene, so to speak. As I will attempt to demonstrate, architecture goes beyond being a neutral or passive environment in which the advent of the subject takes place; rather, we need to think of architecture as an active participant in that advent and, as a result, an active component or constituent of that always-becoming subject-to-be. For Foucault, the subject is formed through the intervention of a succession of disciplinary sites—the home, the school, the barracks, the prison, the hospital, etc.—which are best read as active parties to and participants in that emerging subjectivity. Importantly, we don't need to actually experience these institutions as individuals in order for them to have their effect of subjectification; it is enough for them to simply exist as architectures. This expansion of the subject beyond the physical limits of the body is not limited of course to architecture: the wire constitutes the subjectivity of the funambulist; the mitre is the identity of the bishop. Again, these relationships go beyond the common-sense idea that we are shaped by our environments, that we are in part a "product" of the situation of our childhood, including its architecture, to suggest instead that that "we" includes, in a direct manner, that architecture. "We" are not in this model constituted of a pure interiority, "we" are not point-like, but rather, speaking topologically, take the form of regions with fuzzy edges, of always-moving and shifting clouds. We recognize that even within the *cogito* I am already an exteriority, the I that thinks is exterior to the I that describes that thinking, and both are exterior to some inaccessible core I; properly, *cogito, ergo sum* should be rendered in English as "I thinks, therefore it is." Within this framework, architecture must be seen as having a second, almost opposing role: through the mechanism of the enclosure, through the architectural invention of inside and outside, architecture produces the effective fiction of the interiority, stability, unity, and separateness of the self.

The Law of the Line, then, is the primordial law of separation and enclosure imposed on humans in all times and places. It is the Law of the Father as formulated by Freud, emphasized by Melanie Klein, reformulated by Lacan, raged against by Guy Hocquenghem. It is the law, necessary and eternal, that generates separation, separation in the first instance from the mother, producing as a corollary affect the possibility of the binary division of male and female (among other binaries), then, through the instigation of inside and outside, enables the production of an inside and outside, that is *of the self*. There is an all-too-clear teleology: without the Law of the Line, that is to say the Law of Architecture, we could not exist as subjects, we could not develop selves. We are interiors produced as and through architecture.

The Law of Architecture is all too convenient for those who enforce and police it, for those who formulate and promote it, for those who benefit from its prescriptions and proscriptions, its articles, provisions, regulations, and bylaws. Is it pure coincidence that the law, at least as formulated by Freud and reformulated by Lacan, guarantees heterosexuality, exiling all other sexualities to forms of perversion, of sickness, of outlaw, to the outside? Isn't it precisely heterosexuals—and particularly heterosexual men—who benefit from this law?

I want to reformulate the Law of Architecture in slightly different terms, perhaps thinking it through from the point of view of the outlaw. To start with, remember that the Law of Architecture is also the Law of Property (of Propriety): by drawing a line on the ground, we claim ownership over that piece of ground; by drawing a line around something, we claim ownership over that thing. This is a primal move: we draw a line around ourselves, we claim ownership of ourselves. The Law of Architecture is a staking of a claim, an insistence on ownership of land, of livestock, of cities, of men, workers, armies, and most importantly of women. And this reminds us, too, that the Law of Architecture is a law (perhaps like all laws) always founded in violence, and by three levels of violence in particular:

1. Domestication: this is not simple enclosure, but also a violence that changes the being enclosed, often genetically through breeding. Cattle and plants but also men and women—and mostly women.

2. Exile: violence to those who are forced outside.
3. Appropriation: the violence of theft, which is the violence of property.

The Law of Architecture guarantees ownership and control by the male, by the father: the ownership of women guarantees the owner access to sex, the ownership of his children guarantees his right to maintain ownership even after his death. The Law of Property, instituted through (male) violence, protects the property of the (male) lawmaker. The Law is first drawn by the first man—or at least the first to turn sporadic and petty thievery into the permanent expropriation of wealth. The Law is kleptogenetic, that is, born by theft, and architecture supports the law by serving as theatre, hiding the theft, creating an illusion of permanence, benevolence, naturalness.

The Law of Architecture establishes children, like their mother, as property of the father: the law produces Lineage. The child separates from the mother but never, even in adulthood, leaves the possession of the father. The child is required to increase the wealth and property of the father. Homosexual children place themselves outside the law even as they are placed outside the Law, deny Line and Lineage, refused to play the parts the Father has prescribed, threatening the continued existence of the law itself. This is a situation that cannot be accepted: there can be no outside to the law. Outside of the law is only exile and death.

But there can be no law without its outside.

To place oneself (and one's self) outside the law is to steal the property of the father. The homosexual's person, body, thoughts, desires, past and future, *are both stolen property and thief*; homosexuals steal their own selves, the selves that have only come into existence through the effects of the Law; and beyond that they steal future generations—steal, indeed, as Lee Edelman (2004) has claimed, the future itself in the sense of all the future generations of bodies that belong to the father; all homosexuals are murderers who kill their own children and their children's children. The homosexual is always and already, then, both thief and stolen goods. The male homosexual is worst of all: he betrays his brothers, that is, betrays the world of men, by calling its supporting Law into question. The homosexual troubles the very notion of the binary division, that most architectural of concepts, by calling into question the most basic of the binaries, the male|female separation.

The homosexual, then is anti-architecture, the non-entity that exposes the fabrication of the line of enclosure, that brings to light the theft that is immanent in the production of inside|outside, the theft that initiates society, the theft without which the world cannot continue in its current form. The homosexual is always the Thief in the House of Architecture: the dangerous non-force that threatens to expose the kleptogenesis of the world.

Chapter 2

The Cellular Self

It is too frequently omitted that, regardless of the efforts architects make to leave them behind, the said architects exist for that, for building walls. And walls, my word...are made to envelop a void.
—Jacques Lacan, *Talking to Brick Walls*

As Lacan points out, there is an immanent connection between architecture and voids: if architecture is in principle the construction of walls, the drawing of lines, those lines and those walls, in the end, have the purpose of forming voids—or, as Lacan (2017b) might suggest, those walls are formed around voids that pre-exist the construction of the walls or the drawing of the line. We might think of architecture, then, as the making-visible, or reification, of an always-already existing but invisible emptiness, an emptiness that is so important that we need to bring it into physical presence. Architecture in this case tames the void, brings it under our human control, cloaks its power. And of course, since it is Lacan who is making this statement, the implication is that there is more at stake in this discussion of the architectural void than the quotidian need for functional space, or even for the twentieth-century architectural preoccupation with the design of space (although, as Lacan again rightly points out, space in fact is the one thing that cannot actually be designed).[1]

In each age, it seems (although this is not a scientific survey) there is a characteristic void, a primary emptiness expressed through iconic architectural form, that serves to structure the remainder of its universe, a void that often must remain inaccessible to humans. This primary void, at least in the West, is normally expressed by the simplicity and perfection of its form. For the Egyptians this void was the tomb; for the Greeks it was the temple, or, more precisely, the ναός; in medieval Europe, it was the unknowable space of the divine represented on this earth by the light-filled interior of the cathedral. The Renaissance and the Enlightenment did away with the unknowable void in its entirety and replaced it by the point-at-infinity and the grid, the mechanisms by which humankind could see all; we could say that for the Renaissance, the primary void was visible not in a particular building or building type, or indeed in any building at all, but rather in the architectural drawing.[2]

2.1 Giovanni Battista Piranesi, *Le carceri d'invenzione*, title plate, 2nd ed., 1761. (Princeton University Art Museum)

For the modern world, the characteristic void was the prison cell.[3]

In order to make this case, I will start with a consideration of the two most important prison projects of the eighteenth century, two projects separated by roughly forty years that demonstrate a remarkable change in thinking about penal architecture. The first of these projects was the *Carceri d'invenzione*, a set of sixteen images of imaginary prisons drawn by Giovanni Battista Piranesi (1720–1778) and published in two primary editions, the first in 1750 and the second in 1761 (Figure 2.1). The *Carceri* present an impossible world of disorder, gigantic stone vaulted interiors leading away beyond vision, filled with giant machines of all kinds, stairways and bridges leading nowhere, smoke, darkness, and the tiny figures of lost human beings. This is a vision, perhaps, of madness: there is no order here, no discipline. The second of these prison projects, produced a generation later, presents a radically different proposition. I'm referring here to the famous Panopticon project of Jeremy Bentham (1747–1832), first designed in 1787 (by Bentham's brother, Samuel, 1757–1831) and a more famous version from 1791, with a design by the architect Willey Reveley (1760–1799; Figure 2.2). The Panopticon presents a scenario of perfect mechanistic order and clarity based on a geometrically simple plan. In essence, individual cells would be organized in a circular form, with a guard tower, providing a view into all the cells, located at the centre of the scheme. Prisoners, isolated in their cells, would be always susceptible to observation, but would never know if they are being watched, with the result, in Bentham's thinking, of always guaranteeing good behaviour. Although Bentham does not tell us this directly, one major aspect of bad behaviour that the Panopticon is defined to prevent is just that of the "solitary vice," masturbation. For Bentham, masturbation was among the most intolerable of undisciplined behaviours; masturbation, again for Bentham, was a considerably more dangerous problem than sodomy.

In *Discipline and Punish*, Michel Foucault provides a masterly analysis of the workings of the Panopticon as a diagram of power, an analysis that has positioned the Panopticon, although admittedly without its architectural trappings and circular plan form, as central to

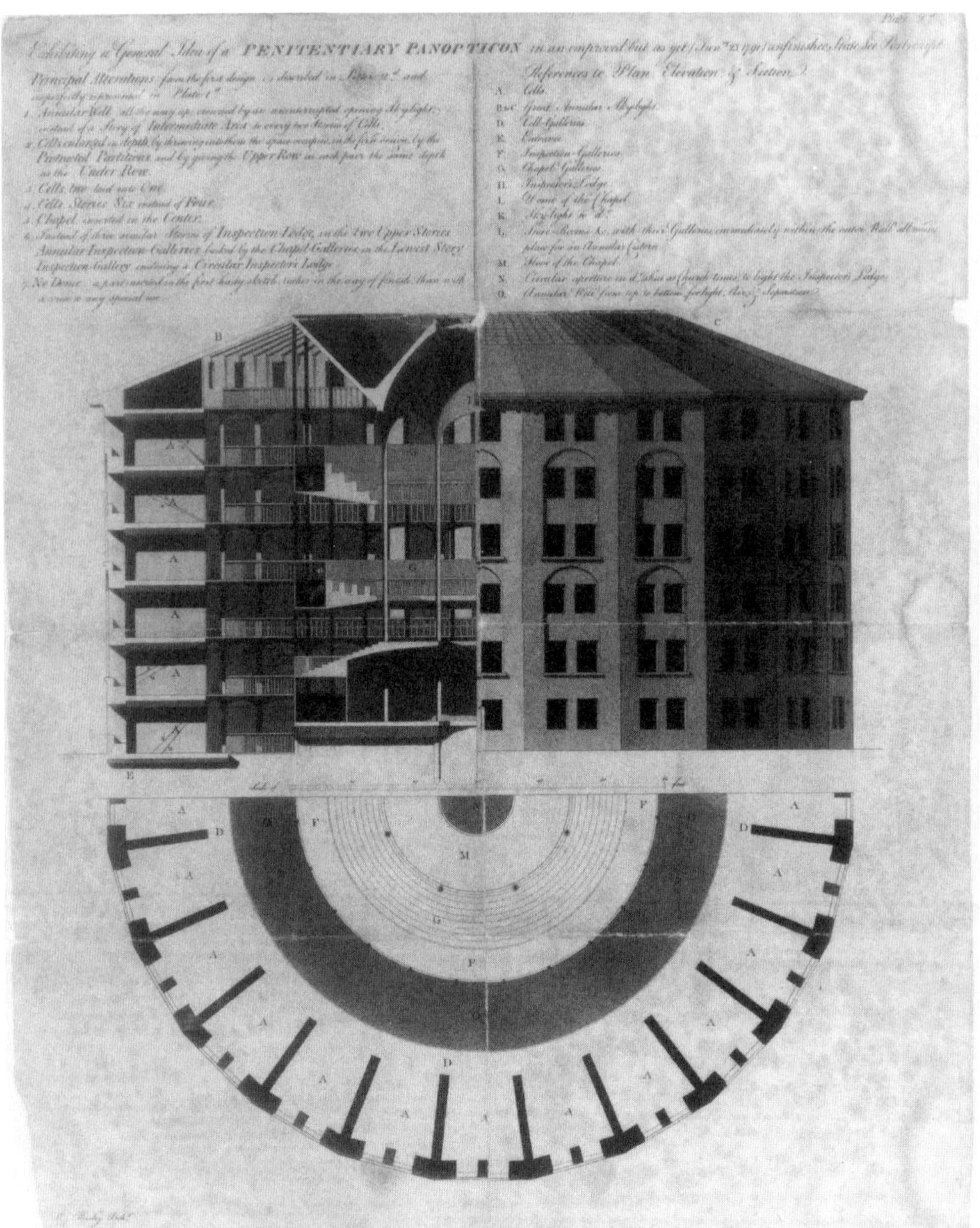

2.2 Jeremy Bentham and Willey Reveley, Panopticon, plan and section, 1791. (The Bentham Papers, UCL Library Services, Special Collections)

our contemporary world. It's not my intention here to enter into this well-trodden argument, but rather just to make a quick observation, also not lost on Foucault. While Piranesi's *Carceri* show us a world in which the individual is lost in a space that is gigantic beyond comprehension, the Panopticon focuses all attention on each particular inmate through the simple mechanism of the cell. As Foucault puts it, "the crowd, a compact mass, a locus of multiple exchanges, individualities merging together, a collective effect, is abolished and replaced by...a multiplicity that can be numbered and supervised" (1979, 201). Accustomed as we are today to the image of the cell as the normal and expected scene of the prison, with bare concrete walls and a small, barred window high up out of reach, it is difficult to recognize how innovative, if not radical, this move was. Indeed, I would like to discuss some innovations in the Panopticon that are characteristic of modernity in architecture, and which together provide a strong case for recognizing this project as the first truly modern architectural project. First, the Panopticon overtly recognizes the building as a mechanism; traditional architectural considerations of symbolic effect and composition are either ignored or subordinate to the pedagogic and functional role of the prison. The Panopticon is not round in order to express a symbolic meaning (we can contrast this with Étienne-Louis Boullée's Cenotaph to Newton, of 1784, for example), but simply because this is the most effective geometry for the desired optical effects. Of course, this situation can also be seen in earlier buildings, such as the Southwark playhouses of the sixteenth century, buildings that also express a certain proto-modernity as a result.

In addition, the Panopticon, as Foucault mentions in the citation above, clearly recognizes the importance of the individual subject. Not only has "the crowd...been replaced by a multiplicity," already a hugely significant move, but each element in that multiplicity is understood as manipulable. Each prisoner can be individually reformed through the twin techniques of inspection and introspection, and each cell in the Panopticon provides an interior that figures and configures the interiority of the prisoner it contains. The Panopticon thus prefigures a whole series of developments critical to modernity, including the rise of the individual, an awareness of the integrity and separability of the self, and the construction of a psychological interiority as well as mechanisms for seeing into that interiority, for mapping and where necessary correcting it, through the work of Freud and others.

Finally, the Panopticon establishes a new for methodology for architectural production, a methodology that developed into a primary modus operandi for modern architecture: *cellular repetition.* Pier Vittorio Aureli and Maria Shéhérazade Giudici (2016) have shown that around the middle of the eighteenth century, architectural practice saw a shift in its planning techniques from subdivision (or what I would call *disposition*) to *composition*. Disposition, at its root, involves separating various functional and symbolic areas of a building program and then placing them in some relationship on a site, while composition is grounded in a concern for the geometrical relationships between spaces and their ability to generate an overall pleasing building form. Composition perhaps reaches its high point as architectural orthodoxy through the work of the architect and pedagogue Jean-Nicolas-Louis Durand (1760–1834), and dominated the work known in the nineteenth and twentieth centuries as Beaux-Arts architecture. Cellular repetition, on the other hand, became a dominant logic in early twentieth-century modernism, such as in the modernist urban and housing schemes of Ludwig Hilberseimer (1885–1967) and Le Corbusier (1887–1965), in which the building, or the city, is produced through a seemingly endless reproduction of identical or near-identical units at multiple scales: rooms, apartments, houses, apartment buildings, neighbourhoods.

Although Jeremy Bentham made use of the Panopticon to further ideas of prison reform, it was already clear to the Benthams that the system could also be usefully applied to other areas of concern. Samuel Bentham, in fact, designed a school of arts for the training of craftsmen in St. Petersburg using panoptical principles in 1807 (Steadman 2007). Foucault makes much of the general deployability of power relationships inherent in the panoptic diagram as a founding principle of the modern disciplinary society, and of course I'm making the same claim for the notion of cellular repetition (Foucault 1979). However, before moving on to look more closely at the development of this mode of production in the broader world, it is important to stress the obvious: that the modern notion of cellular repetition found its first use in prison design. This is not an entirely new reading of developments in nineteenth-century prison architecture; Robin Evans made the case in his masterful 1982 work about early modern British prison design, *The Fabrication of Virtue: English Prison Architecture, 1750–1840*, that now common architectural technologies such as ventilation, sound control, and plumbing, as well as an entire technical apparatus and attitude that went with these technologies, found their first use in the development of prisons, reaching an apogee at Pentonville Prison (1840–42) in London, designed by Captain Joshua Jebb. My argument here takes Evans's position one step farther: while the methodology of cellular repetition, along with its necessary technologies, could be (and indeed was) put to use in service of a broad range of architectural and urban problems, it is my hypothesis that it could never entirely shake off its history: traces, uncanny traces, even *queer* traces, of its origins in penal architecture would remain.

The Queerness of the Prison

In contemporary culture—and I think it was the same in modern culture—we tend to think of prisons as queer. This is certainly true for the non-sexual meanings of that word: to those of us who live our lives "on the outside," prisons are strange, bizarre, unfathomable spaces, spaces that we don't understand (or if we do it is only through film and television depictions), spaces that operate under inscrutable and unknowable systems both official and unofficial, rules that are perhaps adapted from but nevertheless foreign to those by which we live our lives (or are the ways we live our lives adapted from the rules of the prison?), socialities that are beyond our ken. In this sense the prison seems to us like Piranesi's etchings—a great space of unknowable dimensions in which we, as people, are lost. So the prison is to us doubly strange: strange in its abnormal order, its rigid sense of time (see, for example, Michael Hardt's 1997 essay "Prison Time") and strange in its seeming anarchy, its lack of social order, its lawlessness. To put this even more simply, the prison is strange (queer) because for us in the normal world it is *other*: it is a world apart, a heterotopia in Foucauldian terms, a rigorous inside that is a rigorous outside.

On the other hand, if the modern prison can be considered queer in the sense of being a space of the other, the prison in the modern world is also a queer space from a sexual point of view. For evidence of this status, we can cite the continued presence of the prison in the gay (and lesbian) erotic imaginary, the number of queer pornographic movies set in prisons, the number of gay bars and sex clubs with names such as "Cell Block" and so on. Mainstream media representations of prisons invariably have at least one queer storyline; we need only think of the unusual number of lesbian or trans characters in *Orange Is the New Black* or the Australian comedy *Rake* in which the show's lead, Cleaver Green, is required to rebuff, over and over, the amorous attention of a cellmate. Or the words of recently released (bottom) Mickey Milkovich, on the American TV comedy *Shameless*, "If I wanted to fuck guys, I would have stayed in prison." Or...well, it seems to me that we would be hard pressed to find a prison episode in popular media that did not include some reference to gay sex, even as simple as "he's too cute for prison" or "make sure you don't drop the soap."

Why is it that the prison plays such an important role in the queer imaginary? Part of this is of course the homosocial construction of the prison system (itself a construction of modern penal practice), but it must be pointed out that other homosocial situations (barracks, sports teams, gyms, boarding schools) do not have quite the same intensity of queerness as the prison. In the case of the prison, these two aspects of queerness reinforce each other. The absolute otherness of the prison (and of the prisoner) produces its association with that most absolute of possible others: the homosexual. The absolute nature of power relationships within the machine of the prison mirrors the popular image of the violence of gay male anal intercourse. The penetration of the gaze of the director of the Panopticon is as much a violation of the prisoner's being as any penetration of the body.

Regina Kunzel, in her 2008 discussion of nineteenth-century American prisons, has pointed out the ways in which homosexual relations (although the term itself is anachronistic) were a central defining feature of these early prisons. As Kunzel puts it, "Rather than peripheral to the workings of the early carceral regime or the regrettable byproduct of sex-segregated incarceration, same-sex sex was constitutive of the modern prison, informing the preoccupations of its designers, determining its modes of secrecy, and structuring the intimate culture that would come to take shape there" (2008, 16).

As Kunzel constructs the narrative, the development of single-sex institutions was at least in part a reaction to the rampant sexual activity, consensual and otherwise, as well as attendant problems such as drunkenness and prostitution, in existing prisons housing mixed-sex populations (2008, 21). It would not be hard to conjecture that one argument for the cellular system, although probably most often unspoken, was to eliminate the possibility of same-sex carnal activity. The new prisons constructed at the beginning of the nineteenth century, most famously Auburn Prison in Auburn, near Syracuse, New York, and Eastern State Penitentiary, originally named Cherry Hill State Prison, in Philadelphia, Pennsylvania, were designed not simply to punish inmates, or to deprive them of liberty, but also to reform criminals and prepare them for a return to society. The fundamental methods used to attain this goal were an insistence on an extreme and regular discipline, useful work, and isolation of inmates from each other and often from all human company. Isolation, sometimes carried to extremes (prisoners at Auburn were not allowed to look at each other, even when eating beside each other), had a dual stated goal: to allow the inmate ample time with his thoughts, to consider his actions and to repent; and to prevent various forms of corrupting influence among diverse prison populations. One of these corruptions, although often left unspoken, was that of same-sex sex.

Cellular Growth

Of course, neither Piranesi's *Carceri* nor Bentham's Panopticon were built projects. However, the transformation from prisons designed to hold many prisoners in the same space to those designed around solitary isolation appears to have taken place almost immediately following the publication of Bentham's work, at least in Western Europe and North America. Images of British prisons from the seventeenth and eighteenth centuries invariably show crowded scenes, often with the prisoner's wife and children accompanying him to incarceration. A look at the plans of London's notorious Newgate Prison, rebuilt in 1790, shows wards instead of individual cells, gathered around three courtyards: one for male felons, one for female felons, and one for debtors. Newgate was famous as an example of "terror architecture," a form of "architecture parlante" that was expected to act as a deterrent by the very form, material, and decoration of the prison. Just a year later, in 1791, Sir Robert Adam (1728–1792) developed the plan for Edinburgh's Bridewell Prison based explicitly on the Panopticon (although it is not clear to what extent it would have functioned optically as a panopticon), incorporating individual cells arranged in a semicircle (for more information, see Evans 1982).

The 1820s saw the construction of several important prisons, especially in the United States, all designed on the cellular model. The North Wing of Auburn Prison incorporated individual cell blocks arranged back-to-back within a larger volume (Figure 2.3). Eastern State Penitentiary, which opened in Philadelphia in 1829, contained a series of cell blocks radiating out from a central hall, in a modified version of the Panopticon (guards had panoptic vision of each cell block, but not of each individual cell; Figure 2.4). Eastern State and Auburn became famous within circles of prison reformers, theorists, and builders for the Philadelphia and Auburn systems, respectively, which elaborated operationally on the cellular system: at Auburn, inmates worked, exercised, and ate in common areas, albeit in enforced silence, while at Eastern State prisoners were confined to their cells at all times, being provided with the required facilities to carry out work in their cells. Both systems originated from the theoretical position that in order to reform or improve convicts, solitude was necessary. The prisoner must be allowed to reflect on their crime and to obtain a state of penitence: hence the invention of the term *penitentiary*. According to Gustave de Beaumont and Alexis de Tocqueville, both New York State and Pennsylvania discovered that solitude without work was not

2.3 Stereoscopic image showing an interior view along the prison cells of Auburn Prison, a maximum-security state prison in Auburn, New York, ca. 1895. (Photo by Archive Photos / Getty Images)

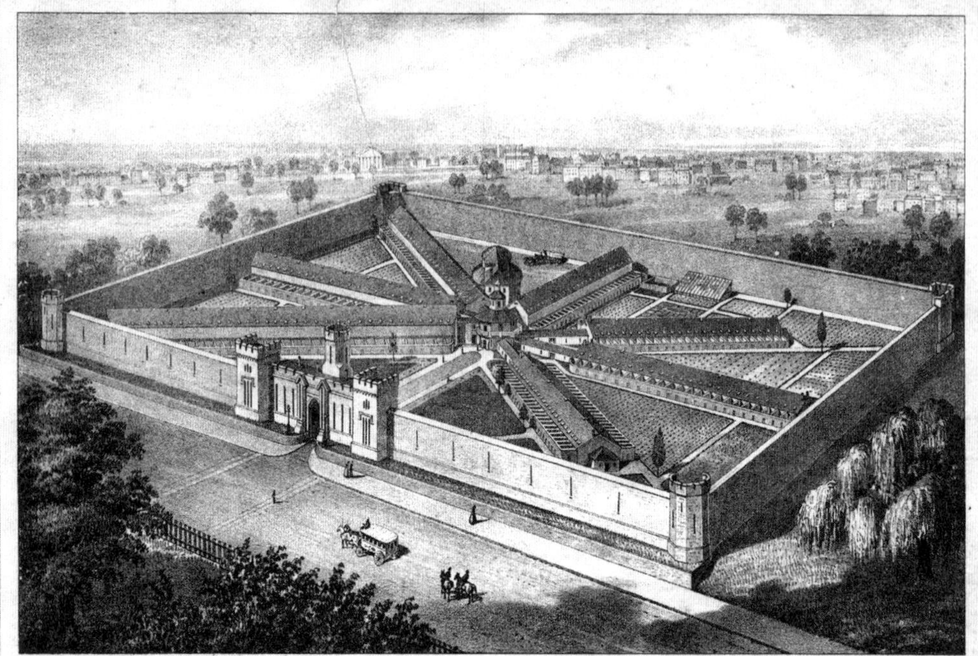

2.4 Samuel Cowperthwaite, *The State Penitentiary, for the Eastern District of Pennsylvania*, 1855. P.S. Duval & Company Lithography, Philadelphia. Photograph. Copyright holder: Richard Vaux. (World Digital Library; Library of Congress, https://www.loc.gov/item/2021670376/)

effective in producing penitence, but rather "this absolute solitude, if nothing interrupts it, is beyond the strength of man: it destroys the criminal without intermission and without pity; it does not reform, it kills" (1833, 41). Both the Philadelphia and Auburn systems arose, as a result, as means to interrupt that solitary introspection with the useful activity of work. The debate between the two systems was rather intense; according to commentators of the period, the Auburn system was understood to be more humane but more difficult (and expensive) to operate; discipline, and silence, needed to be enforced by guards, often with the use of a whip. The Philadelphia system, on the other hand, was seen to be more *terrible*, although easier to manage (the walls did all the work), but much more expensive to build as cells needed to be larger in order to incorporate space for work.

Modern Prisons in France

The situation in France showed a similar development. We can take, for example, the Bagne de Brest (Brest Prison), a massive prison built in 1748 to house galley prisoners. The *bagne* was designed primarily as a very long and large open space in which prisoners were held in common (chained at night, by the ankle, to a long bar). Contemporary interior images of the *bagne* are reminiscent of the *Carceri*, although not as extreme.

The first generation after the French Revolution saw a number of confiscated religious establishments turned into prisons, including the Abbaye de Clairvaux (Clairvaux Abbey), which became the Maison Centrale de Clairvaux (Clairvaux Prison) in 1808; the Couvent des Ursulines de Poissy (Convent of Poissy), reopened as the Maison Centrale de Poissy (Poissy Prison) in 1817, and the Abbaye Royale de Fontevraud (Fontevraud Abbey), redeveloped as the Maison Centrale de Fontevraud (Fontevraud Prison). This last was situated within an existing Royal Abbey (the tombs of Plantagenet kings and queens of France are located here) whose founding dates back to the eleventh century, appropriated at the time of the Revolution, and reinvented as a prison by Napoleon, its spaces adapted in the early nineteenth century for correctional use, opening its doors in 1814 (Prigent 2017).[4]

Despite the early date of the opening of Fontevraud, and despite the lack of a clear formal diagram resulting from the adaptation of the abbey for the purposes of incarceration (although it has been pointed out by numerous authors that the transformation from abbey to prison merely exchanged one voluntary form of incarceration for another involuntary form), it would be a mistake to imagine that Fontevraud was not connected to or indeed an important part of the development of the modern radically instrumentalized carceral regime we have been discussing. The initial conversion works were overseen by the engineer Charles-Marie Normand (1766–1838), of the Ponts et Chaussées, and included, among other things, the establishment of a ring road and a unifying square plan for the ensemble (Mathurin and Stalder 2016). A comparison of the plans of the site before and after the establishment of the ring road and the square plan show clearly that this was not an obvious or straightforward addition to the site, but rather the direct imposition of geometric will (Figures 2.5 and 2.6). Tantalizingly, in 1821 "the architect Durand" carried out work on the abbey church, adding several floors of dormitories and workshops into the volume (Bertreux 2016). It is tempting to conclude that this is none other than Jean-Nicolas-Louis Durand, architect and—more importantly—very influential teacher and writer on architecture in the first decades of the nineteenth century, and whose teachings developed the grid as a primary tool for the instrumentalization of architecture and its submission to an effectively neutral and mechanistic geometry (we have already encountered Durand in relation to composition some pages back). Although we have no proof for this identification, and although Durand is a relatively common surname in the area around Fontevraud, it is not unreasonable to consider that the work carried out by Normand already shows distinct traces of the influence of J.N.L. Durand. A comparison of the plan of Fontevraud as developed by Normand with plate XIX of Durand's *Précis of the Lectures on Architecture*, which illustrates a design for a prison in a large city, engraved by Charles-Pierre-Joseph Normand, shows an unmistakable and immediate family relationship (Durand 2000; Figure 2.7). A review of the plan clarifies that the dominant design methodology at work here is that of composition, unifying the disposition of the religious complex. However, although there were cells in the prison, many prisoners were housed in *celles à poule*, latticework "chicken cages," and others slept in large dormitories; the cell, and cellular repetition, were not the dominant design strategies at work.[5]

The cellular system arrived in France some twenty years after the opening of Fontevraud Prison as a result of two delegations sent to the United States to review the new penitentiaries. The first of these was the famous journey by Alexis de Tocqueville (1805–1859) and Gustave de Beaumont (1802–1866), which resulted in Tocqueville's best-known work, *Democracy in America* (1835). Although the tour of prisons that was the official purpose of the journey seems to have been a bit of a pretense for Beaumont and Tocqueville, their report *On the Penitentiary System in the United States and Its Application in France* (1833), which recommended the establishment of a penitentiary system in France, was well received and proved highly influential. As a result, in 1836 the Département de l'interieur (Ministry of the Interior) commissioned the jurist Frédéric-Auguste Demetz (1796–1873) to carry out a second follow-up mission to the United States in which he was charged with verifying the findings of Beaumont and Tocqueville and evaluating the longer-term effectiveness of what were, at the time of the earlier visit, quite new systems, as well as more carefully evaluating the financial implications of the two American systems (Blouet and Demetz 1837). The architect Guillaume-Abel Blouet (1795–1853), who had recently completed supervising the construction of the Arc de Triomphe, accompanied Demetz to provide financial information and technical drawings of the prisons.

Blouet was already a well-known architect at that time, although his story is not so well known today. Blouet attended the École des Beaux-Arts, in the studio of Pierre-Jules Delespine (1756–1825), from 1814 to 1821, when he was awarded the Grand Prix de Rome (Middleton 1993); Henri Labrouste (1801–1875), whose career is today much better known, placed second in this competition. In Rome, Blouet focused on archaeological work (notably on painstaking drawings of the Baths of Caracalla), and this work was followed by his appointment to an archaeological expedition to Greece; on his return to Paris was appointed to the post of Architect of the Arc de Triomphe.

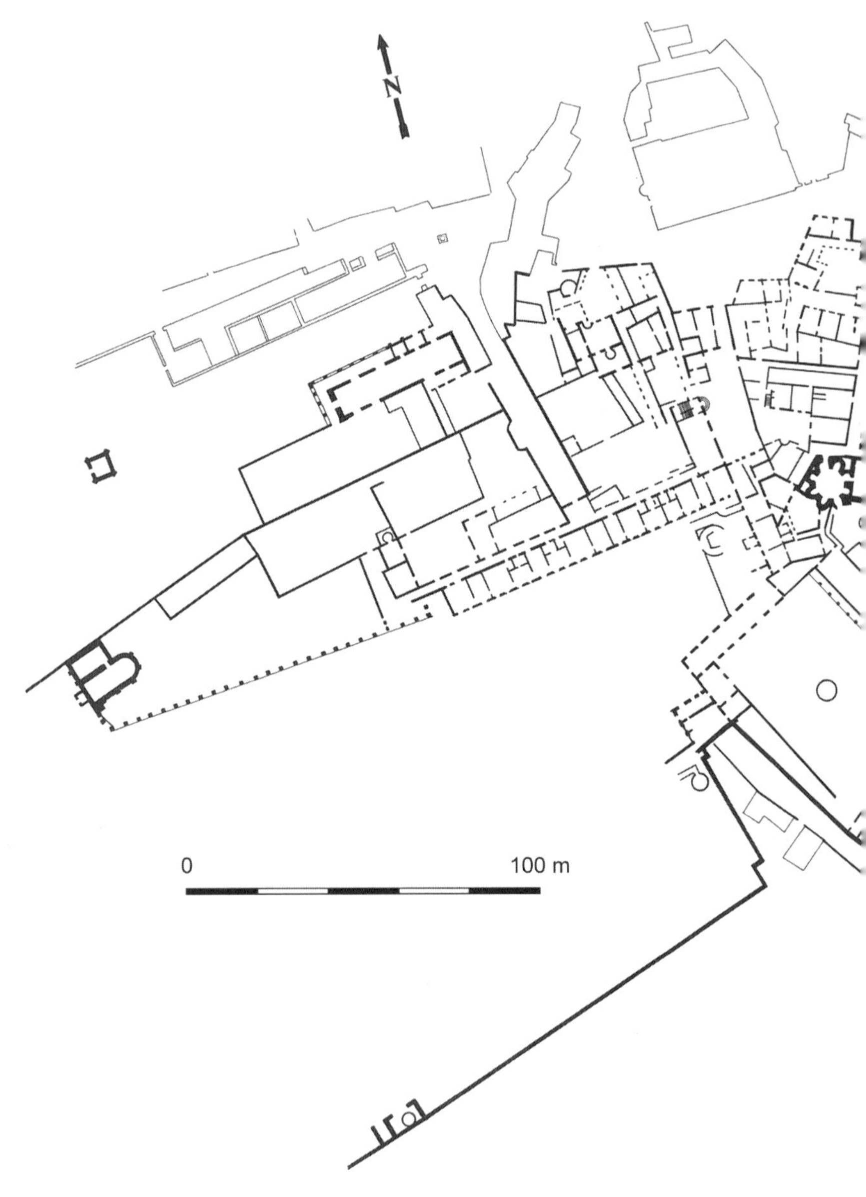

2.5 Fontevraud in the middle of the eighteenth century.
(© Conservation du patrimoine. Département de Maine-et-Loire)

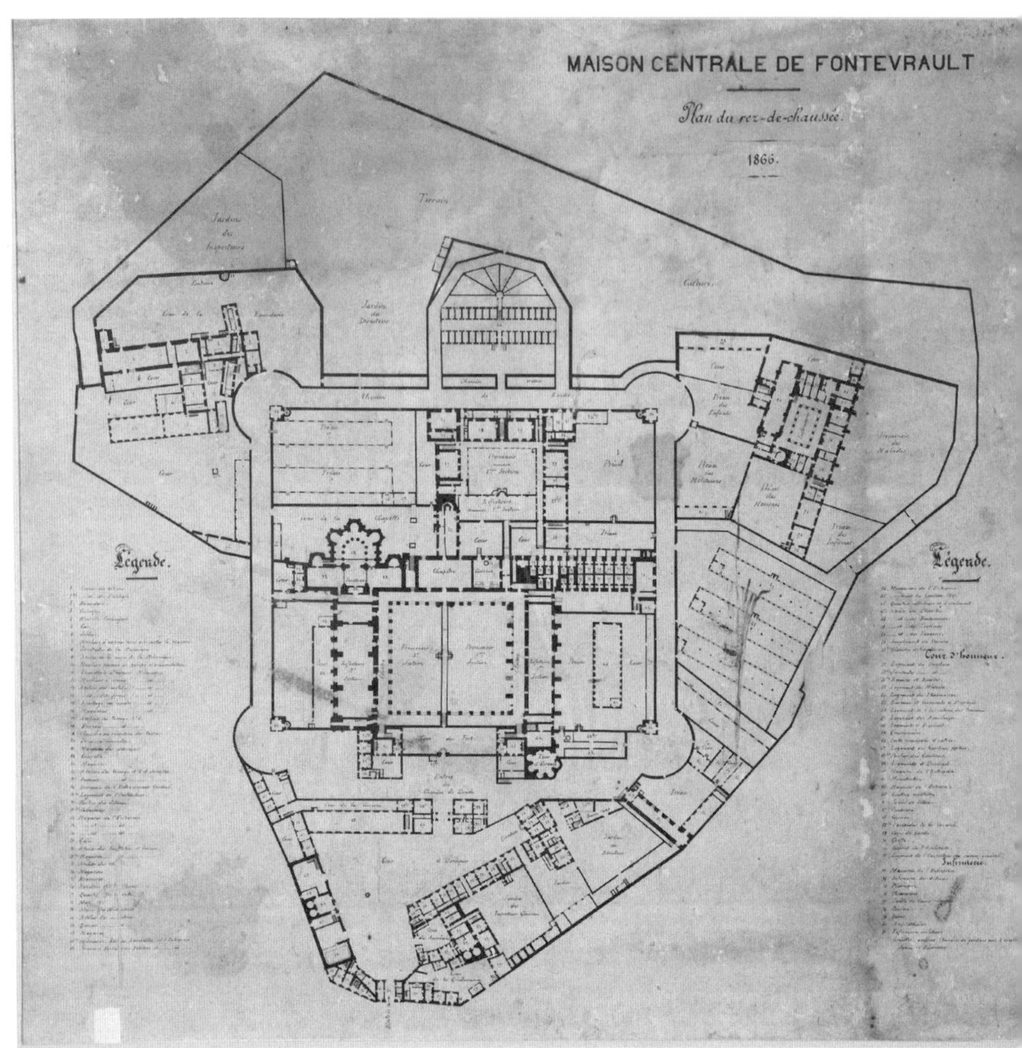

2.6 Ground floor, Fontevraud Prison, 1861. (© Région Pays de la Loire - Inventaire Général. Patrice Giraud (reproduction), 2012)

As Robin Middleton (1993) notes, there is little in Blouet's career to this point to suggest why he was chosen for the journey to the United States, or, for that matter, why he would accept it. In any case, Blouet's subsequent work, including his report on returning from America, bears little resemblance to his earlier work; somehow, he had become a radical humanitarian, interested not in classical form and statuary but in a utilitarian theory of architecture. This turn of positions is set out clearly on the second page of his report of 1837:

> Ils [the Americans] ont pensé, avec raison ce me semble, que, dans les édifices de ce genre, la première condition à remplir par l'architecte, c'est de pourvoir au besoin réel. Le strict nécessaire donne la forme, d'où il résulte que cette forme, qui n'est pas arbitraire, est toujours la meilleure et la moins dispendieuse. Point d'inutilités décoratives ni de luxe architectural, et je suis convaincu que, tout en satisfaisant à la rigoureuse économie, l'art trouvera toujours sa part, et qu'il en résultera pour l'édifice le caractère le mieux approprié et l'expression la plus convenable. (Blouet and Demetz 1837, 4)
>
> They [the Americans] thought, rightly it seems to me, that, in buildings of this type, the first condition to be fulfilled by the architect is to provide for real needs. Form follows from strict necessity, from which it follows that this form, which is not arbitrary, is always the best and the least expensive. There is no useless decoration or architectural luxury, and I am convinced that, in satisfying rigorous economy, art will always find its part, resulting in the building having the most appropriate character and most suitable expression. (Author's translation)

Blouet is here speaking specifically of the design of prisons. However, it is easy to see that this concept can be extended to become a theory of architectural production as a whole, and indeed, as Middleton points out, Blouet sought in later writing to interpret even classical Greek architecture as agreeing with this dictum. Of course, there is a remarkable resonance between this statement and architectural thinking of

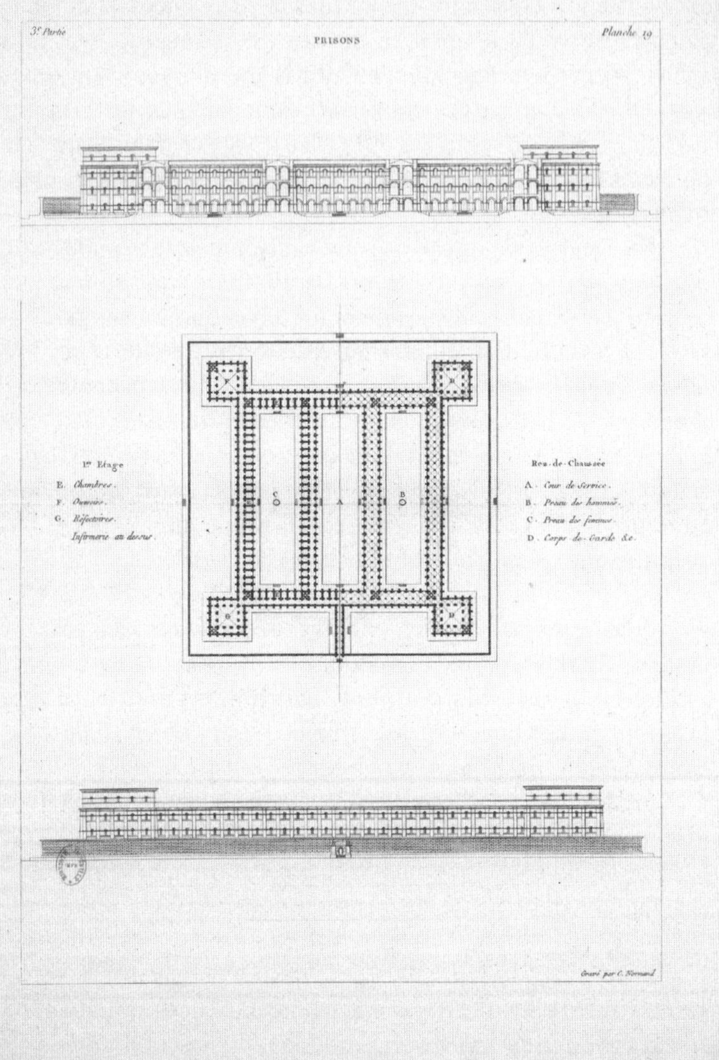

2.7 Jean-Nicolas-Louis Durand, *Précis des leçons d'architecture données à l'École polytechnique*, Plate XIX, Prisons, 1825. (Bibliothèque Nationale de France.)

a hundred years later—one could, for example, sum up Blouet's statement as "form follows function." One could, it seems, count Blouet as one of the first of the truly modern architectural thinkers, or at least a thinker whose work prefigured the thinking of the modern masters of the twentieth century. Or, from another perspective, and in keeping with Foucault's notion of the carceral society, we can note the degree to which the lessons of prison design form the theoretical basis for high modern architecture.

Even before the trip to America, Blouet held a position of some authority and influence within architectural circles in France. In 1825 Delespine passed away, and Blouet took over as *patron* of his studio at the École des Beaux-Arts, remaining in this position until his death in 1853. In 1846 he was appointed Professeur de Théorie de l'Architecture at the École, and the next year published a revised and "completed" version of Jean-Baptiste Rondelet's *Traité théorique et pratique de l'art de bâtir* (Blouet and Rondelet 1847), among the most important architecture texts of the early nineteenth century, often used in complement with Durand's *Précis*.

As a result, Blouet (and his ideas about a pragmatic architecture) would have had significant influence on a generation of French architects. In the world of prison architecture, he had equal influence, consolidating his belief in the power of the cellular system and in particular of the Philadelphia system. In 1839 he was appointed Inspecteur General des Edifices Penitentiaries, a post he held until 1848; as part of this role he issued a series of directives in the form of circulars to local authorities on the design of prisons. In 1841 he published *Instruction et programme pour la construction des maisons d'arrêt et de justice: Atlas de plans de prisons cellulaires,* along with Harou-Romain (Nicolas-Philippe Harou) and Hector Horeau, which he followed up in 1843 with *Projet de prison cellulaire pour 585 condamnés précédé d'observations sur le Système pénitentiaire*. Here again we see Blouet's preference for the Philadelphia system of total isolation, in what we have to read as a powerful claim for the disciplinary potential of architecture: "A Philadelphie, les murs sont la punition du crime; la cellule met le détenu en présence de lui-même; il est forcé d'entendre sa conscience; il veut éloigner

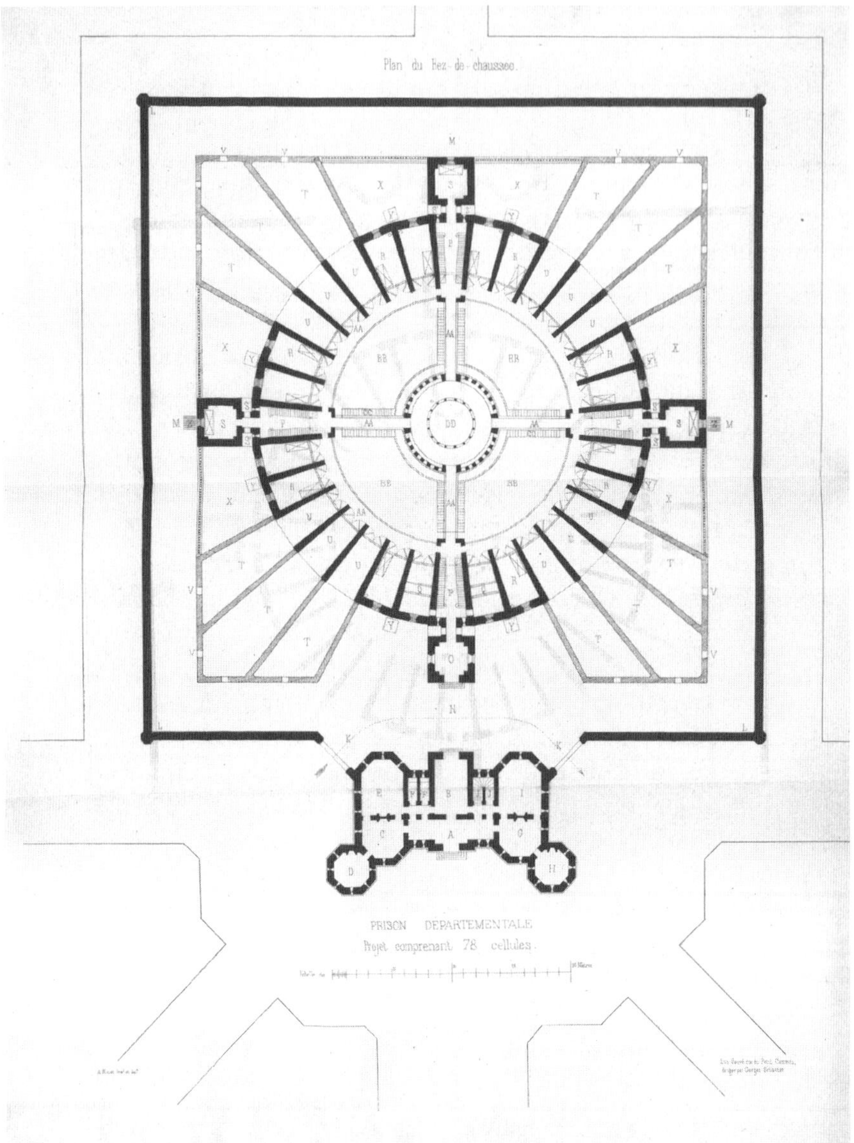

2.8 Guillaume-Abel Blouet, Harou-Romain, and Hector Horeau, *Instruction et programme pour la construction des maisons d'arrêt et de justice: Atlas de plans de prisons cellulaires*. Prison Departmentale, 1841. (Brown University Library)

ce persécuteur acharné; le travail que ses mains n'avaient peut-être jamais connu s'offre à lui moins redoutable; c'est un ennemi dont il va se servir pour en combattre un autre qui lui semble plus à craindre" (Blouet 1843, 9). (At Philadelphia, walls are the punishment for crime. The cell puts the inmate in the presence of himself. He is forced to listen to his conscience. He wants to remove this fierce persecutor; the work that his hands had perhaps never known is presented to him less formidable, as an enemy that he will use to fight another who seems to him to be more fearful.) At the same time, we see Blouet discussing the prison in terms that are remarkably similar to those that the so-called modern masters would use in the following century, with a careful attention to the health of occupants in terms of heating, ventilation, and plumbing. For example, "Les cellules, rangées sur trois étages, seraient de capacité suffisante pour les besoins des détenus, pourvues de tous les accessoires nécessaires à leur habitation et disposées dans tous leurs détails de manière à être chauffées, ventilées et parfaitement saines" (Blouet 1843, 52). (The cells, organized on three floors, would be large enough for the needs of the prisoners, provided with all the furnishings needed for their inhabitation, and arranged in all their details so as to be heated, ventilated and perfectly healthy. [Author's translations]) It would be easy to imagine Le Corbusier speaking in precisely these terms about one of his urban housing projects, with their focus on light, air, and sanitation.

Cell and Self

By the middle of the nineteenth century, a cellular typology had come to dominate penal architecture across the continent of Europe as well as in North and South America and Australia. In the popular imagination, the cell is today an inevitable part of the prison story, and images of eighteenth-century prisons such as the *Carceri* are difficult for us to even recognize as prisons. Of course, the ultimate solitude of the Philadelphia system is today nothing more than a myth, as contemporary prisons, at least in the Western world, have moved towards systems closer to that of Auburn (although without the enforced silence) or even to dormitory-style sleeping arrangements; in the United States, this is very clearly the result of the current regime of mass incarceration.

It should be clear, though, that the movement towards cellular systems was not confined to the work of prisons. By the late nineteenth or early twentieth centuries, we can discern a number of spatial developments that have taken on aspects of the cell: the bedroom, the office, the cubicle, the treatment room, the dorm room, the suburban house, the apartment, the hotel. Of course, most or all of these spaces existed prior to the nineteenth century, but at this time (and partly because of an expanded interest in the *interior* as a design category connected to the rise of a bourgeois class) each developed a certain codification and specificity that in many cases mirrored, with some temporal delay, the transition from the prison ward (a space for the common use of a relatively undifferentiated collection) to the penitentiary cell (a space that recognizes and makes use of the specifics of the individual). These spaces share a number of formal and cultural attributes that arguably first arose, as a coherent architectonic system, with the prison cell.

First, and as already discussed, these voids are designed for the individual—or, occasionally, for the *individual* couple or the *individual* (that is, nuclear) family—in contrast to earlier spaces (wards or dormitories) designed for a common experience, often among strangers. Prior to the mid-nineteenth century it was not uncommon for beds to be shared between strangers in inns, for example; consider the opening of *Moby Dick*, in which the narrator Ishmael shares a bed with the Polynesian Queequeg, an idea that today would strike one as decidedly strange. More critically, perhaps, the emergence of the individual space coincides with the emergence of individualism as a philosophical and political doctrine claiming that the foundation of society must be seen in the individual, that society can only be understood as an aggregation of individuals, dating from approximately the 1820s in the thought of the Saint-Simonians in France. The development of the individual cell, bedroom, or office presupposes, parallels, and produces a world in which each person is recognized as an individual with their own rights, duties, desires, and expectations and in which the needs of the individual—of each individual—are important for the functioning of society. For each individual, for each fundamental unit, there is now a unique and identifiable interior: without this interior, without a cell, the individual can no longer be properly said to exist.

Second, such spaces present themselves as not only *for* but *of* the individual occupant. That is, they are on the first level pure interiors, without, in principle, an exterior aspect (or, in any case, the exterior is unknowable to the interior).[6] Nor is the interior ever really knowable to the exterior: despite Bentham's machinations, the cell consistently maintains a certain degree of obscurity.[7] They are interiors that are *of* the occupant in the sense that penetration from the exterior by any other person, outside of a few very controlled situations and protocols, is to be understood as a violation, as though it were a penetration of the body: to be, in theory, impossible. The hotel maid can only enter when the guest is not present, the younger sibling cannot enter the room, another patient can't come into the examination room when your pants are down. Further, it is an interior the character of which is due to the additions and accretions that express the individual: think, for example, of a teenager's bedroom adorned with posters of favourite bands and athletes, or indeed of the prison cell plastered with magazine photos of women or of race cars. This is even true, in the most minimal of ways, in the doctor's consulting room: where you choose to place your clothes, how you sit on the edge of the table. In short, the cell is not simply a container, a refuge, or an expression of the individual self, but rather is both that and also an inseparable part of that self.[8]

Third, these spaces are designed to manipulate, heal, and produce the individual self: in this sense they are all corrective or penitentiary spaces. Fundamental to the operation of cellular repetition is an understanding of the malleable individual, able to adapt to particular normative formations (consider the contemporary hotel room: queen-sized bed, dresser, closet, bathroom, desk, side chair, television, telephone) and indeed retain upon leaving an impression of that organization of space. The inner structure and organization of the replicable cellular space thus has the ability to moderate and transform, or, in the phrase used by Sara Ahmed (2006), *orient* the individual. Cellular repetition thus presupposes and produces a particular type

2.9 Sauvé and Faivre, Mettray penal colony, Mettray, France: a general view, 1844. Lithograph after Alexandre Thierry. (Wellcome Collection)

of individual with particular and precisely understood characteristics. Proceeding in lockstep with the investigation and codification of the cellular interior in the nineteenth century was of course an equal dissection, exploration, and classification of that other great interior, the psychological and especially the sexual interior of the self, with, among other things, and to paraphrase Foucault, the invention of the homosexual (and the simultaneous invention of the heterosexual), the treatment of hysteria (the hysteria around hysteria), and the intense concern for childhood sexuality (especially masturbation). From this point of view, we can see that the nineteenth century is bookended by two great interiors that are about the interior: the individual cell at Auburn, and Freud's consulting room in Vienna.

Fourth, and partly as an accommodation to the previous characteristics, cellular voids are in all cases perfectly interchangeable and adaptable. They are designed as ideal combinatorial elements, able to be assembled together into easily constructed and managed blocks (cell blocks, apartment blocks, suburban blocks). As such they present relatively simple geometric forms, most often rectangular prisms; where variety is allowed, it is contained within strict typological rules. In most cases the cell has no exterior as such, the exterior faces being subsumed by those of the agglomeration; evidence of the interior identity is reduced, often by code or covenant, to no more than the symbolic, in the form of a nameplate, which itself is often further reduced to a number. Temporally, the cell is equally adaptable, able in its simplicity to accommodate (within limits) the personality of its occupants, as is abundantly clear to anyone who has experienced the uncanniness of revisiting a former residence. By the early twentieth century, these characteristics of the cellular model had developed into an entirely new methodology for architectural and urban design, as we can see, for example, in the urban schemes of Hilberseimer or, for that matter, those of Le Corbusier.

To summarize my argument to this point, there was a co-development over the course of the nineteenth century on the one hand of the individual, of the modern self, of the disciplinary subject, and on the other of the modern cellular interior, capable of mechanistic repetition and agglomeration. These two developments cannot be properly separated, but must be understood as co-dependent effects, and both have their roots in the penal reform movement of the late eighteenth and early nineteenth centuries, with Bentham's Panopticon as its symbolic origin. Both developments, in other words, start from a position that assumes a deviancy and criminality on the part of its users, a deviancy and criminality that remains fundamental to the diagram of the self (and especially the sexual self), a deviancy and criminality that must be suppressed, corrected, and erased *through the mechanism of architecture*. The walls themselves are the punishment of crime.

Mettray

If Blouet is not well remembered today, this is probably a result of the very small number of buildings that he actually designed. Blouet's position as inspector general of prisons prohibited him from acting simultaneously as architect in his area of greatest expertise, although some sixty prisons were designed and built by other architects under his watch. However, Blouet did serve as architect for one important project in this story, the Colonie Agricole et Pénitentiare de Mettray (Figure 2.9).[9]

On his return to France after their study tour of American prisons, Demetz set about arranging for the founding of an internal colony for juvenile delinquents near the town of Mettray, near Tours, and Blouet was hired as architect, with the colony opening in 1840. The physical form of the colony as designed by Blouet is characterized first and foremost by a sense of order. As one contemporary account puts it, "uniformity, order, and symmetry reign throughout the little village" (Thomson 1856, 427). A large central square, with a chapel at its head, faces the entrance to the colony. Flanking the entrance to the square, opposite the chapel, are two buildings: the director's house and the school at which instructors were trained, a critical component of the Mettray system (Thomson 1856, 429). Ten other identical buildings are arranged on the two sides of the square; these three-storey buildings were the pavilions in which the colonists lived and worked, known at Mettray as *houses*. On the lower floor of these houses were the workshops in which the colonists who did not work in the fields learned their trades; the second

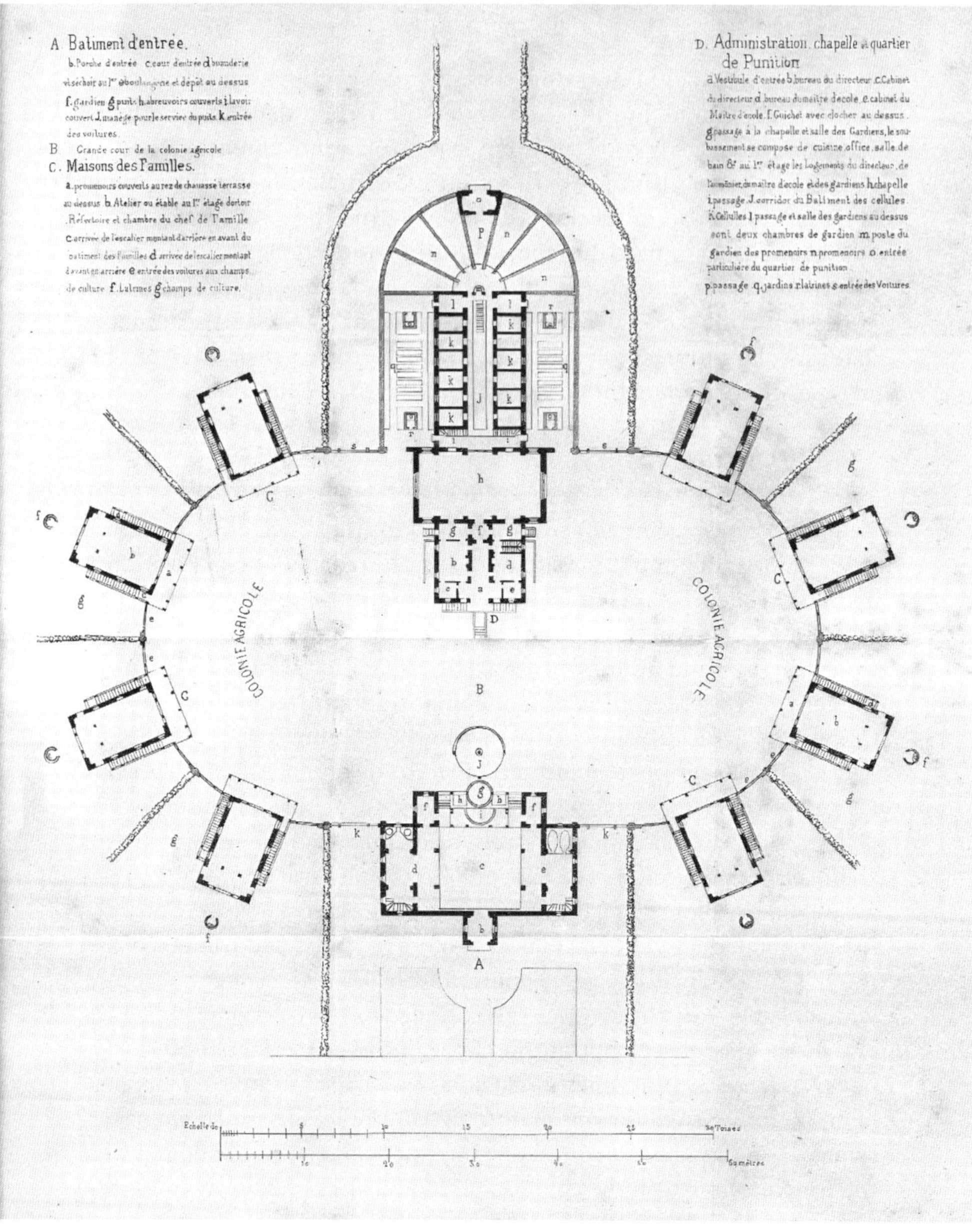

2.10 Guillaume-Abel Blouet, Mettray colony, preliminary site plan, 1839. (Archives Départmentales d'Indre-et-Loire, Cote 114J617)

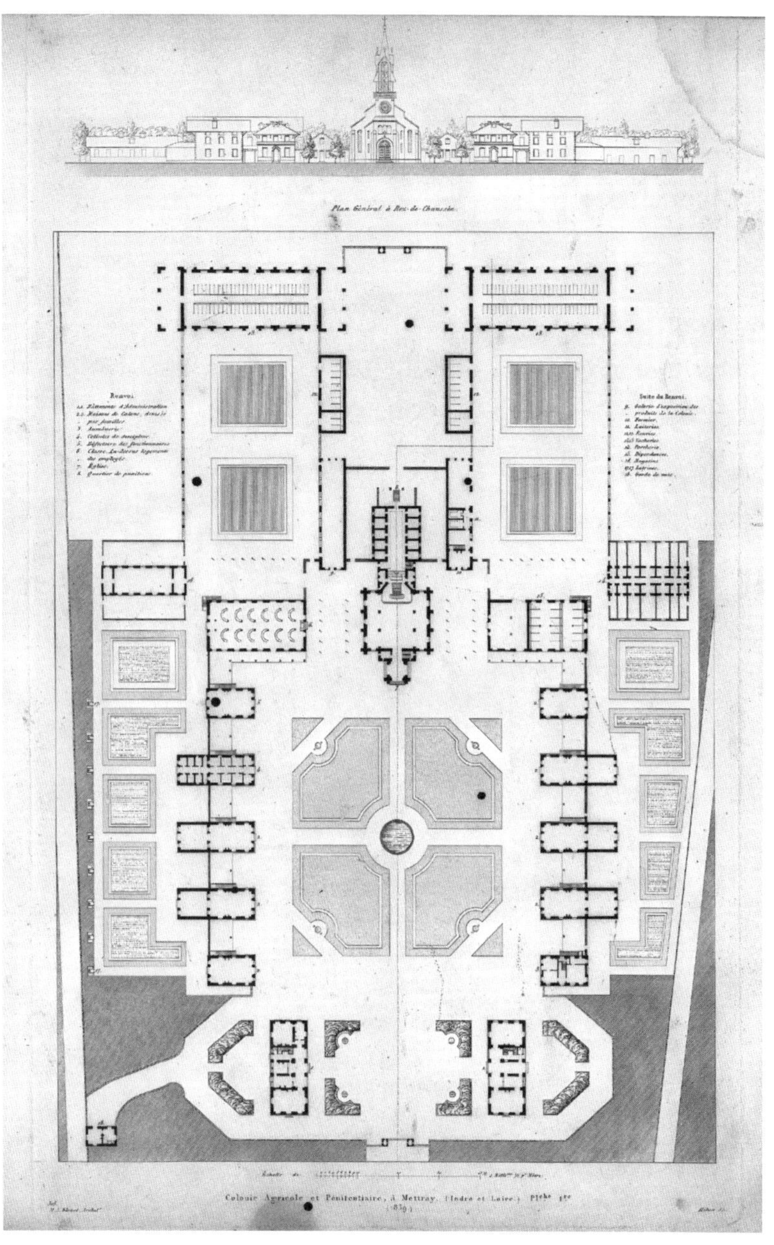

2.11 Guillaume-Abel Blouet, Mettray colony, final site plan, 1839. (Archives Départmentales d'Indre-et-Loire, Cote 114J66)

2.12 A family of colonists at Mettray, 1903. Postcard. Photographer not known, possibly Hamel. (Wikimedia Commons)

1903
Hamel

floor contained a room that functioned during the day as a mess hall and at night as the dormitory; and the third floor contained a separate dormitory for the younger children (Thomson 1856, 428).[10]

Blouet's plan for Mettray is not at all like the various projects for cellular prisons that he produced around the same time. The overall sense of harmony and order in the composition place the colony squarely in the tradition of the École des Arts. An early, preliminary plan, in particular, in which the project takes the figure of an ellipse, is an obvious reference to Claude-Nicolas Ledoux's plan for the ideal city of Chaux, built in the 1770s, complete with a dominant Bâtiment d'Entrée blocking entrance into the square (Bergdoll 2000, 99–102; Figure 2.10). The location of the director's residence (and office) in the centre of the court, more or less at the focal point of the ellipse—the position of privilege from which all the colonists' houses could easily be surveyed—also shows the influence of Ledoux's unbuilt, post-revolutionary plans for the completion of Chaux.

In the final, built project at Mettray, the panoptical quality of the overall plan was radically diminished (Figure 2.11). The administration buildings were moved one to each side of the central axis, leaving the entrance unencumbered and the main courtyard free of building, and the circular form of the overall plan replaced by a square. The colony is clearly centred on this open space of the square, which stands out as a space for (organized, communal) activity, dominated symbolically by the church at the north end. This shift in the plan shows a move away from an externally disciplined sense of order maintained through surveillance toward an internal sense of discipline maintained through communal activity, which was precisely Demetz's aim.[11]

Although the chapel is the most impressive single building in the colony, it is the *houses* taken as a whole that dominate the space (Figures 2.12 and 2.13). Colonists at Mettray were not lodged in cells, and reformation through the penitence of solitude was not the mechanism at play. Rather, each *house* at Mettray was occupied by a *family* of sixty colonists, presided over by one adult and one or two *older brothers*—older colonists charged with keeping order. The colony, thus, was organized in explicit imitation of a family structure. Demetz

2.13 A family house at Mettray. (Photograph by the author, 2005)

quite intentionally took on the family structure as metaphor for that of Mettray, as is pointed out by the following comment in a report made twenty years after his death: "The structure of his work set out to imitate the family, under the direction of a human father and the protection of the heavenly father" (De Witt, quoted in White 1993, 64). This was not capricious or accidental. After all, it was because of the failure of the boys' biological families that they found themselves "at risk" (Dekker and Lechner 1999, 41). Stephen Toth (2019) discusses at length the strategies used by Mettray's administration to break or obviate the bonds of family, such as forbidding visits, particularly from unwed mothers. This family-based structure is key to an understanding of the role of Mettray in the modern world.[12]

However, we should pause for a moment to consider what the founders of Mettray would have meant by *family*. Jean-Louis Flandrin (1979), who has traced the usage of the word *famille* in the eighteenth and nineteenth centuries through an investigation of dictionary entries, points out three essentially different meanings of the word. The first has to do with *lineage*, descent: the Bourbon family, the Hapsburg family. Although the outgrowth of biological events, this meaning of the word is essentially political in nature, related to property or alliances. Illegitimate children are not part of the family in this sense. The second meaning is most closely related to the English word *household* and would include any number of people living usually under the same roof and under the legal disciplinary control of the father of the house. Family in this sense could include unmarried (non-nuclear) relations, as well as servants. The third meaning is that of the nuclear or natural family, composed of father, mother, and offspring. Flandrin points out that prior to the Revolution, most dictionaries listed *household* as the primary definition, while listing the natural family as the third or even fourth definition. By the 1830s, however, dictionaries were beginning to list the natural family as the primary definition. By the 1860s, if not before, this natural family was generally understood to be the basic building block of society. This was a result, on one hand, of the naturalization impulse that formed part of the Enlightenment project (Flandrin 1979) and, on the other hand, of an instrumentalization of the nuclear family as a mechanism for promoting order by nineteenth-century social engineers (Donzelot 1979). At the time of Mettray's founding, its central formative concept, that of the family, was therefore in a certain amount of flux. Demetz's understanding of the term *family* is far from clear. On one hand, the paternalistic, disciplinary family is represented at Mettray by a second institution, separate from the reformatory: the Maison Paternelle. Here, wayward children of wealthy families could be shut up for an indeterminate time period at the will of their fathers (Donzelot 1979; Sauvestre 1864, 64–79; Toth 2019; White, 1993). As well, the notion of the extended family, not all members of which are related by blood, could be seen to be at the root of the Mettray families. The fact that the leaders of each family were called *frères ainés* (older brothers) argues against this notion, however, as does the decided shift away from the centralized, paternalistic early scheme toward the distributed system of the final project. Furthermore, Demetz's stated goals of placing the colonists in a state of nature implies strongly that it is the natural family that he had in mind. In the end, and pending further research, we should say that at Mettray, family meant both household *and* natural family.[13]

Contemporary accounts of the colony were invariably positive, even enthusiastic in their reviews. One typical account is *Une visite à Mettray*, written by Charles Sauvestre and first published as a series of columns in the Paris journal *L'Opinion nationale* in 1864. Sauvestre, a skeptic, agreed to visit the colony in December 1863 and returned to Paris a convert. The resulting columns (later published in book form, to be sold "au profit de la Colonie de Mettray") are effusive in their appreciation of the work of Demetz and Blouet. In part, this appreciation is based on several anecdotes relating to former colonists that attest to the positive results of the experiment; however, in the main, this appreciation seems to come from first-hand observations of the colony. Sauvestre is most impressed by the sense of order, made evident from the moment of arrival at the colony. Having arrived on a Sunday, Sauvestre was immediately treated to the *grand musique*, the weekly performance of the colony band in the main square. The comparison between colonists working together to make music and the disorderly play of urchins on the streets of Paris is unmistakable.

2.14 Sauvé and Faivre, Mettray penal colony, Mettray, France, the refectory, 1844. Lithograph after Alexandre Thierry. (Wellcome Collection)

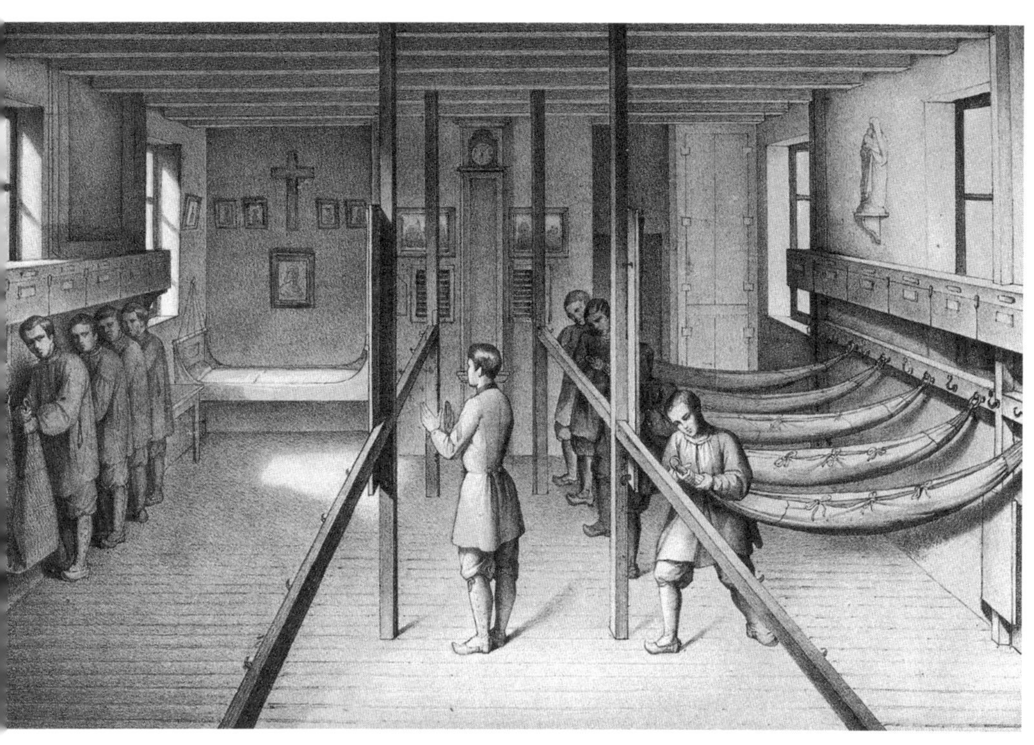

2.15 Sauvé and Faivre, Mettray penal colony, Mettray, France, a dormitory for inmates of the penal colony, who operate the system for setting up their hammocks and putting them away, 1844. Lithograph after Alexandre Thierry. (Wellcome Collection)

2.16 Sauvé and Faivre, Mettray penal colony, Mettray, France, a dormitory for inmates of the penal colony, who climb into their hammocks, 1844. Lithograph after Alexandre Thierry. (Wellcome Collection)

Order is then shown to pervade every aspect of the colonists' activities, as a rigorous daily schedule is followed (Toth 2019, 53–54). Sauvestre titled the column in which he discussed this routine "Système d'Éducation" (1864, 25), clearly making the argument that the adoption of routine, of discipline, is a critical pedagogic component (Thomson 1856, 428).[14]

Sauvestre (1864) was equally impressed by the extent to which the physical form of the colony had been developed to reinforce this imposition of order and discipline. As a prime example, Sauvestre discussed the room used for both sleeping and dining. Every morning, the colonists were required to make the transformation by taking down hammocks and putting in their place long tables, hinged to the wall (Sauvestre, 1864, 44; Figures 2.14 to 2.16). The houses were, therefore, quite literally machines; I am tempted to say, despite the anachronism, *machines for living in*. As with any machine, it is the product of the machine process that is critical at Mettray: although the ability to make double use of the space was economical, it is clear that the opportunity it provided to enforce a rigid, precise discipline, to be carried out in a clockwork fashion, was equally important. The correspondence between the productive intent (the establishment of order and discipline) and the machinery that produces (the architecture of the colony) is one to one; the colony both *models* and *produces* order.[15]

Partly as a result of publications such as that of Sauvestre, Mettray became quite well known both in France and internationally. The colony was seen as a model for youth education, and spawned several similar institutions, such as the Nederlandsch Mettray in Holland and Red Hill in England. In the development of modern pedagogical ideas, Mettray is an important signpost. In what is probably the best-known late twentieth-century account of the colony, in the last chapter of his *Discipline and Punish: The Birth of the Prison*, Michel Foucault (1979) argued that this influence of Mettray extends beyond the arena of education into the public realm in general. Noting that Mettray presents a model in which disciplinary structures are not confined to penitential institutions, but are an important part of everyday life (precisely the shift we have noted between the preliminary, elliptical plan for the colony and the final, square plan), Foucault dated the origin of a carceral regime—that is, a world in which disciplinary structures are universal, characteristic of modern Western society—to the founding of Mettray. For Foucault, the key point here was that at Mettray, the distinction between punishment and discipline is blurred. As Foucault put it, "The carceral 'naturalizes' the legal power to punish, as it 'legalizes' the technical power to discipline" (1979, 303).

Cells and Houses

Among the most intriguing aspects of Mettray, especially given the theoretical position I have taken in this chapter, is the relative absence of cells, the replacement of the cell as the fundamental unit of the facility by the house. Why would Blouet, the staunch if not single-minded supporter of the cellular system in France, choose to abandon this system in one of his few built projects, and certainly his most famous? How does this development force us to reconsider the idea of the cellular self?

There are of course obvious reasons for setting aside the cellular system at Mettray. First, Mettray was not understood as a prison, but rather as a colony; the ideas that drove the cellular system around isolation and solitude may well have been seen as antithetical to the idea of the colony, that is, to the idea of developing a new society. Second, there would have been a tacit understanding that the colonists were, in this instance, children: rather than being designed for the reformation of the adult, as a cellular prison would have been, Mettray was designed for the formation of the child or youth. Hence, we can imagine that colonists were grouped into "families" in order to take advantage of the nurturing formative function of the natural family as well as the more disciplinary function of the paternal family. This dual nature of the family is thus key; it could be argued that by the late decades of Mettray's existence, the paternalistic understanding of family had faded, leaving only a weak and ineffective and obviously false natural family.

In any case, we can state that the inhabitants of a single house at Mettray were not a more-or-less random collection of individuals, as we might have seen in the wards at Newgate. Nor were they individuals gathered together out of simple expediency or for bureaucratic purposes. Rather, the colonists were understood as a social unit, a family, whatever we take that word to mean. The plan of Mettray, then, is not a return to pre-Benthamite conceptions of incarceration, but rather the development of a new form, an evolution of the cellular type on a larger scale, larger in that the inhabitant of the cell is no longer the single individual, but rather the single social unit, the single family. The houses at Mettray bear all the primary qualities of cells: they are geometrically simple, they are repetitive modules, and they are capable of fundamentally infinite extension. They also bring together two great movements of the early nineteenth century, the development of the individual as fundamental particle for the construction of the state and the development of the family as machine that produces that individual. Each of these basic objects, individual and family, has its own architectural counterpart, the (monistic) cell and the (mechanistic) house.

We can see Mettray, then, as a predecessor—although probably not a conscious precedent—of the great suburban developments of the later nineteenth and twentieth centuries, providing a crystal-clear link in that chain between the penitentiary cell and the contemporary condo tower. These houses, too, designed to house single-sex families, add to the never quite vanishing queerness of the house.

The Contemporary Cell

In sum, the cell, in its theoretical manifestation in Bentham's Panopticon as well as its material realization at Eastern State Penitentiary and Auburn Prison and the countless modern prisons that followed them, stands as the fundamental architectural manifestation of the modern individual, the essential prototype of the unitary and interchangeable modern subject, the primary building block of modern architecture. As it spread from penal architecture to the civilian world, the cellular concept brought with it its conceptual origins, marking all quotidian spaces with its penitential history and identifying all modern selves as prisoners.

In our contemporary world of late capital, cellular repetition has become the dominant mechanism for the construction of reality, so dominant that we no longer see it as anything but the way the world is structured. It is of course the modern technique of production par excellence, congruent with the dumb machines and production lines of the nineteenth and twentieth centuries, with the rise of the nation-state and its demands for control and for soldiers, and the demands of capital for an easy multiplication of profit.

Today, of course, we live in a very different world from that of the 1840s, or even that of the 1920s: David Harvey's world of late capitalism, Jean Baudrillard's world of simulacra, Alain Badiou's world of the pornographic era, and dozens of other formulations. It is not my goal here to try to untangle this mess of contemporary thinking about our time. Rather, I want to just raise the question: has the cell been supplanted as a characteristic void for our era? Are we able, finally, to move beyond the disciplinary model of the world and the self that we inherited from Bentham?

There is no doubt that the contemporary cell (the bedroom, the apartment, the office) is a very different entity from the classic cell of Auburn and Eastern State. First of all, we can recognize that, as Deleuze (1992) and others have pointed out, we no longer live in a disciplinary society, but rather have moved into a society of direct and often internalized control; the cell, as the primary mechanism for the establishment of discipline, has faded in our imagination if not in our lives, supplanted by the systems that control us, locate us, connect us, track us, and identify us: our tax status, ISP address, vaccination record, passport, credit rating. In this world, as Deleuze tells us, the enclosure does not go away, but becomes malleable: "Enclosures are moulds, distinct castings, but controls are a modulation, like a self-deforming cast that will continuously change from one moment to the other, or like a sieve whose mesh will transmute from point to point" (1992, 4). Formally, the classic model of the cell that I have discussed above, the cell with rigid, impermeable walls that identify a void, an emptiness that itself models the clear void of the self, gives way to a very different entity, one that has perhaps more in common with a biological cell than a prison cell. This contemporary cell is, first of all, far from empty. Rather, we understand it as filled with criss-crossing flows of information and energy, concepts, and contiguities. Neither is the cell bounded by impermeable walls. Indeed, the walls of our contemporary enclosures are defined as such by their permeability, by their insubstantiality, and our cells are no longer mechanisms of isolation but are rather defined by connection and proximity-at-a-distance. Our cells have ceased to act as replicable, self-contained units and operate now as nodes in multiple overlapping networks. We are no longer contained by our cells, but, rather, our cells present us with loci from which we can operate in a wider world.

It should be no surprise then that cellular repetition has lost its primacy as the generating impulse of contemporary architecture, overtaken by the mechanisms of machine intelligence. One need only look at the buildings of Frank Gehry, Zaha Hadid, and a few others to recognize that the world of cellular discipline is long gone—and these, of course, are the architects of a past generation, precursors to a coming world in which design is the province of artificial intelligences, in which each void is produced in its own form for its own purposes, in which each individual is produced to maximize the whole. What will emerge as the dominant void in this unimaginable world?

At first he notices only a soft rumbling, like a warning in the belly of the beast, a soft mourning in the nether regions of the prison, like the machine is trying without success to digest its most recent prey. The thief opens his eyes, as the narrow bed begins to shake. In the distance there is a keening: he can't quite hear it, but he knows it is there, somewhere, beyond the edges of his cell. Something falls from the wall, one of his newspaper clippings, then another, then another, then he realizes that the walls and the ceiling are themselves starting to peel apart, not falling like stones would, but peeling like layer after layer of images, as though the wall is nothing more than the layers of clippings and pictures of rough murderers and tough boys he covered it with. He closes his eyes, hoping the story of the fall will end, but with no luck: when he opens them again the flakes of images have gotten smaller, the prison is falling around him, falling softly, in the form of letters falling like snow in a blizzard of not-yet-words. And on each letter, he can see, is a tiny version of himself, blurry, speaking his truth, making his meaning—is this what has become of the keening?—to the void, to the flurry, swirling in great blustery gusts, falling, falling. He sits up, erect, worried and hurried. On one letter he is telling the story of the necktie and the noose, on another the story of a powerful and beautiful whore, on another that of a beggar walking forever on a high, high tightrope, an artist in his studio, young men fighting for their lives, two brothers making love before they murder each other, would-be women drinking in seedy bars, thinking in speedy cars, winking at needy tars. A thought comes to him: the letter always arrives…

The snow stops. The world is black. Nothing remains but the steel frame of his bed and some tiny glittering lights in the distance. The thief walks slowly out into the void, carefully following the endlessly unspooling line of the story.

Chapter 3

La maison, ce n’est pas une prison

House

The Villa Savoye, located in the Paris outer suburb of Poissy, is perhaps the most studied and most influential building of the period between the two world wars (Figure 3.1).[1] The Villa was designed by Le Corbusier and constructed between 1928 and 1931. It sits on a roughly square patch of open ground surrounded (at the time of construction) by forest. The house was designed as a country retreat for the Savoye family: Pierre, co-founder of the Gras Savoye insurance company; his wife, Eugénie; and their son, Roger. The Savoyes allowed Le Corbusier considerable flexibility in terms of design and program, and the open site allowed him to produce a building that put into construction the principles for the modern dwelling that he had been developing in his work for the previous decade. In summary, these principles are listed as Le Corbusier's well-known "Five Points for a New Architecture": pilotis, the roof garden, the free plan, the strip window, and the free façade (Sbriglio 2008).

The Villa as constructed could be described as a white box raised on slender columns or pilotis. The first floor, which was the domain of the Savoyes, is square in plan, with the various rooms clustered around a large terrace. The ground floor is essentially the domain of the car, containing the garage and accommodations for the chauffeur and the maids; the horseshoe plan form of the ground floor is derived from the turning radius of the car. A ramp and a spiral stair serve as means of communication between the two realms.

The Savoyes moved into the Villa in the summer of 1930 and immediately began to notice problems with the building, including numerous complaints about faulty wiring, leaking roofs, and an inadequate heating system, which may have contributed to Roger's worsening health (according to Jacques Sbriglio, Roger spent 1933 in a sanatorium; 2008, 107). By 1937, after a series of increasingly strident letters of complaint from Mme Savoye to Le Corbusier, the family abandoned the Villa.[2]

After the Savoyes left, the building fell on hard times, although the exact circumstances are difficult to determine. According to Sbriglio, the Villa was used for a time as a hay barn, and was requisitioned by both

3.1 Le Corbusier, Villa Savoye, 1931.
(Photograph by the author, 2005)

the German and American armies. Various sources claim that it was used as a field hospital, as an ammunition depot, as a stables. After the Second World War the Savoye family maintained ownership of the house, but did not repair the damage that the war years had caused; one writer claims that they had been sent to concentration camps during the war, and were no longer able to afford to live as before (Walker 2013). By the 1960s, the house had fallen into serious decay. As Bernard Tschumi wrote in his 1977 essay "Architecture and Transgression," "Those who in 1965 visited the then derelict Villa Savoye certainly remember the squalid walls of the small service rooms on the ground floor, stinking of urine, smeared with excrement, and covered with obscene graffiti" (2001, 73).

In 1965 the Villa was formally purchased by the French state and named a historical monument. A careful renovation process followed, and the Villa is now open to visitors.

If the Villa had a short career as a house, it has had a significant afterlife among architects and students of architecture, influencing the development of modern architecture in ways both subtle and not so subtle. This influence is due in the first instance to Le Corbusier's intense program of promotion of the work (arguably, of self-promotion), including its promotion during his lecture tour to South America in 1929, described in *Precisions* (Le Corbusier [1930] 1991), and as the feature building in the film *Architecture d'aujourd'hui*, and the Villa played a starring role in Philip Johnson and Henry-Russell Hitchcock's blockbuster exhibition of 1932 at MoMA in New York, *Modern Architecture: International Exhibition*. Although the technical deficiencies in the building were also well known—a 1935 article in *TIME* talked about the leaking roofs and the problem of too much glass, and the abandonment of the Villa by the Savoyes probably added to the turn away from International Style modernism in the 1960s, led by figures such as Tom Wolfe—the building continued to influence architectural thinking well after it had gone into serious decay. To mention just a few examples of the Villa's presence in architectural discourse, Colin Rowe's (2009) seminal essay from 1947, "The Mathematics of the Ideal Villa," consciously linked the Villa Savoye formally and compositionally to Andrea Palladio's Villa Rotonda, causing a shift in architectural thinking about modernism; Tschumi's 1977 article, mentioned above, used the Villa and its decay as a way to think about transgression and, later, violence in architecture; and Beatriz Colomina's 1992 article, "The Split Wall: Domestic Voyeurism," in her important book of the same year, *Sexuality & Space* (1992a), featured an in-depth analysis of gender in Le Corbusier's representations of the Villa. The Villa Savoye can be linked back to utopian architectural positions through the attention to compositional perfection as well as the clear statement of principles on which it is founded, reminding us more of the Phalansteries—but also of the Benthamite ideal prisons of Blouet—than of the Villas of Palladio. What is more, the Villa continues to be fertile ground for a discussion and investigation of issues that remain of concern today: issues around the body, around representation, around transgression and violence, around architecture. Indeed, although he doesn't mention Savoye in the article, it is intriguing that Andrew Holder's important 2017 article, "Five Points Toward a Queer Architecture; Or, Notes on *Mario Banana No. 1*," is implicitly based on a reading of the Villa Savoye.

The essays by Colomina and Tschumi begin to tie the unusual history—and to a certain extent the unusual formal and material elements—of the Villa to the questions around queerness that we are engaged in here. It seems to me though that there is already and always something strange about the Villa Savoye. There is, for example, the sheer and stark objectness of the building, so different from other houses of its time, even other houses by Le Corbusier, like the Maison Garches. Or the strange, disorienting quality of the ramp, a disorienting quality that Le Corbusier comments on positively; one emerges at the top of the ramp as if into some strange new domestic utopia. Or the strange doubling of stair and ramp. Or the (over-)emphasized role of plumbing: the tiled bath and chaise longue open and next to the bed in the master bedroom, the presence of a lavatory in the grand entry. The clearest way to grasp the strangeness that is inherent in the building, though, is to look more closely at the principles that the Villa embodies: Le Corbusier's "Five Points for a New Architecture," which constitute a radical overturning of the key theoretical tenets that had guided architecture for centuries—possibly for millennia. These five points systematically call into question, rebuff, overturn, *queer* the most fundamental principles of architecture: the status of the ground, the differentiation between interior and exterior, the solidity of the wall,

3.2 Le Corbusier, Villa Savoye, 1959. View of terrace from inside the salon. (Photographed by René Burri. © René Burri)

even the role of the human—all the characteristics that propose firmness, solidity, authority for architecture. Villa Savoye provides an alternate (and very queer) vision of architecture, a modernist image of dissolution, of weightlessness, of groundlessness, of unhomeliness, a vision provided at the very foundational moment of modern architecture.

House-Machine

In a 1930 film about the (early) works of Le Corbusier, *Architecture d'aujourd'hui*, directed by Pierre Chenal and written by Le Corbusier himself, the Villa Savoye is presented as the primary example of Le Corbusier's famous dictum of modern domesticity: *The House Is a Machine for Living In*. This statement of Le Corbusier's, repeated and discussed in more detail in his best-known piece of writing of the era, *Toward an Architecture* ([1923] 2009), is more complex than it seems and has been widely misinterpreted both within popular culture and by generations of students of architecture. The Villa Savoye certainly looks like a machine, presenting a machine aesthetic stripped, for the most part, of ornamentation, making use of elements such as the famous strip windows and ships railings, but the machine metaphor for Le Corbusier goes well beyond aesthetics—and, one could argue, beyond metaphor itself. Le Corbusier's argument, presented in a beautifully concise manner in the film, is that in the modern age, in the age of the machine, we should consider the house the way we would any other machine. Just as the car is a machine for driving in, and the airplane is a machine for flying in, we should consider the house to be a machine for living in. The implication, of course, is that just as the automobile and the airplane had transformed the ability for people to travel—transforming, in turn, most or all other aspects of life in the modern world, re-forming our patterns of land use, our daily routines, and so on—a machinic consideration of the house could transform the way we live. Daily life becomes a process like any other, a process open to design, a process within the control of the architect. Through the metaphor of the house as machine, the life of the modern man becomes domesticated.

Arguably, and not surprisingly, the Villa moves beyond metaphor to function as a machine—or rather, the functions of the house are developed in a like manner to the functions of a car or a plane, albeit stylized and geometricized. The mechanical operation of the house, its machinic nature, is never as clear as it would be with a car or a plane; Le Corbusier, like his modernist counterparts, was never able to fully separate himself from traditional architectural concerns for composition, geometry, proportion. Still, we can see this machinic quality in the incessant concerns with circulation—the circular route of the car to the garage, the redundant or at least parallel circulation of the stair and the ramp, suggesting both a constant movement up and down and an overriding concern for a healthy lifestyle, made overtly evident in the scenes of calisthenics on the roof terrace in the 1930 film and of course reinforced by the presence of the large solarium on the top level. This concern for health is furthered by an obsession with plumbing—note, for example, the lavatory that sits at the centre of the circulatory system—that derives from a primary concern with hygiene and cleanliness. As Colomina (2019) and others have demonstrated, the modern house-machine has been designed to produce modern, healthy, athletic men and women.

Although Le Corbusier doesn't tell us this in such explicit terms, the Villa is also very clearly a vision machine, a perfect geometric form obsessively and symmetrically windowed on all sides, sited for visual control and surveillance of its landscape precinct. It appears to be a machine designed both to be seen and for seeing from, both designed for and produced by the new technology of film, a house designed to play a starring role in a film. We could suggest that it was inevitable, or necessary, that Le Corbusier would produce a film of the house. Of course, though, a concern with vision has other resonances and other cultural referents, and a connection with, a trace of, Bentham's Panopticon is unavoidable.

This trace of the Panopticon explicitly arises—or fails to arise—in Chenal's film at one particular moment. Narration is accommodated in the silent film through a series of title screens. At one point during the presentation of the Villa Savoye, one of the screens tells us that "*Une rampe en pente douce conduit au solarium*" (A gently sloping ramp leads to the solarium). The text continues with the following extraordinary statement: "*Une maison, ce n'est pas une prison: l'aspect change à chaque pas...*" (A house is not a prison: the view changes with each step...; Figure 3.3). Curiously, in 1935 Le Corbusier and Chenal produced a second version of the film in which,

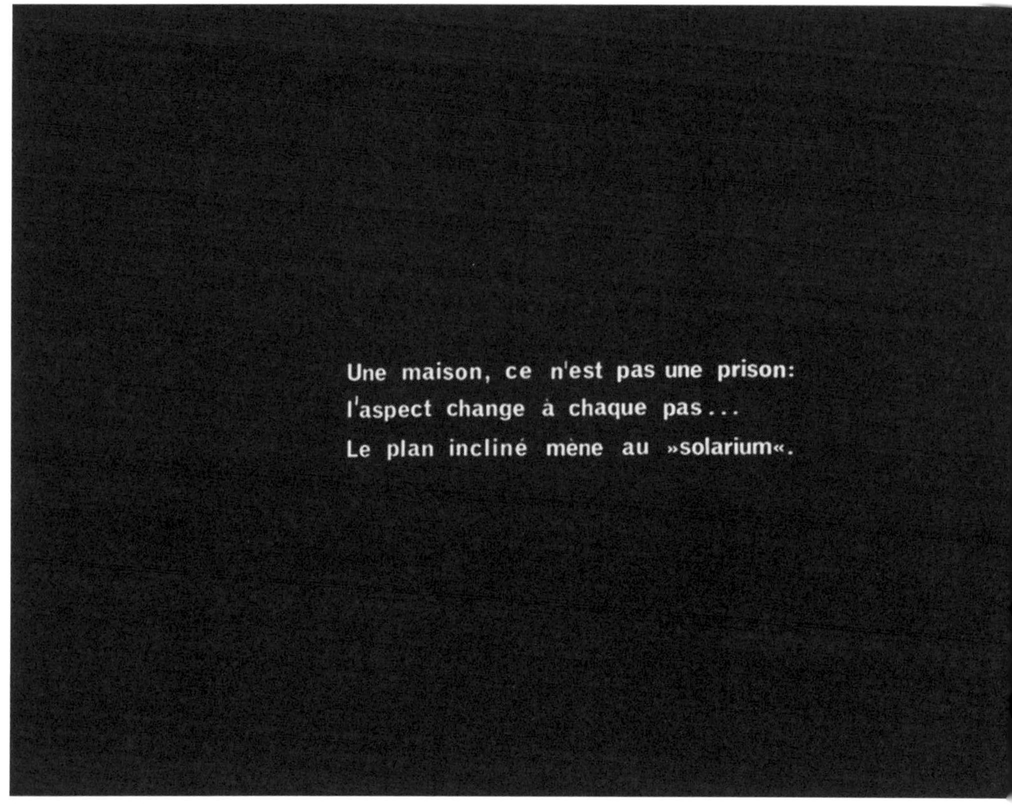

3.3 Pierre Chenal, *Architecture d'aujourd'hui*, 1930. Intertitle. (Centre National du Cinéma et de l'Image Animée [CNC])

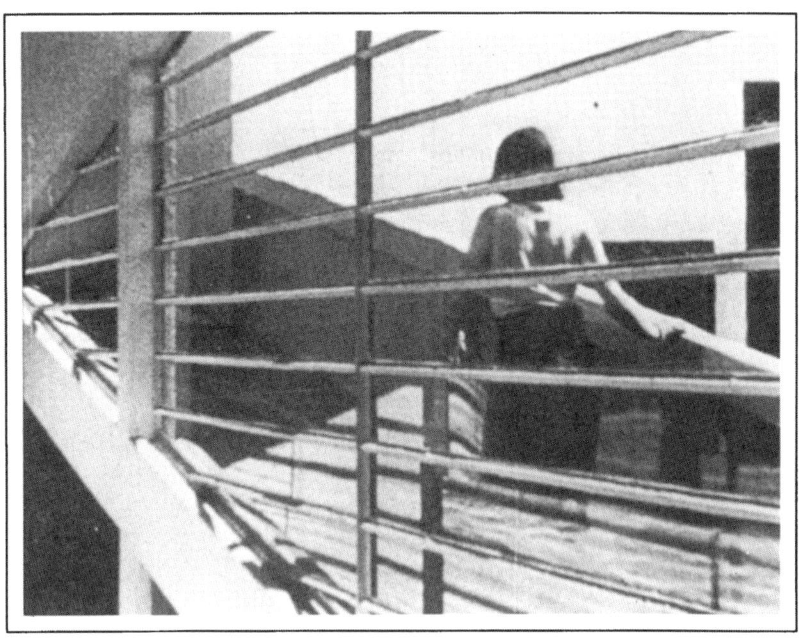

Villa Savoye. Still from
L'Architecture d'aujourd'hui: *"Une maison ce n'est pas une prison: l'aspect change à chaque pas."*

3.4 Beatriz Colomina, *Privacy and Publicity*, 1996. Page layout, p. 292. (Image courtesy MIT Press)

among other changes, this latter text was removed. Veronique Boone (2017), in her dissertation about the films of Le Corbusier, suggests that the text was shortened in order to reduce the problems of translation for an American audience, but my gut tells me there is something more at play. Did Corb realize that he had perhaps said too much, that the resonances between the house and a prison were perhaps too close to call it to his viewers' attention, that the ways in which the camera obsessively surveys the female occupant of the house, seemingly trapped within its geometries, moving incessantly on its circulatory systems, framed (as Colomina [1992b] notes) *behind bars* had too much of the prison in it (Figure 3.4)? Or did Le Corbusier come to realize the degree to which the Maison Centrale de Poissy—the major prison just down the road from the Villa Savoye, which he no doubt would have encountered on site visits to the Villa—had brought the prison as a type a bit too closely into his thinking? Or, conversely, did some astute editor realize that it was simply a typo—that a house is, indeed, a prison?[3]

It seems to me, though, that whatever the chain of events that led to the removal of this text from the film, its very absence is proof of its truth: that the house is, in some way, to some degree, in some universe, a prison. I see hints of this everywhere I look: in the sheer formal strangeness of the house, a rigorously square box, raised up off the ground (according to Le Corbusier, to avoid dampness—contamination), in the centre of an open field, separated in both plan and section from the world; in the windows placed all the way around the building on all sides—long, narrow windows, perfect for seeing out, for surveying, controlling, this open field, for stopping a thief from reaching the house. I see it in the gardener's cottage, with its formal relation to the Villa, floating above the wall, and in the cottage's even more uncanny formal relation to the guardhouse at the real prison, the Maison Centrale in Poissy, just down the street (Figures 3.5 and 3.6).

Architecture d'aujourd'hui leaves us, then, with two bold concepts about the house, one expressed (the house is a machine for living in) and one suppressed (the house is [not] a prison). It's worth noting, too, that Le Corbusier is not referring specifically to the Villa Savoye in making these comments; rather, both statements refer to Le Corbusier's understanding of the role of the house in the modern world. Both concepts are intriguing,

3.5 Le Corbusier, Villa Savoye, gardener's cottage, 1931.
(Photograph by the author, 2005)

3.6 Maison Centrale de Poissy, guard tower.
(Photograph by the author, 2005)

somewhat opaque, and worth examining further. The two concepts—house as machine, house as prison—have a clear complementarity, not only from their structuring role in the film, one overt and present, the other notable for its near absence, but also, as we have discussed in the previous chapter, from the historical role of the prison-as-machine as the founding project of modernity in architecture. Although I referred to the concept as suppressed above, we might be more precise in categorizing it as *repressed*, a perhaps intentionally forgotten truth about the origins of modernity, or, as Slavoj Žižek (2004) might call it, an unknown known.

In the remainder of this chapter, I want to examine these two concepts in a little more depth, starting with the idea of the house as a machine. What might we uncover if we were to take Le Corbusier literally in his claim that the house is a machine for living in? What, exactly, does this machine do? How does it function? I will start this discussion with an examination of the great thermodynamic engines that changed the world on all fronts in the nineteenth century.

The Carnot Cycle

Both the modern house, as epitomized by the Villa Savoye, and the modern prison, as described and analyzed by Michel Foucault (1979), have been described as machines.[4] There is no question of course that Le Corbusier and Foucault, when using the term *machine*, do not have exactly the same thing in mind; for Le Corbusier, as we have seen, the term *machine* is primarily a metaphor, or at most used to present and propose a similarity to the dominant machines of the early twentieth century: the automobile and the airplane. The word *machine* designates a new and radical means of thinking about architecture not in terms of its eternal compositional or material characteristics, although those did not cease to have importance, but in terms of its effects, its production. Critically, a machine for Le Corbusier is open to evolutionary change through the medium of conscious design. Foucault, on the other hand, uses the term to designate an element of an apparatus or *dispositif*, an effective, active node within an overarching structural network constructed through the workings of power.

The *Cambridge Dictionary* defines a machine as "a piece of equipment with several moving parts that uses power to do a particular type of work." This is a remarkably straightforward, extremely general, and not all that useful definition, applicable to all manner of devices, from locomotives to spaceships, from computers to political organizations. We might generalize the definition even more to describe a black-box machine, which is concerned less with the structure of the machine (having several parts) and more with its effects (to do a particular type of work). A black-box machine can be described as an intermediate between its inputs, which are typically energy and material, and its outputs: typically, a product of some kind (and we can be quite generic in terms of what defines a product) and waste. These four external linkages (material, energy, product, waste) are necessary components of any machine. We can see this, for example,in the two most dominant machines of the eighteenth and nineteenth centuries: the steam engine and the guillotine (here, again, we see the dialectic of production and discipline come into view). The latter has as its inputs the body of the nobleman and the ferocious energy of the mob, and as outputs the construction of a new order and the waste material of the corpse. The steam engine can be described just as simply on a schematic level: think of a locomotive with the inputs of a collection of passengers in Rouen and power in the form of a coal furnace, a product in the form of workers in Paris and waste in the form of heat (and of course other waste products and other frictions). The operation of the engine is slightly more complex than that of the guillotine, from a technological point of view. In 1824, in *Réflexions sur la puissance motrice du feu et sur les machines propres à développer cette puissance*, Sadi Carnot first defined an energy cycle that later came to be called the Carnot cycle (Carnot 1960). The Carnot cycle is a reversible energy cycle (theoretically the only such reversible cycle) that uses the first and second laws of thermodynamics to derive work from a system.[5] The Carnot cycle was important from a theoretical point of view in the effect it had on the development of thermodynamic theory. It was also important from a more practical viewpoint, however, in that it had immediate application: the Carnot cycle describes the workings of a steam engine. This was not lost on Carnot, who included drawings of several steam engines, including those of the inventors James Watt (1736–1819) and Jacob Perkins (1766–1849), in his treatise.

We could cite a number of generalized machines that operate on the principles of the Carnot cycle that came to dominate the nineteenth and early twentieth centuries, such as steam engines, of course, with locomotives that drastically redrew the landscape of Europe and then the rest of the world, but also less obvious technological advancements: capitalism, Hegelian dialectics, Freud's Oedipus, Haussmann's Paris, bourgeois society as a whole. While it may seem surprising to describe some of the items on this admittedly ambitious list as thermodynamic engines, my suggestion here is that the fundamental logic of the Carnot cycle found its way into the foundations of many divergent aspects of nineteenth-century life.[6] Further, like any Carnot cycle engine, these systems were constrained to less-than-perfect operation, inevitably leaving behind waste products of various forms and various materials, producing an alternate and often invisible anti-modernism. Michel Serres sums up the world produced by Carnot in three principles, readily extended beyond the world of thermodynamics tout court: *difference*, the principle that wherever difference is found it is available (and will inevitably be mobilized) as a motive force for production; *reservoir*, the principle that we need a storehouse of energy as well as a set of techniques to maintain difference; and lastly, *circulation*, a means of moving across and through difference (1975, 66). Sexual difference, for example: in a machine world, sexual difference becomes a resource that can be put to work, even if we are not immediately clear what the output might be (surely it is not as simple as the production of more bodies). A set of techniques must be developed to define, clarify, survey, maintain, and enforce that sexual difference, and a means of circulation of fluid across the divide that marks the sexual difference must be identified. It makes no difference that these terms and practices pre-existed the machine world; in the machine world they all take on a new, more distinct, more sharply defined character.[7]

Serres, though, misses or ignores the fourth fundamental component of any effective Carnot cycle process of any *difference engine*: any system that operates outside of the purely utopic, any system that operates with non-zero power, must, as a consequence, produce waste. With the development of thermodynamic machines came the introduction of unavoidable waste on a large scale; the resultant need for a whole science of waste management had, and continues to have, significant repercussions for the development of society. The degree, type, materiality, place of origin, method of production, and above all means of disposal of this waste will vary from system to system. How can we define the waste products of the sexual difference machine?[8]

Bachelor Machines

A bachelor machine is a fantastic image that transforms love into a technique of death.
—Michel Carrouges, "Directions for Use"

In undertaking a machinic analysis of the Villa Savoye, the concept of the Bachelor Machine, as described by Michel Carrouges in *Les machines celibataires* of 1954, is potentially useful (Carrouges 1975). In this work, Carrouges noted a few machinic images in literature and art that shared particular morphological and functional similarities, and proposed the Bachelor Machine as a type, basing his description first of all on Marcel Duchamp's *Large Glass*.[9]

Carrouges provides us with a clear formal schematic of the Bachelor Machine. First, like the *Large Glass*, or for that matter the Villa Savoye, the Bachelor Machine is always comprised of an upper and a lower portion (Carrouges 1975, 23). The upper part of the machine is the realm of the feminine (the bride, in the *Large Glass*: Mme Savoye's boudoir in an early, unbuilt project for the Villa [Le Corbusier 1966]; the world of the family, in the built version) while the lower area is that of the masculine (the bachelors in the *Large Glass*; the world of the chauffeur, of the car, at the Villa Savoye). Something—a message, a fluid, an energy—passes between the two sections of the machine. The Bachelor

Machine is thus an image of a sort of steam engine, a sexual Carnot cycle, an energetic cycle in which male and female are both stuck, and both implicated; a cycle in which the sexual potential energy implicit in the difference between the male and female is used to generate work.

It's rather easy to jump to a somewhat obvious conclusion: The Villa Savoye, or indeed the modern house in general, is a Bachelor Machine.[10] Alain Montesse, writing also within Carrouges's volume, makes this conclusion explicit: "Structurally, a Bachelor Machine looks like a 2-storey arrangement, the lower storey being occupied by a reclining man who is the victim of various torments coming from the storey above" (1975, 110). The Bachelor Machine shares the structure of a house, at least of a typical two-storey house (such as one a child might draw), which locates the feminine (as exemplified by the site of sex, of the intimate, the bedroom) in the upper storey, with the lower storey (containing workrooms, study, dens, garages) as the realm of the social, the masculine. In other words, the Bachelor Machine is explicitly the house understood as a mechanism that uses the sexual difference of male and female in order to obtain work: a sex machine. And we could certainly draw the section of the Villa Savoye to accommodate this reading. The section of the house makes it clear: the realm of Madame Savoye on the upper floor, held up off the ground, kept virginal and clean (unsullied by the dirt of the world) but also kept prisoner by the stiff, erect and white piloti-cocks of the undeniable masculine presence on the ground floor, in the realm of the chauffeur, and the incessant circulation—up the ramp, down the stair, up the ramp, down the stair—connecting these gendered energies.

The Bachelor Machine, then, is explicitly the house understood as a mechanism that uses the sexual energy of male and female to obtain useful work. The house is thus both participant in and constructor of an economics of sexual desire that is, because of its necessary connection to the role of the family, explicitly a heterosexual economics.[11] Focused as it is in production—that is, reproduction—there is no obvious way for people of queer sexualities to participate in this economy. Worse still, the queer individual diverts sexual energy away from the family, in other words, away from work useful to society. Queerness, in this conception, is a source of friction. In other words, the homosexual steals energy. From the point of view of the modern world, to be homosexual is already to be a thief.[12]

Waste Products

The implication of course is that the primary role of the house as a societal machine is nothing less than the production of heterosexuality (and we may as well say at the same time the production of homosexuality). Such a reading is in line with the gender performativity theories of Judith Butler (1990) or the thoughts of Sara Ahmed (2006) around the construction of the heterosexuality in her *Queer Phenomenology*. Within this reading, queerness is waste, the queer individual is nothing more than the waste product of the imperfect Carnot cycle of the house, and the prison is nothing more than a technique of waste management.[13]

As I have mentioned above, the introduction of Carnot cycle mechanisms into society on a large scale brings to the fore the necessity for an entire scientific discipline of waste management. Waste, and the generation of waste, is a necessary and unavoidable component of any thermodynamic machine (arguably of any machine, even abstract machines). From this perspective, the prison can be understood as one of a series of techniques developed for the management of the waste products of the house—including the waste product of the homosexual. Waste management raises several salient questions: how can we identify waste and distinguish it from products of value?[14] What techniques can we develop to efficiently separate waste from non-waste and to deal with waste? Waste must be made invisible, not allowed to pile up in the streets (Laporte 2000).[15] The question of "away" is raised: waste must be removed from the system in question in order to not accumulate and become unhealthy and unmanageable. Waste might be contained (nuclear waste), or transported to some other jurisdiction, or incinerated.[16]

There are three critical points that need to be discussed in relation to the question of waste. The first is that waste does not disappear; this is a reformulation of the second law of thermodynamics, or a restatement that there is fact no outside to any system. Nor does waste reenter the system ready to be reused. Rather, waste accumulates, particularly if left on its own. We should not be surprised, then, to see a continual expansion of prison systems in the developed world. Eventually, given enough time, waste containment mechanisms will become cancerous and fail in any given system.

The second point that needs to be stressed here is that waste is not a pre-existing enemy to be defeated; rather, waste is produced as part of the normal workings of the machine, a necessary counterpart to its productive operations. The thief is produced by the machine of property, and neither can exist without the other; the homosexual is produced by the machine of the bourgeois family, and neither can exist without the other; the prison is produced by the machine of the house, and neither can exist without the other.

Third, the waste receptacle cannot be thought of as a static structure—it too is a machine, or rather a whole set of contradictory and incommensurable overlapping and interpenetrating machines.[17]

Waste, dirt, filth: these are all concepts that are bound together in our reading of the Villa Savoye. The issue of waste management, of the separation of dirt and filth, is announced at the Villa in the entry hall by the obvious presence of the washbasin; dirt is to be removed before entering the house. This epitome of cleanliness is reinforced, of course, by the presence of the open bath in the master bedroom, as cleanliness becomes a ritual enabled by the house-machine. But the struggle against dirt is advertised much earlier, before one reaches the interior, as the dominant structural move of the house—the elevation on pilotis—is undertaken in order to lift the house above the dirt and moisture of the ground. The Villa is to be a structure in which dirt, filth, and waste are rejected, kept out, *abjected*. Expulsion, elimination, ejection: these are the techniques by which dirt is dealt with in the Villa. Filth is not allowed inside, and if it somehow finds its way, it is rapidly moved out through the mechanism of plumbing. As Colomina (2019) has demonstrated, these moves are connected to an important strategy of health in the modern house. What an irony, then, that the Savoyes felt the need to abandon the house specifically because of the failure of the house-machine and the growing illness of their son. How strange, too, is Savoye's afterlife of abandonment, of excrement, of abjection. Savoye maintains an intimate connection with waste in its origins, in its operation, in its ending: it is an abjection machine that in the end is itself abjected, an *abject object* that stands before us, confronting us with our own abjection.[18]

House|Prison

Now, a critical analysis would doubtless destroy the appearance of solidity of this house, stripping it, as it were, of its concrete slabs and its thin non-load bearing walls, which are really glorified screens, and uncovering a very different picture. In the light of this imaginary analysis, our house would emerge—permeated from every direction by streams of energy which run in and out of it.

—Henri Lefebvre, *The Production of Space*

The last few sections provide a bit of a basis for understanding this second relationship, that between house and prison. The relationship is indeed alluded to on several occasions in the previous pages, in discussions around friction, theft, product, and waste. In this section I would like to take a more direct approach to the question, asking what we might understand by Le Corbusier's statement, *Une maison ce n'est pas une prison*. Based on what we have discussed so far, it seems that there are three potential readings of this situation: that house and prison are identical, or at least isomorphic, that house and prison are homomorphic and homogenic twins; that house and prison are complementary entities, component parts of a larger system, that indeed cannot exist one without the other; and finally, that house and prison are transforms, distorted images of each other as seen in a funhouse mirror.

The ways in which the modern house and the modern prison—what we, today, think of simply as *house* and *prison*—are homomorphic are both multiple and indisputable. From a classical modernist point of view this should come as no surprise, since the house and the prison share essential programmatic needs: both typologies are developed around the quotidian needs of the human body. Both house and prison provide facilities for consuming food and eliminating waste, for sleep, for exercise (to a certain degree), for hygiene, for work, for socialization. Both structures act as representations and extensions of the body, representations and extensions that are intimate and totalizing in a way that other spaces and other structures are not. What is more, both typologies are constructed around primary disciplinary principles, the discipline of the state on the one hand and the discipline of the family on the other. One could argue—this goes to the heart of this reading of Le Corbusier's phrase—that these two disciplines are not so very different, especially within the context of the modern world and even more especially, perhaps, in that of nineteenth-century France, as I have shown in my discussion of Mettray in the previous chapter. And although we are tempted to see this resemblance in one direction only, as a paternalization of penal discipline, a recourse to the discipline of the family understood as natural and unquestionable, both my analysis of the family in French laws of the early industrial world and Pier Vittorio Aureli and Maria Shéhérazade Giudici's (2016) broader and deeper analysis of domesticity (the very word is connected explicitly to the word *domination*) suggests that we should look in both directions. We have here not father and son, but two brothers, or perhaps cousins, sharing a common progenitor. It is in this sense that these two typologies, now understood as so divergent, are homogenic—that is, that they share the same origins, whether we think of those origins as mythic scenes of violence in which the prison and house are born in the same moment as a place for the Man to keep his women locked up and secure, or, specific to the modern types, historical in that both the modern house and the modern prison have their origins in the notion of the cell and the invention of the individual psyche. It is perhaps no surprise that this connection remains clear in the slang term "the Big House," that is, the jail: this is, after all, an apt description for a prison. This suggests perhaps that we can think of the prison as a type of house—or maybe that we should instead consider the house a type of prison.

One could argue, I suppose, that the primary difference is that the prison keeps one confined, while the house does not. Is it not the case, though, that the house keeps us confined in ways that are perhaps more subtle and less obvious than those of the prison? I'm not referring here so much to obvious forms of confinement—the confinement of the elderly, for example, or of the sick, the infirm, of children, especially teenagers (especially, arguably, gay teenagers), and even less of instances in which houses have become not more real but less savoury places of confinement—house arrest, abduction, abuse—but rather of the ways in which the house keeps us confined to its own web, confined through mortgages, through the effects of land and property ownership, and the demands that come with property of being proper. The house can be, like Auburn, a prison with walls, but it can also be, like Mettray, a prison without walls, a prison that keeps us confined through its own internal gravitational pull.

The undeniable fact remains that while the house and the prison have many characteristics in common, a common origin, a certain commonality in terms of function, there remains, it seems, some difference between the two forms, some difference that makes the phrase "the house is a prison" a phrase that shocks. If the modern house and the modern prison are both machines, both descended from the ur-machine of Bentham's Panopticon, if both have identifiable inputs and outputs worked on via a black-box or Carnot cycle mechanism, they remain in some important ways different machines. Indeed, while we can easily describe the house as a sexual Carnot cycle and can easily identify the hot and cold reservoirs pertaining to the gender binary (even if I must admit that the identification of hot and cold as female and male appears, to me, strange and arbitrary), it is not so straightforward to identify these reservoirs in the prison; in any case, there is no a priori binary that can be developed to produce the cycle. Where can we find hot and cold in the gender-segregated machine of the prison? What cycles can be developed, what can be produced? The useless machines of nineteenth-century prisons, the treadmill, the crank, the punishment cell, all these mechanisms used to produce useless work from the bodies of these prisoners, all these machines suddenly make sense as part of the defunct, non-productive mechanism of the prison. If the component machines of the house produce bodies as well as discipline through the motive force of pleasure, the prison lacks all three of these components: it does not act through pleasure, but only through fear and pain; it destroys bodies rather than producing them; and it fails in the production of discipline, producing in the end only submission, hatred, and death.

There is, though, another way of considering the relationship between these two machines, a way which recognizes their complementarity—that is, the way in which these two entities combine to form an even larger machine connected not so much by structural similarities as by the systems of flow that hold them together. Gilles Deleuze and Félix Guattari, in their work together and separately staring in the 1970s, developed a mode of analysis that prioritized a consideration of machines over a consideration of structure. In his article "Machine and Structure" of 1971, Guattari claimed that "a machine is inseparable from its structural articulations and, conversely, that each contingent structure is dominated...by a system of machines" (1984, 111). Further, the "structural process encloses the subject," while for the machine "the subject is always somewhere else" (112). What matters when considering machines is therefore not the relative positions of bodies in relation to the mechanism, but rather the ways in which the machine controls the various flows of energy, money, words, and so on that pass under it. In *Anti-Oedipus*, Deleuze and Guattari (1983) frame the idea of a machine in precisely this way, as an entity that sits on top of and stops, or constricts or redirects—or indeed amplifies or even produces flows, as an entity connected to other machine-entities, producing unending circuits of flows of every possible type.

In the case of our two machines, house and prison, it is clear that the linkage, the flow between the two systems takes the form of waste: that is, that the prison collects and processes the waste products of the house-machine. As I have mentioned already, this waste takes the form of bodies incapable of further participation in the cycles that comprise the house-machine, the cycles of reproduction, on the one hand, and the cycle of production—that is, of capital—on the other. Beyond the flow of bodies, though, there are other complementary flows involved here, such as the flow of property vertically, let us call it, that is temporally, or the various horizontal flows (money, power, bodies, objects, fear, pain, and pleasure) between and around the gravitational masses of properties. Each building, each property, each house, and each prison operates as a Carnot cycle reservoir, or like a gravitational black hole, creating a whole universe of frantic activity. The question, then, is not so much to decode hot and cold reservoirs in the prison as to understand the pure difference that connects instead of dividing house and prison, the difference that binds them in a universe of complementarity. House-machine and prison-machine need each other, rely on each other, in order to exist.

But what types of flows would connect and bind the house-machine and the prison-machine? We could not do better in answering this question than to consider the architectural elements we have already uncovered: violence, the essential constitutive and constituent violence of architecture, the violence of the line, the violence of ownership, the violence of separation; and sex, or rather the disciplining of sex, or maybe even the way architecture constructs and produces sex, identity (including sexual identity), and especially gender as an essential aspect of that ur-violence. And, of course, the way in which architecture produces the family as a byproduct of that violence. So, in addition to the flows of energy that Lefebvre (2004) highlights in his discussion of the house, we see many other flows: flows of money, property, power, alliance, blood, sperm, energy, water, air, shit, DNA, religion. A closer look would reveal that each of these flows—and the perhaps infinite others that we would discover—is itself multiple, doubled or tripled or quadrupled with additional flows moving in the same channels, passing their own messages; and these flows merge and connect, becoming indistinguishable one from the other, then separating again. Flows attract and repel, combine and mutually annihilate, accelerate and slow down. And each machine contains, in addition to its recognized mechanism and function, one or two or thirty additional unseen, unrecognized, unplanned-for mechanisms and functions, operating on partial flows or on multiplicities of flows. Likewise, products of these flows, circuits, and machines come into and move out of being, anticipated and unanticipated, solid and ephemeral, recognized and unseen, canny and uncanny. House and prison flow through and over each other, oscillating in and out of phase, combining and separating, and always producing.

House and prison, in their role as complementary structures, take on and distort characteristics of each other in order to attract, engage, and mobilize the various flows that move between them. If the house is a sex-machine, then the prison too takes on this attribute, the prison becomes itself a sex-machine. And if the prison is a discipline-machine, or a vision-machine, so too is the house. No attribute of one element in this couple can be missing from its partner, even though its presence is cloaked, its aspect distorted. The components of the house-machine map, one to one, onto those of the prison-machine.

House and prison can be understood, then, to be nothing more than divergent representations of the same institution as seen from opposite sides of the architectural binary. Of course, I am not claiming here that there is any mathematical function that could turn a house inside out, like a glove, to become a prison. The best we could say, perhaps, is that one side of the transform emphasizes familial love, while the other emphasizes hatred. One focuses on discipline, while the other hides and obfuscates its disciplinary methods. One is a raw expression of the law (the Law of the Father, the Law of Architecture), while the other is a more subtle acceptance of that same law. One view concentrates on the politics of the monad, the enclosure of the self, while the other interrogates from the position of the binary. Strikingly, it is not always easy to identify which of our building types takes which position in the transform, which is house, and which is prison.[19]

Chapter 4

On Stained Sheets

Three things made solitary sex unnatural. First, it was motivated not by a real object of desire but by a phantasm; masturbation threatened to overwhelm the most protean and potentially creative of the mind's faculties—the imagination—and drive it over a cliff. Second, while all other sex was social, masturbation was private, or, when it was not done alone, it was social in all the wrong ways: wicked servants taught it to children, wicked older boys taught it to innocent younger ones, girls and boys in schools taught it to each other away from adult supervision. Sex was naturally done with someone; solitary sex was not. And third, unlike other appetites, the urge to masturbate could be neither sated nor moderated. Done alone, driven only by the mind's own creations, it was a primal, irremediable, and seductively, even addictively, easy transgression. Every man, woman, and child suddenly seemed to have access to the boundless excesses of gratification that had once been the privilege of Roman emperors.

—Thomas Laqueur, *Solitary Sex*[1]

If we are to take seriously questions about queer architecture, we will need to understand what sex is, and more precisely, the mechanisms by which sex enters architectural thinking. This question—how does sex enter architecture?—is another difficult question, and one that will require some picking away at, some unpacking, in order to answer. It is my position here that one of the roles of architecture is precisely to hide and obscure the presence of sex in buildings and, by extension, within architecture itself. One of my ambitions is to break open the vault, to bring to light the various ways in which buildings are repositories, containers, and producers of sex, and in which architecture serves to discipline, support, and conceal these mechanisms. Still, we can make a quick and provisional hypothetical sketch of four such mechanisms here.

First, we relate to, occupy, approach, think about, use buildings in a sexualized manner. This is encompassed in our unavoidable bodily relationships with buildings—entering, being inside, touching, and so on—and our bodily functions that are staged, contained, and hidden by buildings—eating, fucking, shitting, sleeping, etc. As a result, buildings become libidinous objects, and carry at least a residue or trace of sex. Within this latent sexualization of buildings, architecture has the role of disciplining and organizing these sexual traces. Some traces are repressed or desexualized, while in other cases the architecture will produce/present official or appropriately organize sexualities.

Second, architecture, in its bilamellar relation to building, creates a gap, a kind of unknown knowledge. There are things about buildings that we are not supposed to know and things we are supposed to know, and one job of architecture is to distinguish between those two categories. Hence there is an unknowable void, an uncanniness, at the heart of every building, an uncanniness that resonates with the uncanniness and lack of relation of sex.

Third, buildings (and architecture) are the result of the same power systems in human society that structure our sexual relationships. Or, rather, buildings (and architecture) are the mechanisms that produce and maintain those sexual relationships. This is most clearly seen in the organization of the family house, but is also present in buildings of all kinds, buildings that mirror the sexualized structures in which we live. Architecture again has the role of disciplining, masking, hiding, and sometimes selectively and strategically revealing these relations of power, gender, sex.

Finally, according to Lacan, desire is always the desire of the other. Indeed, the existence of the other is the fuel that drives sex; without (an) other, there would be no desire, no sexuality, no sex. Architecture, though, has the primary role of ordering, hence of separating. Architecture's primary responsibility is the production of the other, of structuring our world into binaries: inside|outside, nature|culture, work|leisure, you|me, master|slave, male|female, cis|trans, top|bottom. This aspect of architecture, its function of separation and especially of separating inside and outside, both literally and figuratively, has been analyzed by Elizabeth Grosz (2001). What this suggests, though, is not only that architecture has a relation to sex, that sex does indeed enter into architecture, but in fact that architecture has an important role in controlling, organizing, and disciplining sex.

However we structure the relationship, one thing is clear: Architecture always has a relation to the erotic. After all, sex always happens in relation to buildings: in bedrooms, on kitchen tables, in offices, in cheap motels. And even when sex happens out of doors, in the park or in the wilderness, the *frisson* is always the result precisely of that outside-ness. Quite aside from the physical location in which sex takes place, a location that I would suggest ties sex and architecture from the start (architecture takes on the smell, so to speak, of all that sex), our erotic scenes are inseparably tied up with places; it is this link that makes the classic brothel, the house of illusion, so powerful. As any watcher of pornography will tell you (that is, anyone), that is, anyone, our erotic desires are intimately bound up with architectural scenes: the boudoir, the dungeon, the locker room, the doctor's office, the prison—and on and on. All places of power, that is, all places touched by architecture, are settings for the erotic; architecture is never neutral, when it comes to the erotic, but always an actant in the erotic assemblage.

In previous chapters we have discussed the house as the corollary of the family, as a machine structured for reproduction and therefore formed around heterosexual intercourse. Here, in order to dig a little deeper into the relationship between sex and architecture, in what follows I will investigate first a different type of house, more explicitly connected to sex: the brothel (whorehouse, seraglio, house of pleasure, house of illusions). Following this, I will consider architecture's relationship to a different, non-reproductive sex act: masturbation.

The House of Illusion

Brothels, as we are all aware, are an ancient institutional and architectural type. In an earlier speculative interlude, I suggested that the brothel precedes the house, and while this may or may not be true chronologically, I believe it to be true conceptually. Other writers have traced the origin of the brothel to the institution of temple prostitutes in the ancient world, suggesting that the brothel itself maintains some traces of divinity (Simons 1975). Still, these buildings, with few exceptions, have been markedly understudied from within the discipline of architecture; indeed, it is difficult to find any sustained architectural analysis or coherent history of brothels, and I won't be providing that history here either. In part, of course, brothels are understudied for quite understandable and quotidian reasons. First, most brothels operate through a modicum of discretion; however fantastic or ornate the interiors might be, the exteriors are often plain and ordinary, designed to meld into the background. What's more, one imagines that there is little documentation of brothels, as these were not, after all, buildings designed for posterity. And few great architects designed brothels—that we know of. In what follows, though, I hope to suggest at least one other reason for this aporia.

One notable exception to this is probably the best-studied brothel project of the past few hundred years, the Oikéma, or Maison de la Passion (Oikéma, or House of Pleasure), designed by Claude-Nicolas Ledoux (1736–1806) as part of his unbuilt project for the ideal city of Chaux. In the 1770s and 1780s Ledoux produced several important official works of architecture, including a series of customs houses or *barrieres* for Paris (1785) and the Saline Royale (Royal Saltworks) at Arc-et-Senan (1774–79). With the advent of the revolution, Ledoux was seen as closely connected to the ancien régime and was imprisoned from 1790 to 1793. While imprisoned, he began working on the project for Chaux, publishing the work in 1804, in the first volume of his collected works, *L'architecture considérée sous le rapport de l'art, des moeurs et de la législation* (Figure 4.1). Chaux took the plan form of a complete circle, or rather oval, of which the previous Royal Saltworks project comprised the southern half. In addition to the buildings in the circle, Ledoux produced schemes for a number of additional buildings that would be needed for the city to function smoothly. These included, among other buildings, numerous houses, a *pacifère* (building for peacefully resolving conflicts), a portico, a stock exchange, a market, a church, a *panarèthéon* (school of moral philosophy), and most importantly for us, a public brothel, the Oikéma (Figure 4.2).

Most commentators on the work of Ledoux mention the Oikéma, although few go into any depth in the discussion. As Paul Holmquist put it in his 2016 article about the Oikéma, "of all the institutions proposed by Claude-Nicolas Ledoux for the ideal city

4.1 Claude-Nicolas Ledoux, Ideal city of Chaux, 1804.
(Alamy Images)

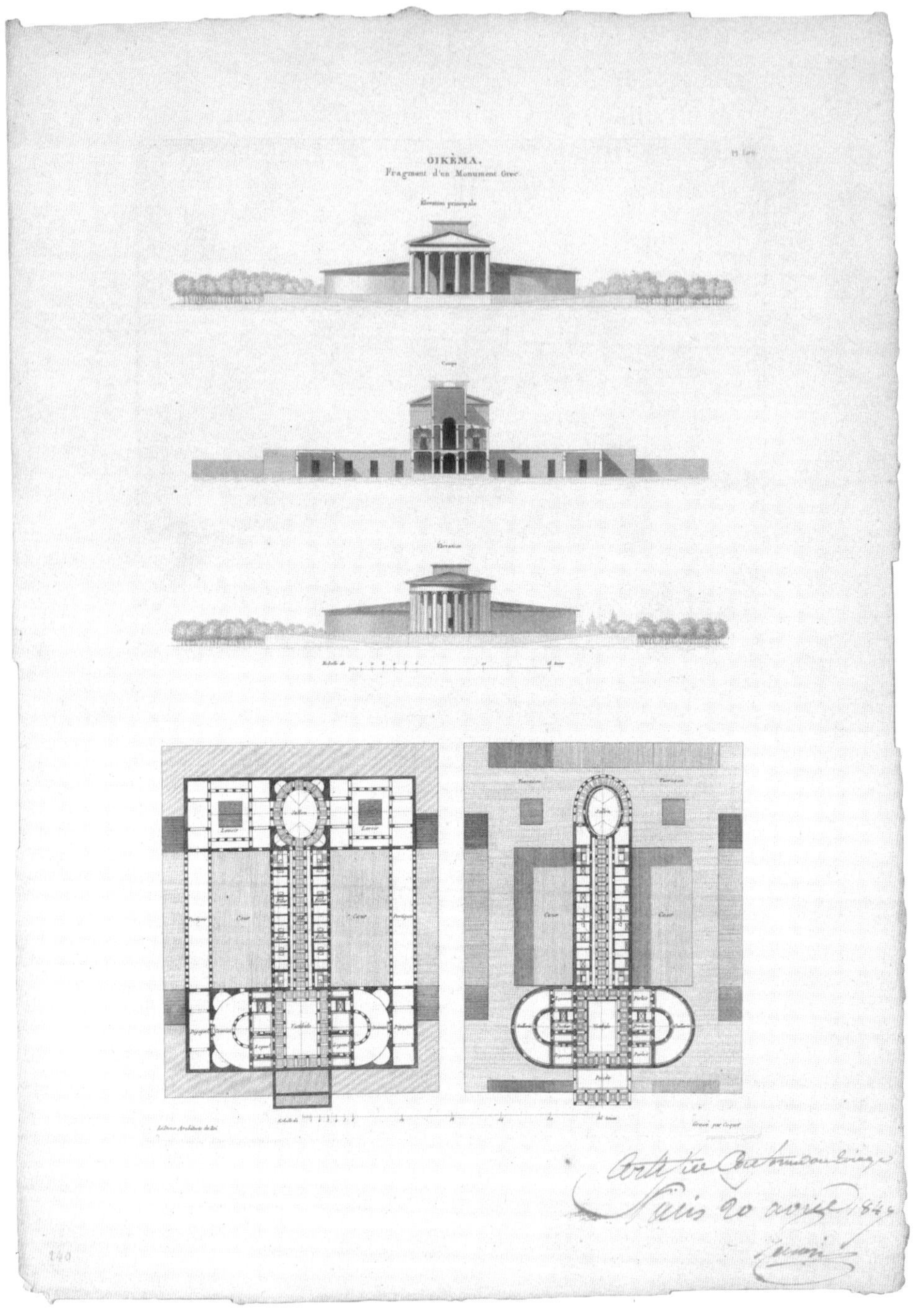

4.2 Claude-Nicolas Ledoux, Ideal city of Chaux, Oikéma, or House of Pleasure: elevation, section, and plans, 1804. (Bibliothèque National de France)

of Chaux, none has resisted interpretation more than his enigmatic 'workshop of corruption,' the Oikéma" (96). Indeed, if one is to discuss the city of Chaux based on Ledoux's drawings, the Oikéma is not really possible to pass up, if only because of its very clearly phallic plan form. Anthony Vidler, for example, in a passage on the Oikéma and a precedent project, the Maison de Plaisir (House of Pleasure) designed for Montmartre, in which Vidler focuses on Masonic symbolism and rites of initiation, writes, "in both cases...Ledoux retained an overriding figurative dimension that was secret—known only to the architect because hidden in the plan—but that nevertheless spoke of its function. Both plans were witty plays on an obviously phallic theme" (1987, 109). In his 1995 book *Building Sex*, Aaron Betsky takes a slightly more explicit reading of the building: "This was the place where young men would gather when they were ready to become adult citizens. Their rite of passage was to lose their virginity to specially trained young maidens. The whole building was shaped like a penis, its central axis culminating in the chamber of manhood, its spaces filled out with chambers of pleasure. Here Ledoux brought the erection of a grand order back to its social basis: the assertion of male power over women, the world, and themselves" (106). Even Paulette Singley, in her 1993 paper "The Anamorphic Phallus Within Ledoux's Dismembered Plan of Chaux" is caught by this image: "Seen and unseen, such apparent duplicity is equally manifest in Ledoux's unbuilt projects for a House of Pleasure in Paris and for an Oikema [*sic*] in the Ideal City of Chaux wherein these two designs operate as calligrams read under erasure...Explicitly phallic configurations embedded within the plans, these premature erections remain expertly concealed from all but the select initiates privileged to view Ledoux's sumptuous etchings" (176). Singley, as one might imagine given the topic of her paper, goes into considerably more depth in her analysis of the Oikéma than did Vidler or Betsky. However, even this lengthy analysis remains stuck on the level of iconography; rarely does Singley venture outside of these constraints to ask what was actually going on in this project. After all, it's easy to simply understand this as a joke—why would the eminent "Architect du Roi" Ledoux design a public brothel as a significant part of the ideal city of Chaux that would be, in effect, his life's work? And why would he choose to draw, clearly and openly, a penis among the etchings that would comprise his architectural legacy?

The Oikéma also connects in several ways to other aspects of the discussion between the prison and the house that we have been following. We note, first of all, that this project is roughly contemporaneous with Bentham's Panopticon, and stands as another early modern project that seeks, explicitly, to engineer aspects of society—in this case, the sexuality of society. And of course the Oikéma is a sort of prison, or perhaps better workhouse, confining in this case the "maidens" who are employed in its cell-like rooms (we can imagine the length of the phallus increasing infinitely as the need for more and more cells grows). On the other hand, these rooms offer a kind of abstracted and simplified domesticity, a machinic engine that is intended to produce, in the end, a domesticated sexuality. The Oikéma, and in a way all brothels, thus present for us aspects of prison, machine, house—all the concepts around which this book is formed.[2]

Architectures of the Phallus

The key structural feature of comedy in general [is] the appearance of the phallus, the comic "coming out" of the hidden signifier pertaining to the fundamental structure of the symbolic order and to its power relations.
—Alenka Zupančič, "Power in the Closet (And Its Coming Out)"

In order to uncover a bit more of what is at stake in these drawings, it will be helpful to consider the role of the phallus in discourse and in signification. For this I will draw largely on the work of Jacques Lacan, and in large part as interpreted by Slovenian thinker Alenka Zupančič, and in particular her paper "Power in the Closet (And Its Coming Out)," published in 2016.

The phallus is a central concept in Lacan's thinking. The phallus is not precisely or simply a penis—we could say that it is in fact everything about the penis except the penis, a representation of all of the connotations, fantasies, desires, and so on connected with the penis. Plus, of course, the penis—Lacan on occasion referred to the penis as the *real phallus*, that is, the phallus as it exists in the register of the real. The phallus, psychologically, is much more than the male sexual organ: it stands for our notions of power (power to penetrate, to inseminate, but also power *tout court*); it stands for, it embodies, sexual desire, and not just male desire; it stands for sexual and gender difference, not for masculinity, but for difference itself, and since difference is the basic means by which signification works (thank you, Saussure), the phallus stands for signification itself. The phallus is, so to speak, the lynch-pin that holds the human symbolic experience together, the fundamental object that guarantees signification, that promises order and structure, the final reference to which all chains of reference reduce. As Zupančič puts it, "it [the phallus] functions as a hidden presupposition (and reference) of the signifying order, guaranteeing its meaning" (2016, 220).

This situation is strange enough in itself—why should it be that the phallus, a *dick*, has this critical function? Isn't this some sort of mad gynophobic delusion?—but even stranger to come to grips with is Lacan's notion that, in order to maintain this position, to guarantee signification, the phallus must remain hidden. The arguments for this hiddenness of the phallus are far too complex and intricate for me to do justice to here; one excellent source for more information is Ellie Ragland-Sullivan's *The Logic of Sexuation* (2004). However, in crude terms, we could say that the *must* in the previous sentence is not a logical must but rather a psychical must—there is simply too much at stake, the potential consequences are simply too traumatic, for the phallus to be revealed.[3] In Zupančič's reading of Lacan, the arrival of the phallus on stage (in the theatre or on the stage of everyday life) results in a crisis or disruption of signification, leading to comedy, or distraction, or both.

The emergence onto the political scene in 2016, just at the moment of publication of Zupančič's essay, of Donald J. Trump, serves as a useful case in point. It is Trump, more than any other contemporary figure, that makes clear the relationships between the phallus, political power, and comedy. First, in contrast to previous generations of leaders, Trump brings the phallus back into play in contemporary politics with a vengeance, and in a way that makes it clear that he, and he alone, has the phallus. By putting the phallus on stage—and not just any phallus, his own phallus—Trump simultaneously proclaims his power and turns the world of politics into farce, abolishing in the process (this is an amazing confirmation of Lacan's position) any possibility of signification or discourse. In the face of this chaotic comedic scene, neither traditional political discourse—now revealed as castrated—nor traditional political comedy—which only adds to the chaos of the new scene—maintain any power of opposition. Within this scene, only the "prick of great stature," only the man who is not afraid to proclaim loudly the presence of his own phallus, of his own virility, can promise to "Make America Great Again," to restore the virility of a nation which until now did not realize it had been lost.

In Zupančič's scheme, then, we have to conclude by suggesting that Trump (along with Berlusconi, Bolsonaro, and others) presents us with the coming out of the closet of power, the coming out to power of power, the emergence of a power that is not afraid to not just reveal but proclaim its brutality, its untruthfulness, its avarice. This is a power that resides openly in sexual organization, in the power of the phallus.

Where does this discussion leave us, in terms of our analysis of LeDoux's Oikéma? First, I would point out that the appearance of the phallus (and we must be clear that this is a phallus, not a penis, despite Betsky's comments) in Ledoux's engravings is a classic example of placing the phallus on the stage. The plan etching is highly incongruous within the context of the volume, leading to immediate reactions of shock, surprise, and titillation; the comedic effect, while unable to quite gain a foothold here, is nonetheless undeniable. Plus, of course, it results in an immediate distraction: the figure of the phallus becomes the overriding question of the analysis, as we have seen in the three commentators quoted above, foreclosing the possibility of a more nuanced or considered analysis.

Such an analysis might start by considering the question of the brothel itself during the post-revolutionary and early Napoleonic years in France. As Paul B. Preciado (2015) has pointed out, there were several proposals for public brothels just before the Revolution, notably those put forward by Restif de la Bretonne and by the Marquis de Sade. Ledoux himself produced a project for a public brothel of gigantic scale to cover the top of Montmartre in 1787. In 1804 a Napoleonic decree required prostitutes in Paris to be registered and to undergo frequent medical examinations, which led in short order to the development of state-licensed brothels. These institutions, such as the famous Le Chabanais, flourished in nineteenth- and twentieth-century Paris under what became known as "the French system." The brothels were finally closed in 1946 after the end of the Second World War (Conner 2017). In this context, Ledoux's Oikéma seems markedly less shocking than it otherwise might—and also, perhaps, somewhat more prescient.

As Preciado points out, Restif's proposal resulted largely from concerns about the spread of syphilis; the enclosure of prostitutes in brothels, where their health could be monitored and their activities controlled, was intended to ensure the health of the general population. Sade, on the other hand, was more concerned with the safety of the inmate of the brothel, that is, the libertine. The primary diagram of the brothel in either case was the enclosing wall, the rigid separation between interior and exterior. The Oikéma did not follow either of these models; rather, the institution was intended to operate as a means of purifying the youth who would visit it, turning them back to virtue through exposure to vice, like some sort of inoculation, enabling them to enter properly into marriage—that is, to participate fully in an ordered society. Interior and exterior are not separated in the Oikéma, but rather flow one into the other as parts of a single mechanism. It is no wonder, then, that Preciado understands the project as an early and powerful example of the formation of the biopolitical state, as it positions sexuality, and especially control over sexuality, right at the core of the construction of an ideal society.[4]

From this point of view, we can see that the brothel is far from "witty play" or from a throw-away one-liner of a project; rather, this project is conceptually central to the ideal city. The phallus, then, operates as pure distraction, as a giant sign that says "there is nothing to see here, this is just a joke, don't bother looking." The phallic form prevents us from seeing the true radicality in the project.

There are, however, some other signs that might point us to what's going on here. To be up front here, I have to say that I am not a Ledoux scholar and much of what follows is pure speculation. Still, there are some things that strike me as strange; for example, Ledoux signs his drawings "Le Doux, Architecte du roi" (Ledoux, Royal Architect), some fifteen years after the Revolution and eleven years after the suppression of the Académie Royale d'Architecture (Royal Academy of Architecture) in 1793. The use of this title, albeit in small lettering, in a volume of revolutionary designs and dedicated to the emperor, Napoleon, must be considered meaningful; although Ledoux's motivations are questionable, he is nonetheless aligning both himself and his work with the ancien régime. In addition, Ledoux was fifty-three years old at the time of the Revolution, that is, just hitting the prime of his career as an architect; unable to build any further works, he must have been fully aware that these drawings, never intended to come to fruition in built form, would be his final statement for posterity. It seems to me that we need to think of these drawings as a message, a letter, from the old world, represented by the *architect du roi*, to the new world in the form of the emperor.

What is the meaning of this message? Is this a blueprint for an ideal future society? A manifesto, with extended middle finger, for resistance to the new post-revolutionary world? Or perhaps a note of warning, from the old world to the new? Of one thing we can be sure: Ledoux was not so deranged as to think, like Vitruvius, that this work was the path to new commissions, that flattering the emperor was the way to more success. His precise motivations for producing this work, in the senses I've laid out above, were likely unknown or at least unclear to Ledoux, but he offers a hint in the form of the phallus.

First, of course, the project for Chaux does claim to be a plan for the ideal city and hence for the ideal society. This is a society that needs the Oikéma to function, in order to tame the raw sexual impulse and turn it to social good, or, as Preciado (2015) points out, a society in which biopolitical control is fundamental. In Preciado's reading, we might say that it is in fact biopolitics that acts as the phallus in nineteenth-century society, the mechanism that guarantees the meaning of society, constantly growing even as political forms in France changed back and forth over the majority of the century, the mechanism that must remain veiled, invisible, the unacknowledged engine of society, the phallus that is veiled and made almost unreadable precisely by the overt image of the (penile) phallus. Second, the phallic image stands out like a middle finger, like a fuck you, not so much to the reader as to the personage to whom the work has been dedicated, Napoleon. The presence of the phallus turns the work into comedy, into farce, and its dedicatee into a rube. This gift offered to Napoleon (and perhaps to the future) is a gift of power, first the gift of architectural power, but then also the gift of power that is always contained and represented by the phallic symbol. Like every phallic symbol, like every phallus, this gift is a flawed power, an impotent phallus, because—and this in the end is one of the fundamental differences between phallus and penis—every phallus is separated from its body, that is, every phallus is a castrated penis, an impotent power. Emil Kaufmann understood this concern of separation in his 1952 study of Chaux, but, as a formalist, he did not make the links to power or to impotence. And, of course, the image of castration in post-revolutionary France cannot help but suggest the guillotine, and in this particular case the separation of the king's head from his body. The appearance of the (castrated) phallus at this spot in the treatise, at the place that speaks clearly of order and especially psychosexual order, cannot *not* be the image of a world in radical disorder, a world governed by a radically impotent power, a world that has lost its possibility of meaning.[5]

Oikéma is an interesting name for Ledoux to give this project. In the original Greek, *oikēma* signified a dwelling but was also used to designate a prison or a prison cell; according to Holmquist, *oikēma* could also be used to describe a "place of debauchery" (2016, 98). Hence the Oikéma brings together the three architectural strands that make up my narrative in this book: house, prison, sexuality.

The analysis of the preceding few pages also solidifies the schema that I have been developing that sex (and its spin-offs of gender, sexuality, and procreation) sits at the core of the construction of society as a whole, and that architecture serves the role of hiding or veiling that generative impulse. Preciado's work, discussed earlier, in identifying the Oikéma as an early biopolitical project, recognizes sex *in architecture* as key to the development of the modern state. We could say, in other words, that sex acts as the phallus of any building project: to quote Zupančič out of context, sex "functions as a hidden presupposition (and reference) of the signifying order, guaranteeing its meaning" (2016, 220). The emergence of the phallus, of *sex* and especially of *sexuality* into visibility, into explicit presence, immediately produces a crisis of meaning, a state of disorder.

It should be no surprise, then, that around this same time, as the biopolitical regime was beginning to find its feet, one particular form of sex that was radically resistant to control became something of a cause célèbre, even, I would argue, within the realm of architecture: masturbation.

Architecture and the Masturbation Problem[6]

In the first half of the twentieth century, masturbation was understood as something of a crisis of civilization. As Thomas Laqueur points out in his 2004 study of masturbation, *Solitary Sex: A Cultural History of Masturbation,* by the 1930s the notion of masturbation as the cause of physical illnesses had been largely debunked (only to live on as an urban myth). For Laqueur, masturbation as a result was transformed from an urgent danger to public health into an even more pressing danger to society as a whole. As Laqueur puts it, "No longer a threat to health, sex with oneself could represent a rejection not only of socially appropriate sexuality, not only of appropriate sociability, but of the social order itself" (2004, 359). Laqueur traces the genealogy of such attitudes towards masturbation in Western Europe back to the anonymous publication in London, "in or around 1712," of a pamphlet titled *Onania; or, the Heinous Sin of Self Pollution, and all its Frightful Consequences, in both SEXES Considered, with Spiritual and Physical Advice to those who have already injured themselves by this abominable practice. Onania* identified, or, as Laqueur claims, invented, a new approach to masturbation: while in previous thinking masturbation was considered a sin, damaging perhaps to the soul, from 1712 on it increasingly came to be understood both as a disease and a vice, damaging to the body and eventually, as we see in Sartre's comments, to the social order. By the mid-nineteenth century, onanism was understood as a plague that the modern world would need to eradicate, as the modern vice par excellence.

Laqueur's analysis of the literature around masturbation, especially that from the eighteenth and nineteenth centuries, identifies three lines of thought around the evil of masturbation, three modalities by which onanism is understood by the mid-nineteenth century to be abhorrent. In each case, the problem is seen to reside not so much in the physical act or in the physical effects of masturbation, but rather in the mental activity, the thoughts, that accompany and give birth to the acts. First, masturbation is understood to be based not in the desire for a real person, or indeed for any real object; it is a product solely of the imagination, and results in purely imaginary effects. In Freud's words, cited by Laqueur, "Masturbation contributes to the substitution of fantasy objects for reality" (2004, 210). As such, solitary sex results in a false pleasure, artificial, counterfeit, and fraudulent; worse, it contributes to the dissociation of the masturbator from the reality of the world. Second, masturbation is both solitary and secret; in Laqueur's phrase, it comes to be understood "not as *a* but *the* solitary vice, not as a but *the* secret sin" (224), the vice that epitomizes all secrets and, in fact, from which all secrets flow. "This vice's solitariness and secrecy went beyond the merely antisocial or morally reprehensible; the act was outside the pale not just of this or that but any possible social order" (225). Indeed, masturbation seemed to provide a definition for the idea of the private, to create it as a category. As a secret, private vice, it was autarkic, a self-contained economy of production and effect. Third, precisely because it needs no external support or stimulus, because it can be carried out any time and any place, and because it is a thirst that is never capable of being sated, masturbation is understood as the very figure of excess and wastage. It is an unregulated and unregulatable vice, a harmful addiction that will sap the energies of the onanist and cause harm to those around him. As Laqueur points out, eighteenth- and nineteenth-century Europeans understood masturbation to be *unnatural* in all three of these modalities, and it was precisely this unnatural character of the act that made it so abhorrent and so in need of extermination or at least control. Looking back from today's viewpoint, though—that is, with 2020s vision—and especially from a viewpoint that has as its aim an understanding of how masturbation might relate to architecture, how architectural and onanistic discourses might become (perhaps promiscuously) entwined, I would argue that the real problem with masturbation in the nineteenth century was that masturbation, in all the modalities that Laqueur has identified, is *undisciplined*. And in the modern world, architecture was, if anything, the art of discipline.

The undisciplined character of masturbation provides a clue to the relationship, in the nineteenth century, between architecture and masturbation.[7] This is certainly a strange relationship, one that is not immediately obvious, but there is no doubt in my mind that such a relationship both pertains to and is of importance in understanding the modern world. Indeed, as I have already pointed out, the idea that the prison cell, the architectural mechanism for the discipline of the unruly subject, was simultaneously the setting par excellence for masturbation, forms an incredible problem at the core of modernity, the problem of the private versus the social, of the politics of surveillance, which has dogged architecture to the present day. We can see this relationship in the basic structure of arguably the best known of all disciplinary architectures. As mentioned in chapter 2, Jeremy Bentham's Panopticon was designed to change the behaviour of prisoners in their cells by the removal of privacy. The Panopticon, in other words, was designed first and foremost to prevent masturbation (Bentham, as Laqueur points out, thought masturbation to be a greater problem than sodomy).

Laqueur's positioning of masturbation as imaginary, solitary/secret, and excess provides a suitable framework to construct an understanding of this strange relationship. First, masturbation, as Laqueur stresses, is a practice founded in the imaginary. As such, we can think of masturbation as operating in distinct opposition to architecture, which presents itself—arguably in all times and places—as a discipline concerned entirely with the real, with solidity, permanence, structure. The worlds produced by these two practices, architecture and masturbation, are therefore at root incommensurable, apparently completely independent; the very difference between the practice of the construction of the imaginary par excellence and the practice of the construction of the real par excellence renders invisible the presence of any relationship at all.

At around the beginning of the nineteenth century, however, this situation became more pronounced, as architecture adjusted to new political, social, and economic developments. During this process, architecture came to understand its primary task less as the representation of power (of the church, of the state, of money) and more as the construction of a new world. This is an effect of the transition stressed by Foucault from a sovereign power, rooted in necropolitics (the power to give death), spectacle and symbol, to biopolitics, rooted in the art of living. Architecture, in other words, transitioned from providing an image of the power of the sovereign, the church, the state, and instead became concerned with the production of mechanisms, *dispositifs*, for the construction of the modern, docile subject. Such a concern of course expands its boundaries: Architecture would no longer be concerned simply with the design of buildings (if it ever was), but will take up, through the design and construction of those institutions that shape the modern subject, the modern economy, and indeed the modern state, the design of the world as a whole. Architecture came to stress its productive role, denying, at least in discourse, its representative role. As a result, we can see the development of several issues that bear directly on the relationship between architecture and masturbation:

1. Architecture must deny the role that fantasy plays in its process. Architecture takes on this task by redefining itself as a discipline and a profession, through the twin institutions of the architecture school and the professional association, aligned in both cases with modern technological, economic, and bureaucratic structures. Underlying methods of fantasy image construction are subordinated to technological methods.

2. Architecture stresses its productive role in society over its representational role. Here I mean primarily architecture's role in the construction of the economy, through the production of direct apparatus (factories, warehouses, shops) as well as the ancillary apparatus (houses, schools, colleges, prisons, government administrations). Architecture aligns itself fully with capital.
3. Architecture claims for itself the role of the *only* constructor of environments in the modern world, extending itself to the production of design objects at all scales (from tableware to furniture to buildings to cities).
4. Architecture distances itself (disowns) technologies of the image (painting, theatre, cinema) as well as elements of the fantastic or the image within its own production. The struggle between structure and ornament becomes central to the development of modernity in architecture, as epitomized in the work of the art nouveau architects, Adolf Loos, Louis Sullivan, and others.[8]

Masturbation, of course, falls into conflict of one kind or another with each of these positions: it is the practice based in fantasy par excellence, threatening to expose the fantastic at the core of the architectural discipline; it has no (apparent) effect on the real world, operating on a total internal economy of desire and ejaculation, while producing a fantasy world that at best ignores or at worst has *destructive* effects on the real (as noted in chapter 1, masturbation can be understood as an act of theft); it is an alternative technique of world-creation, potentially producing another fantasy world that operates in parallel to or indeed in opposition to the physical world of architecture; and of course it is the technique of the constant production of imagery.[9]

So far, the relationship between masturbation and architecture has remained abstract. However, the relationship becomes a bit more real when we consider Laqueur's second point: masturbation is both solitary and secret. After all, the secrecy within which masturbation takes place is normally furnished by architecture. Despite the masturbatory production of a fantastic world, the physical act of masturbation is always connected with the architecture in which it takes place: in one's bedroom, in a prison cell, in a public washroom, in the office, in a peep-show booth. All these and of course many more locations have an inescapable effect on the act itself and on its fantasy production. This is in fact a universal: even masturbating outside, in the wilderness, is inflected by the fact of *not* being inside a building. I would argue, too, that masturbating in a space changes our view of that space forever—indeed, changes that space forever. Architecture and masturbation are therefore intertwined as a couple: they penetrate each other, impregnate each other.

Architecture, too, defines the condition of privacy through the development of spaces that are shut away. The model for this condition in the sixteenth and seventeenth centuries may have been the prayer closet, but by the late eighteenth and early nineteenth centuries the prison cell had become the most exemplary form. The nineteenth century, concerned as it was with the disciplining of the body, saw the development and codification of a series of private spaces arguably based on the model of the cell, such as the private bedroom (we could also cite in this regard the development in the twentieth century of the nuclear family and its corollary, the single-family house, each presenting a new and hitherto unknown level of privacy). Such spaces are of course spaces in which masturbation can flourish, spaces in which new techniques of surveillance must be developed in order to maintain discipline, especially masturbatory discipline; we have already cited two such examples, operating at the extreme ends of the nineteenth century: Bentham's Panopticon and Freudian psychoanalysis.

However, architecture's primary mandate through this period was not the construction of the individual (through masturbatory or other means), but the construction of society. The individual was largely understood within architecture as a single, infinitely replicable unit, as demonstrated by the housing schemes of Le Corbusier, the urban planning of Hilberseimer, ergonomic standards developed by Ernst Neufert ([1936] 1980), Henry Dreyfuss (1960), and others, or the post-war tract housing of Levittown. It is pure irony, in the world of the Fordist ideal of the assembly line, or the eugenic ideal of the identical and reproducible superman, that the provision of the infinitely identical cellular living space became the perfect Petri dish for the emergence of the modern, individual, sexual self. This tension between the social and the individual remained a dominant and unresolved tension in architectural thinking through the twentieth century, playing out not only on the domestic scene with the distinction between the open-plan and closed bedrooms, but also in areas as diverse as education (open vs. closed classrooms) and, more widely, the workplace. This is the story of the private office versus the secretarial pool, and is of course a story bound up in questions of race, class, and gender.

Part and parcel of architecture's new role as the constructor of the physical apparatus of society was a concern for the *disciplined* construction of that modern world, for the elimination of excess. To be clear, though, the issue was not with excess as such, but particularly with non-productive, undisciplined excess. Excess, after all, was and remains at the root of the functioning of capital, in the form of surplus value. The disciplinary role of architecture was to eliminate uncontrolled excess that manifested as waste.

It is no surprise, then, that the question of ornament and the related question of rational structure emerged as another of the critical issues of modern architecture. Ornament became a problem for architecture not only because of the imaginary nature of ornament, but also (and arguably more importantly) because of its inefficiency: ornament was not understood to contribute to the productive capacity of the architectural apparatus. We can see this idea played out in the rapid rise and fall of art nouveau; in Loos's influential *Ornament and Crime* (2019), which originated as a 1910 lecture; in the streamlined white houses of Le Corbusier; in Mies van der Rohe's famous dictum of "Less is more." Meanwhile, movements such as Taylorism, functionalism, the *Existenzminimum*, the Maison Dom-Ino, Le Corbusier's urban planning schemes, the Athens Charter of the Congrès Internationaux d'Architecture Moderne (CIAM), and the time and motion studies of Eadweard Muybridge, Étienne-Jules Marey, and most directly (for architecture) Frank and Lillian Gilbreth, demonstrate the importance to modern architecture of developing a scientific, rational approach to efficiency. *As far as I am aware, there are no time-and-motion studies of masturbation.*[10]

Implied in the conception of the modern, and particularly in the architectural modern, is the notion of mechanical efficiency (implied, for example, in Le Corbusier's notion of the house as a machine for living in). There is to be, in a tea kettle, a room, a house, a city, no wasted motion or excess parts. Participation in the machine of society was to be universal and compulsory, with all activities, including sexual activities, contributing to the greater profit. Masturbation, though, as conceived by the moderns, was nothing but wasted motion, undisciplined and undisciplinable.

By the early twentieth century, it was no longer quite so clear that the motions of the masturbator were entirely wasted, that the excess of masturbation was without value. For Freud, for example, in *The Three Essays on Sexuality* ([1905] 1962), masturbation, or at least infantile masturbation, was a valuable, indeed necessary activity, as it formed the genesis for what would emerge as adult sexuality. Furthermore, the mere existence of the supremely private act of masturbation (and equally importantly, its ubiquity) pointed to and in fact was seen to constitute or at least delimit a core of the individual self, a radically private self that is beyond social regulation, and indeed beyond the social. This individual self, in other words, is the waste product of masturbation: the individual self that is, as I have described elsewhere, already an architectural production, the kleptogenetic sequestering of the singular plurality of being, the invention of the private.

The relationship between architecture and masturbation in the modern world (and indeed, I would suggest, in any era) is barely discernable. It is an uncanny relationship that only rarely emerges into the realm of the visible (peep holes, video booths, back rooms). Masturbation is a ghostly presence within architecture, impermanent and immaterial, but a presence nonetheless, a presence that speaks to the fundamental architectural issues of modernity: the rejection of the imaginary, the struggle between the private and the social, and the mechanistic concern for waste and excess. Masturbation and architecture form an unacknowledged, illicit couple. Possibly the clearest and most powerful exposition of this relationship is Vito Acconci's work *Seedbed*, from 1972, in which the artist lay beneath a ramp in the gallery, masturbating as people walked above; Acconci's project shows us that masturbation is always present in any structure.

It is precisely this lack of visibility of the relationship that is important, that in fact constitutes the nature of the relationship. I want to return, briefly, to the question of privacy. For Laqueur, masturbation is the epitome of the private act, the very definition and site of formation, in fact, of the private. However, here I think Laqueur misses the point (although this is probably an unfair accusation). It is not simply the case, as I have described above, that the conflict between the private and the social became a critical architectural issue in the modern world; such an argument fails to recognize that the idea of the private is, in itself, an architectural concept (as is, for that matter, the social). It is not that masturbation is inherently or naturally a private act, but rather that architecture literally makes it a private act and maintains it in a state of mandatory privacy. *It is not that the prisoner masturbates in his cell, but rather, that the masturbator is held prisoner by architecture.*

We could expand this analysis to other sex acts beyond masturbation, to address at last the question of "how does sex enter into architecture": architecture's role is to make private and secret, to hide away and make invisible, and to maintain the private nature of sex. Indeed, I would suggest that this is not simply a role of architecture among other roles—shelter, protection etc.—but *the primary role and purpose* for architecture. Sex is not something added on to architecture, something that a particular work of architecture may or may not have, a question of particulars of form or materiality, but the core of what architecture is about. Architecture's job in relation to sex goes beyond simply holding it, simply being a site for sex acts or sexual fantasies, or even beyond the position of privatizing sex: architecture

4.3 Truck supervisor Bernard Levey standing with his family in front of their home in new housing development, Levittown, New York, 1950. (Photograph by Bernard Hoffman/ The LIFE Picture Collection / Shutterstock)

has the additional task of disciplining sex. Certain sexual practices are allowed by the architecture of any given time, while others, while not necessarily explicitly forbidden, are discouraged, or simply *not present*. We can make use of Sara Ahmed's (2006) concept of orientation in this respect. Take, for example, the Levittown Cape Cod House of 1947, prototypical of the modern house, with its master bedroom and children's bedroom (Figure 4.3). The Cape Cod could be occupied by a single gay man, and the second bedroom repurposed as a guest room, office, and so on; but the house remains *oriented* to the needs of the nuclear family and in turn *orients* its occupants to the corresponding sexual practices. The position of the bedroom at the rear of the house *orients* its occupants to discretion in their sexual lives, *orients* them away from public sexual displays, etc., while the thin walls *orient* the users towards sexual activities that are, relatively speaking, quiet. The single shared bathroom *orients* the inhabitants away from sex in the shower, or bathing together, or watersports. The analysis could doubtless continue, and a similar analysis could be made for any house, and indeed for any building, to understand the ways in which sex is disciplined by architecture. But how then might we affect some architectural dis-orientation?[11]

Masturbation in the Pornographic Era

Masturbation in public or quasi-public settings has a rich history as a conscious or unconscious mode of resistance among queer people and groups: in parks, in toilet rooms, in cinemas, in the back rooms of bars. I don't aim to trace that history here or to analyze the practices involved beyond what might be implied in what I have already claimed. During the AIDS crisis, descriptions and discussions of such practices proliferated, in the work for example of Douglas Crimp, David Wojnarowicz, and (from a notably architectural standpoint) John Paul Ricco. For Ricco, quasi-public masturbation of the type that took place in the back rooms of New York bars in the early 1990s was itself a spatial practice resulting in an architecture that was smelly, sticky, dark, and salty. As Ricco put it in his 1993 essay, "Jack-off-rooms-as-minor-architecture disrupt the heterosexist, bourgeois, marital, familial, domesticating and interiorizing models, imperatives, logics, politics, and spaces, which constitute major architecture(s)" (27). In a preface produced on the occasion of the republication of the essay in 2016, Ricco paid attention to the form of the collectivity that might result from these spatial practices, from these minor architectures. For Ricco, the collectivity that might emerge would be one of *unbecoming*, both in the everyday sense of being unflattering, even abject, and in the philosophical sense of *not becoming*, of a collectivity that does not adhere, does not form identity, does not evolve political or communal goals, a collectivity that, in my terms, was always anti-architectural. It was a collectivity of multiple singularities: "the sex that happened (happens) in the backrooms was (is) sex with, amongst and alongside an incalculable multiplicity of others...When in a backroom you experienced 'an extremely populous solitude'" (Ricco 2016, v). The collectivity, formed from transience and anonymity, is not one that joins together, but one that pushes apart, entropic, and centrifugal in its operations. It has no collective aims beyond ejaculation. Masturbation offers no solutions or, as Ricco put it, "political fantasies or hope for a brighter tomorrow" (v). It does not seek to build new walls. The architecture of jacking-off remains a solitary and non-productive production of sperm.

Architectural Masturbation

The act of formal, visual, verbal or written self-gratification (or any combination of the aforementioned) during the process of, or upon "completion" of designing a building which is commonly post-rationalized to veil a total lack of spatial, theoretical, functional, and conceptual rigour.
—Urban Dictionary

I first drafted these sentences, first stained these sheets, at the height of COVID-19. The pandemic brought into the open more than a few truths, or at least situations, that were not so obvious to us in the past. One of the great ironies, in this time of isolation, is that masturbation is no longer a solitary activity: masturbation has gone online, into that quasi-public space of the internet. This is not exactly new, of course: the image of the masturbator in front of the screen, or in front of the camera, has been more and more with us in recent years, but it has taken this moment of separation to reveal socially *distanced sex as* our new norm, as, really, the only socially responsible and socially acceptable contemporary sexual form. The COVID-19 pandemic has demonstrated the revised place of solitary sex in our contemporary world. Solitary sex is no longer strictly solitary, and the most private of acts is no longer private. Nor is it any longer a product simply of phantasy: masturbation is formed around fantasies provided by the pornography industry, or—which amounts to the same thing—by images of anonymous others, other masturbators, for whom we become pornography in turn. Critically, though, it remains, perhaps more than ever, a question of excess.[12]

In the pharmacopornographic era that we live in, as described by Preciado (2017), masturbation has moved from the periphery to the centre, and is now the fundamental activity that figures the organization of society. Fundamental to this is the question of excess: while earlier eras, the nineteenth and early twentieth centuries, the era of the disciplinary society, the era of the architectural machine, saw excess as waste and without value, the contemporary economy of control, the pharmacopornographic era, understands excess as potential profit. Excess is no longer to be curtailed; rather, excess is to be encouraged. Preciado points out the two primary mechanisms by which ejaculation becomes profit, by which, coincidentally, masturbation becomes work: pharmacological products, especially the birth control pill and Viagra (which, taken together, turn even heterosexual vaginal intercourse into masturbation), and the pornography industry, which ties our masturbatory fantasies into the engine of the economy. Drugs and porn: these are the essential substances that feed our addictions.[13]

Indeed, in the pharmacopornographic era, masturbation, only slightly redirected from its nineteenth-century substance, becomes the central figure for society that, in turn, is restructured along onanistic lines: masturbation, we could say, is the phallus for our contemporary world. Today, society as a whole can be examined following Laqueur's three fundamental characteristics of masturbation. First, society is now

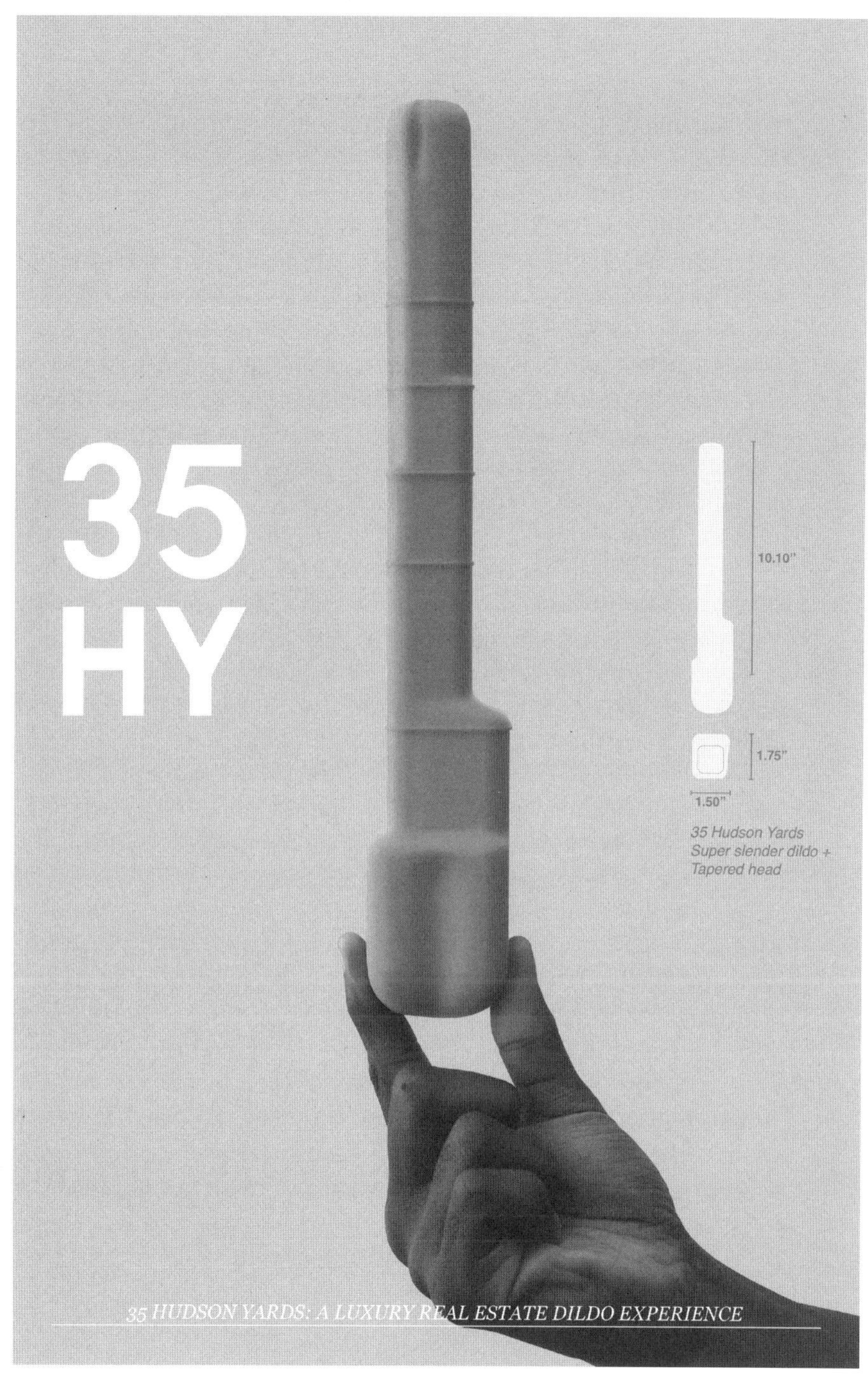

4.4 Wolfgang & Hite, HY 35: A luxury dildo experience. Architectural stuff, 2022. (Image courtesy Wolfgang & Hite)

completely wrapped up in, generated by, and productive of fantasy and the imaginary. We are confronted every day with our current denial of and separation from the reality of our existence, in the form of the lies of Trump and others, the fantasy populisms that only benefit the wealthy, the denial of social and environmental crises—even as people riot in the streets, we are ravaged by a pandemic, and hurricanes and wildfires are out of control. Instead, we, at least those of us in the West, live in a world of our own fantasy, a world of advertising and television, a world of the desire-image. And what is architecture in this world? It is no longer able to take on the role of construction of the real, although of course this cannot be admitted, least of all to architects; today, all architecture can do is play the role of producer (in the sense of the producer of a play or film) of the desire-image. Architecture today, even in its constructed three-dimensional form, cannot be more than image.

Second, our contemporary society is dominated by the solitary. COVID-19 has made that situation clearly evident, but the solitude in which we live is far from caused by the social distancing (the most ironic of terms) wrought by the pandemic. Our solitary existence today, unlike the solitary of past times, is neither private nor secret, but rather both public and evident. Our society is one of atomization, an "extremely populous solitude" in which our energies are focused on self-actualization, on pursuit of personal pleasure, on the development of an imagined self through accumulation of desire-images. Architecture in this world is no longer the arbiter or producer of the private, the secret or the solitary as such, when architecture can be and is penetrated at any moment by technological incursions through its walls, as websites such as Chaturbate bring us into the most private of spaces, into the bedrooms of masturbators around the world. The entire world has now become a back room, a jack-off room, as we spend our lives masturbating.

And, of course, this is a world of pure excess, of insatiable desire for the accumulation of *stuff*: cars, clothes, likes, sexual partners. We are addicted to this *stuff*, literally, our bodies can no longer live without it; it is this *stuff* that we crave, that we yearned for during our weeks and months of social isolation, not the real connections of human to human that this *stuff* represents. It is the representation that we need. And like any other addiction, our need for *stuff* continues to grow, our consumption of *stuff*—our constant onanistic excess—drives our production of capital, enables the proliferation of more and more *stuff*, until, inevitably, we reach a point of overdose. Architecture, far from being the apparatus of discipline, the model of restraint, has become the very figure of excess, of *stuff*, as any view of a contemporary city or walk through a biennale will make clear: the sheer proliferation of more and more formal and material diversity, much without reason or sense, and none of it speaking to its neighbours. Frank Gehry, Daniel Libeskind, Zaha Hadid, Rem Koolhaas: the atomized and atomizing architecture of pure excess, the architecture of ejaculation (Figure 4.4).

In short, architecture's place in the world, architecture's mandate, has been completely overturned. Any calls for a more socially or environmentally responsible architecture are the pure call of nostalgia, looking to regain an image of a lost world. *In the world of masturbation, architecture can only be pornography.*

Chapter 5
Living in Glass Houses

In the final chapter of *Discipline and Punish*, Michel Foucault establishes January 22, 1840, the date of the official opening of the Mettray colony, as the date of completion of the carceral society. Foucault justifies this choice by pointing out, first, that Mettray contained, superimposed on a single site, five primary disciplinary institutional models that together make up the carceral, together with their architectural analogues: the family (house), the army (barracks), the workshop, the school, and justice (the cell). Through the conjunction of these five models, a new regime of totalizing supervision, observation, and knowledge regarding the colonists came into being: "In the normalization of the power of normalization, in the arrangement of a power-knowledge over individuals, Mettray and its school marked a new era" (Foucault 1979, 296). Critically for Foucault, this disciplinary structure, instituted first at Mettray, did not stay within the bounds of the institution, but rather soon spread into society as a whole. The boundary of Mettray proved to be permeable, producing a discipline of discipline characteristic of modernity.

The permeable boundary of Mettray as discussed by Foucault was not just a metaphor: Mettray, as it happened, had no wall.[1] In the first instance, this was likely a pragmatic decision, as the means of producing a satisfactory wall around acres of fields must have been daunting for the founders. In the end, rather than erecting a wall around the colony, the founders instituted a program by which nearby farmers would be paid for the return of any colonists who ran away, thus extending the institution into the surrounding countryside. The dividing line between institution and world becomes blurred, edges cease to be sharp. The carceral society literally spreads beyond the colony, and the distinction between colony and world becomes impossible to locate. It is not so much that the wall is missing at Mettray: the wall is still there, still an effective and highly present boundary.[2] All that is missing is the stone. The corollary effect of Foucault's movement of the discipline of discipline from institution to society is the dematerialization of the wall, an operation that must be seen, from the point of view of architecture, as a fundamentally queer one.[3]

This dematerialization of the wall is of course one of the most critical developments in architecture over the past two centuries, and particularly during the modern era. This process has been in large part caused by the emergence of new technological and hence expressive potential coupled with changing economic realities. In what follows I will argue that this consistent trend to dematerialization also constitutes an opposition to these economic and technical forces, a queering of the wall.[4]

The dematerialization of the enclosure can be understood to derive from the development of new structural materials over the course of the nineteenth and early twentieth centuries, particularly steel and reinforced concrete, which took the place of stone and brick. These new materials demanded a new logic of construction, which can be seen clearly in Le Corbusier's Maison Dom-Ino of 1913. Dom-Ino was not the first project to suggest these constructive logics, which had been developed (primarily in steel construction) in the American skyscraper over the course of the 1890s, but Dom-Ino was possibly the first project to suggest the use of these methods, especially in reinforced concrete, for residential construction. The rationale was simple, if innovative: to develop a logic of housing construction that could be mobilized on an industrial basis. After the war, Le Corbusier would go on to develop these ideas further in his journal *L'Esprit Nouveau* and his books, particularly *Toward an Architecture* ([1923] 2009).

This new constructional logic, like most of Le Corbusier's ideas of this period, is clearly visible in the Villa Savoye, although exigencies of construction did not always allow a full realization of the ideas presented. The building presents as a concrete frame from which the exterior enclosure is hung (this is the basis of the term *curtain wall*). The key and radical concept here is the division of structure and enclosure, hitherto united in the single material entity of the wall, into separate systems, each with its own logic. Enclosure becomes, for the first time, a question on its own terms, not subject to the requirements of structure. Some results are immediately obvious. For example, the enclosure, not being required to hold anything up, does not need to go down to the ground. At Savoye the enclosure is hung a full storey above grade, while in its sister un-house, Mies van der Rohe's Barcelona Pavilion, details at the roof level are presented as though without weight, with wall-like

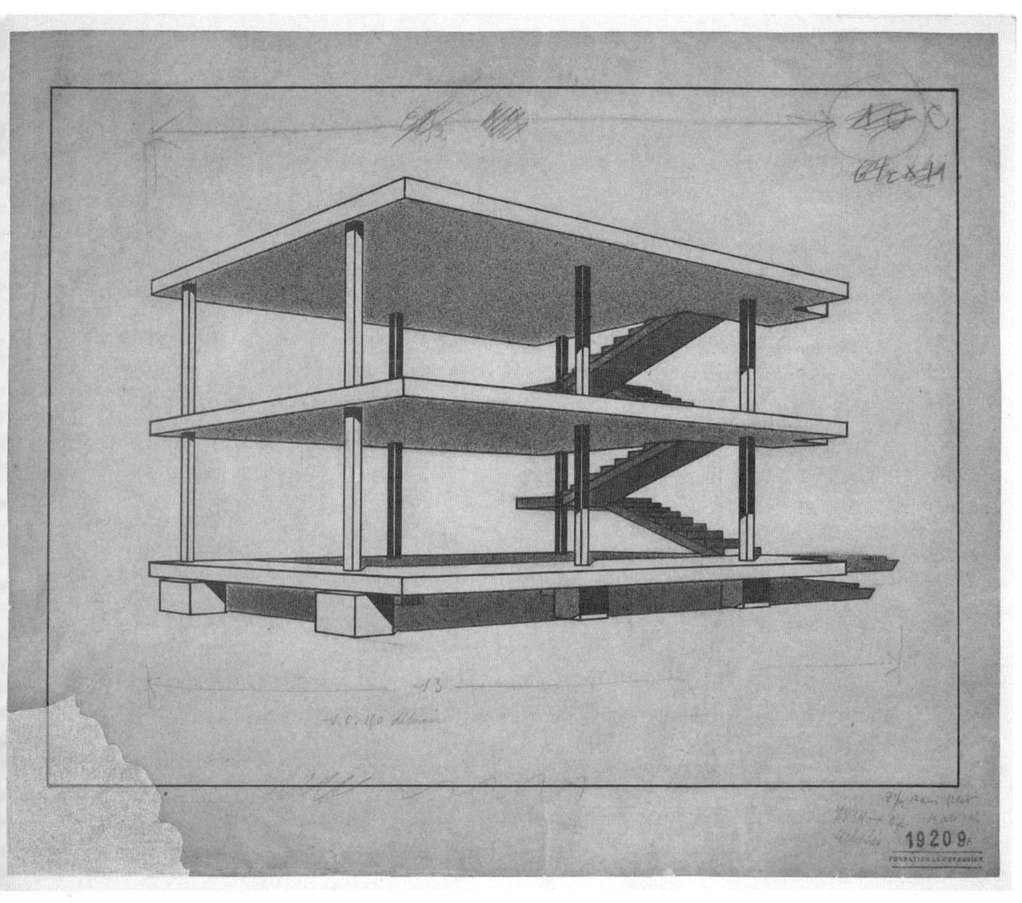

5.1 Le Corbusier, Maison Dom-Ino, 1913. (Image FLC)

objects presented as planar elements slipping under similar roof-like objects. The enclosure no longer has the need for any structural integrity, as Le Corbusier emphasizes with the strip windows, which disrupt any possible structural continuity. Nor is there any need for it to be thick (apart from the requirements of thermal insulation) or heavy: indeed, a lightweight composition would be preferable. Possibly the most critical development is the repetition of the initial move of decoupling of structure and enclosure, understood as a delamination, into a rapid lamination of the enclosure itself, which came to be constructed of multiple specialized layers: interior and exterior finishes, insulation, vapour and moisture barriers, internal substructure, air cavities, and so on. The enclosure, far from being a simple line, became a complex ecosystem of its own. This dematerialization of the enclosure took different but parallel forms in a number of other un-houses; for example, at the Barcelona Pavilion (and also other classic modern houses such as the Rietveld-Schröder House by Gerrit Rietveld of 1924) we see a fragmentation of the enclosure into constituent elements, most often planar. Mies's Farnsworth House (1945–51), in Plano, Illinois, an hour's drive outside of Chicago, more radically separates structural frame from enclosure while fully dematerializing the latter, as the enclosure is reduced to a line of plate glass offering full visual transparency to and from the interior. The glass wall becomes almost nothing, as indicated by Mies's earlier drawings for the unbuilt Resor House—or perhaps better stated, a substitute for nothing. Philip Johnson's Glass House in New Canaan, Connecticut (1948–49), moves steel structure and glass enclosure into the same plane, reinforcing both the nothingness and the somethingness of the glass.

Meanwhile, in the late 1950s through to the 1970s, a few architects and spatial thinkers looked to push the dematerialization of the envelope past the still-solid world of glass. Yves Klein, working with architect Werner Ruhnau, produced several designs for air architectures: projects of an architectural or urban scale that mobilize control over atmospheric conditions to produce a new human sensitivity. Under the air roof, a new and utopian civilization would come into being. Doors would be unnecessary, the concept of secrecy would disappear, and

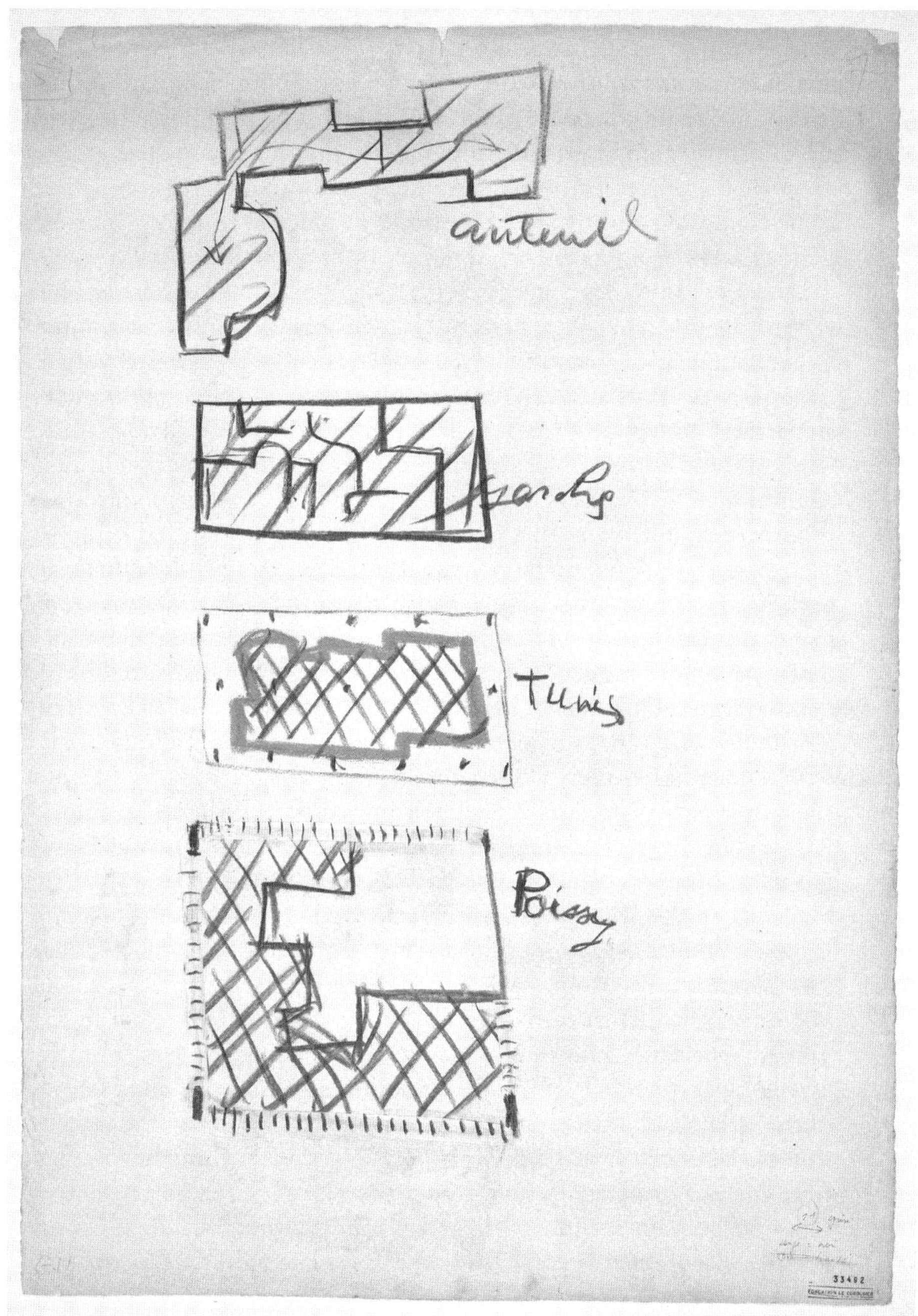

5.2 Le Corbusier, diagram of the four types, 1931. (Image FLC)

inhabitants would live naked in a "new atmosphere of human intimacy" (Klein and Ruhnau 2004, 77). As Klein said, "I would like to speak rapidly about a great architectural project that has always been close to my heart: the realization of a dwelling that is really immaterial but emotionally, technically and functionally practical. This house must be built with the help of a new material, air" (Klein and Ruhnau 2004, 77).

Reyner Banham and François Dallegret's Environment-Bubble of 1965 posited a house of systems, in which the enclosure is limited to the simplest of (plastic) bubbles (Banham 1965). If the envelope is present at all, it is rendered as the simplest possible membrane, a separator preventing leakage between two different atmospheres. Banham and Dallegret place all the weight for controlling the interior environment on interior equipment, drawing the envelope as the most minimal possible line. Although this line represents material reality—the plastic bubble—it remains, nonetheless, as close conceptually to nothing as one could imagine. Henri Lefebvre, in *The Production of Space*, makes this proposition clear: "Now, a critical analysis would doubtless destroy the appearance of solidity of this house, stripping it, as it were, of its concrete slabs and its thin non-loadbearing walls, which are really glorified screens, and uncovering a very different picture. In the light of this imaginary analysis, our house would emerge—permeated from every direction by streams of energy which run in and out of it" (2004, 93). And, of course, this trend to dematerialization has continued, taking the form today of electronic firewalls on the one hand, and ankle bracelets on the other (foot), which convincingly point out that stone is no longer needed in order to prevent escape.

How are we to understand, in terms of this discussion around queerness, the drive to dissolution of the building envelope in the modern world? Despite the utopian goals of connection and intimacy espoused by Klein, we will have to acknowledge first that any removal of the separation of the enclosure is only at best apparent; the separation of the occupants of the Glass House or the Environment-Bubble from their environment is in fact not diminished in relation to that of their predecessors in more normative housing envelopes. Indeed, like at Mettray, Savoye, Farnsworth, and the Glass House all rely on extensive landscape properties to keep intruders away, co-opting the landscape into the building enclosure, ironically thickening, in effect, the enclosure. We could even suggest a theorem: the more insubstantial a building envelope becomes, the thicker its enclosure. In the house without walls, the walls are everywhere; without doors—in reference once again to Klein's projects—one can never leave. Or perhaps we could state this another way: when we grow up in a house without walls, we carry the walls within ourselves forever and wherever.

Second, we can note that the dematerialization of the building envelope has the corollary effect of both emphasizing and disciplining the enclosure, as the complex form of the enclosure of the premodern house gives way to the square at Savoye, the rectangle at Farnsworth and the Glass House, the blob of the Environment-Bubble (and we can even see this in less highbrow houses, such as the rectangle of the Levittown Cape Cod of 1947). Le Corbusier usefully tracks this movement towards the purity of the enclosure in his diagram of the four types, from 1929 (Figure 5.2). These building envelopes speak of unity, integrity, and resolution; no longer able to accept contingency or multiplicity, such enclosures equally demand unity, integrity, and resolution (of identity) on the part of their occupants.

Third, the unified, dematerialized enclosure—the glass wall, for example—places strict demands on the organization of the interior. While the plan may be *free*, unfettered by the demands of structure, it is required *by the very fact of the transparency of the façade* to be highly organized. We can see this development in the movement from the relatively disorganized and contingent plan of the main floor of Savoye to the highly systematic and clear plans of both Farnsworth and the Glass House. And this unified, dematerialized enclosure places equal demands on the house's occupants. Dr. Edith Farnsworth, in discussing her house in *House Beautiful* in 1947, is quoted as saying, "I don't keep garbage under my sink. Do you know why? Because you can see the whole 'kitchen' from the road on the way in here and the can would spoil the appearance of the whole house. So I hide it in the closet further down from the sink. Mies talks about 'free space': but his space is very fixed...Any arrangement of furniture becomes a major problem,

5.3 Ludwig Mies van der Rohe, Farnsworth House,
Plano, Illinois, 1945–51. (Photograph by the author, 2008)

because the house is transparent, like an X-ray" (Barry 1953, 270; Figure 5.3). I want to stress that this aspect of control is a pure effect of the boundary, of the enclosure. This notion of the house as operating like an X-ray is of course a critical idea, as the house, rather than keeping the interior on the interior, penetrates that interior, opening it up and displaying it to the exterior. The envelopes become screens on which are projected a scientific image of the domestic interior. These houses, through their envelopes, produce an uncanny view of what is inside (Figure 5.4). Also intriguing in this quotation from Dr. Farnsworth is the invocation of the closet, the black hole within the enclosure of the house, the lead-lined receptacle of all that cannot be seen by the X-ray of modernity.[5] Paul B. Preciado goes a step further, identifying the house—as well as Johnson's Glass House—as a transparent closet: "This is the mystery of the Farnsworth House, the glass house that had been converted into the 'perfect closet': the more that was shown, the better her secret was guarded" (2019, 17).

For Preciado, Farnsworth's secret was that she was a lesbian, although Preciado admits that "Farnsworth probably did not identify as a lesbian" (2019, 17). Preciado bases this conclusion on the lack of solid evidence of heterosexual relationships in Farnsworth's life (and the lack of solid evidence of a rumoured romantic relationship with Mies), coupled with references in her memoirs to close friendships with women.

In sum, the unified enclosure is a necessary component of the production of, a unified, consistent self, including a unified and consistent sexual identity; multiple selves, multiple or conflicting desires, are not allowed. Dr. Farnsworth must always be Dr. Farnsworth, never morphing into Mrs. Hyde, while Johnson produced a second house—a bedroom posing as a mausoleum—for other aspects of his self. My point here is not so much that the house demands or constructs a uniform identity, not that the modern house banishes the queer (although we will see that the house is also a party to that manoeuvre) but rather that the concurrent dematerialization, unification, and *identification* of the envelope produces, out of a premodern complexity of desires and actions (some geared towards same-sex activities, some not), the modern homosexual—and, indeed, produces the modern heterosexual. *What is more, the production of the modern self through*

5.4 Ludwig Mies van der Rohe, Farnsworth House, Plano, Illinois, 1945–51. Detail. (Photograph by the author, 2008)

this architectural act of enclosure, like any other act of enclosure, is a claim, a hiving off, a separation from the world, a seizing as private property of what was previously common stuff. In other words, self is theft. I steal, therefore I am. Or I am stolen...

I'd like to conclude this section with a brief mention of the dissolution of the enclosure in relation to Gilles Deleuze's (1992) "Postscript on the Societies of Control," first published in French in 1990. Deleuze recognizes that by the time of his writing, indeed already by the time of the May 1968 uprisings, disciplinary techniques in society had shifted from the overt mechanisms described by Foucault (school, barracks, home, prison, hospital) to internalized mechanisms of conformance, a shift brilliantly identified by Preciado in the juxtaposition of the Panopticon with the ubiquitous circular packaging for birth control pills, a shift from external surveillance to internal pharmacological and biopolitical control. Seen from this position, the glass enclosure represents an inversion of the mechanism of the closet and an internalization of the mechanism of the wall. If the stone wall of the prison cell acts both as a corollary of and the necessary productive site for the modern unified self,[6] the glass house, the hall of mirrors, serves perhaps as the model of a fractured, fragile, and disoriented contemporary self.[7]

Two: Screening the Ob-scene

Screens take on significant role in the development of modern architecture. They were a fundamental compositional component, for example, of De Stijl architecture, such as Rietveld's Rietveld-Schröder House of 1924 and reached perhaps a compositional and conceptual apogee in Mies's Barcelona Pavilion of 1929. For Rietveld, working largely compositionally, horizontal and vertical planes are treated equivalently, while Mies maintains a clear hierarchy between *stage* and *screen*. At the Villa Savoye, the plane accounts for two of the five points of a new architecture: the free plan and the free façade, and while these two points arise from the same structural condition—the removal of the structural grid into a separate system—they are important enough to be considered as separate concepts. In what follows, I will consider vertical architectural planes—screens—in terms of their surface effects, while asking, always, a fundamental question: what is behind the screen?[8]

Scene

In June 1966 the *New York Daily News* published a photograph of architect Philip Johnson posed, perhaps seductively, on the lawn in front of his Glass House in New Canaan, Connecticut (Figure 5.5). This is an unusual image of the house for several reasons. First, of course, is the obvious fact that the image includes a human figure; most photos of the Glass House show it without people, either inside or outside the house. What's more, the human in the photo occupies the foreground, relegating the house itself to the position of background—even if, nonetheless, the house remains the real subject of the photo (a second photo in the same article shows Johnson inside the house, seated at the dining table in the distance; Figure 5.6). What's more, the house itself has been posed in a rather unusual situation, with a series of blinds, or screens, drawn across the glass wall behind Johnson, blocking the view of the interior, disabling the transparency for which the house is best known.

Screens are also, of course, extremely familiar devices in our contemporary world. We are literally surrounded by screens, like the one "on which" I am typing these words, the screens of our phones, of our televisions (for those of us who still have such a thing), on almost every piece of equipment, every consumer product we purchase. There are also screens that involve less advanced (although arguably no less effective) technologies: insect screens, sunscreens, windscreens, privacy screens, and so on. These screens act as filters, allowing some information, some light, some wind through, while preventing the passage of other bits: hence the terms *screening* of applicants, COVID-19 *screening*, and so on. Screens provide a double mechanism: on the one hand, they are devices that hide and protect what is behind them, they are both *para-vents* (against the wind) and *par-avants* (that which stands in front); on the other, they are surfaces for the display of information. Although it might be objected that the display function of screens is a recent addition (dating back perhaps to the development of optical devices in the nineteenth century, or to the camera obscura) or that the computer screen no longer has the function of hiding (which is

5.5 Philip Johnson in front of his Glass House, New Canaan, Connecticut, 1966. (Photograph by David McLane / NY Daily News via Getty Images)

5.6 Philip Johnson in his Glass House, New Canaan, Connecticut, 1966. (Photograph by David McLane / NY Daily News via Getty Images)

super-evidently not the case), I will take the position that this ambidextrous character of the screen, its *simultaneous* ability to hide and display, is fundamental to its construction, even if not always evident.

Johnson's Glass House will take on the role of model for the following discussion of screens. We note that the presence of the sunscreens in the *Daily News* photograph is a red herring, an attempt to distract us from (or perhaps alert us to, as this is again the double nature of the screen) the ways in which the glass walls of the house are already screens. In what follows, I will try to clarify what and how these glass screens both display and hide.

Surface

I will start this discussion by considering the screen as a pure surface, that is, as a two-dimensional object with no apparent physical thickness, which acts as a substrate for or holder of an equally two-dimensional image. This starting point is already fraught with difficult conceptions: although, for example, it asks us to ignore the issue of structure, it then goes on to posit a structural role for the "pure surface." Perhaps the biggest problem with this starting point, though, is the invocation of *image*, an idea with a long and complex history and theory that could itself (and indeed does) fill many volumes. The image is also a central concept in the architectural discipline; arguably, it is the key concept, and indeed the main subject, of this book. As W.J.T. Mitchell points out in his important 1984 summary of the thinking around the image, "What Is an Image?," the image is the subject of separate but overlapping discourses in philosophy, literature, psychology, political theory, art, music, and even architecture. While it is my hope that a particular (and perhaps queer) understanding of the image may emerge by the time I have completed this text, for the moment I would like us to limit our consideration to the idea of image in the most everyday sense—that is, the image, so to speak, of a graphic image, projected as pure energy (that is, in a physical sense), on the material but infinitesimal surface of the screen.

Unfortunately, such is the nature of the image that even this tightly constrained and simplistic set-up immediately raises several concerns, objections, or precisions that need to be responded to or specified.

The first of these is the nature of the device that is doing the projecting. The film projector in the cinema projects not an image, but simply a pattern of light of various colours and intensities: it is only when this pattern is seen and interpreted that it becomes an image. We could say, then, that the image is projected onto the screen not by the projection apparatus, but by the viewer, in a sort of reversal of the gaze. This is true even in the case of a painting produced by a human painter, or of a super-intelligent AI-enabled projector: the pattern of light, or pigment, or what have you, only becomes an image on being recognized as such; the projecting device, or the painting, is best thought of not as an addition to the screen, but as part of its apparatus. Second, and consequently, the projection of the image occurs even in the absence of coloured lights or pigments; the blank screen continues to hold an image, even if only an image of blankness (although an image is never blank). Third, it could be argued that this entire line of discussion, of the screen as surface that holds an image, is only and simply a modern or contemporary understanding of screen, dating back perhaps to the Lumière brothers (or to the camera obscura, or to Plato's cave); however, I would argue that these modern projections, these "mad shadows," merely actualize or bring into vision a reality that has always been the nature of a screen.

In Front

As a result of this placement of a viewing subject, whom I will refer to, following the work of Jonathan Crary (1990), as an observer (that is, one who both looks on and complies with), *in front of* the screen (in a simple geometric sense, in the case of an everyday, physical screen), the screen brings into existence a space in front of and adjacent to itself. This space, which I will call a *scene*, is most clearly presented in the theatre, where the scene of the stage literally and clearly sits in front of the backdrop, which takes the form, at least in some traditional theatres, of a painted screen. In the theatre, of course, the parameters of the space in front of the screens, the setting on the stage, are produced in large part, or at least affected, by the image that appears on the screens; we can take Sebastiano Serlio's ([1611] 1982) paradigmatic examples of stage types to demonstrate this. Such an effect is not limited, though, to the theatre, but is instead an everyday if often unnoticed effect in the "real" world: the nature of the imagery on the screens that confront us affects the lived reality and even physicality of the *scene* adjacent. There are obvious examples, designed specifically to produce this effect, especially palaces, courthouses, legislatures, and other "official" buildings of the like; however, we must admit that it is an effect that operates ubiquitously, that architecture-as-screen-and-image produces the spatial effect of the scene in front.[10] The drawn image both precedes and produces the scene of physical experience. The image, in other words, precedes the world: it is the drawing of images that produces a world. This is, of course, the fundamental secret of the architect, whose images produce, literally, the scene of the world, and demonstrates that this architectural technique is more deeply foundational to the world than we may have thought.

A second look at the Glass House, and in particular the photo from the *Daily News* that we have been considering, provides an apt illustration of this connection of screen and scene. In this photo, Johnson lounges on the lawn in front of the Glass House. The lawn here has become more than just a piece of grass: as a result, in large part, of the existence of the house, the lawn has become a particularly designated place, a place to pose, a place that demonstrates Johnson's creative power and wealth, his modern sophistication, as well as a particularly languid sexual presence in keeping with this sophistication. The lawn, stage-like, is carefully composed, designed. The lawn, complete with Johnson, is a scene. Meanwhile, the house sits in the background, anchoring the scene and producing the scene, its glass walls acting as screens that project the image of Johnson's minimalist interior, project precisely this attitude of relaxed, modern domestic sophistication. It is not the screens drawn over the kitchen area that do the work of scene-creation here, but the glass walls themselves. The accompanying photo, with Johnson on the inside of the house (Figure 5.6), operates in precisely the same manner: the camera (and Johnson) is not now behind the screen, but rather again in front of the glass screens, which wrap around the scene in a sort of extended dimensionality, now projecting a bucolic image (Johnson, perhaps apocryphally, once called the walls "very expensive wallpaper"). Johnson, in this image, is no longer the languid wealthy bachelor, but rather the country gentleman, working at his dining table, overseeing his estate. The diagram here is exactly symmetric: a screen that we are always in front of, a two-fronted screen, producing two scenes that complement each other and that come into being simultaneously. These scenes, it is important to note, are tied as by a quantum entanglement; that is, any change to one of these scenes produces simultaneous and immediate correlative alterations in the other scene.

What, though, are these images held on architectural screens, these images that are in turn productive of the world-scene, these images organized, recognized, and *observed* by our observers? We note first of all that they are images developed through complex interplay between architecture and observer, images that both entities are oriented towards, in the sense of orientation used by Sara Ahmed (2006), images that architecture, through its professional, disciplinary, social, authoritarian, material, and processual relations is oriented to hold and display and that observers, through their equally dense networks of relationships (familial, political, educational, sexual, professional, and so on), are oriented to observe. Included in this set of observable images, images that can be both seen and obeyed, images that are able to produce a world-scene, are images related to the sexual construction of a world: images that require, if they are to construct a coherent world-scene, particular sexual practices, desires and orientations; images that, in short, produce a world-scene that allows only those positions. In the photographs of Johnson at the Glass House, we see a virile, masculine sexual subject, posed in front of an image of domestic mastery; the image of Johnson's homosexuality is not present, or rather, is not able to be observed. Somehow, queerness remains behind the screen.

Behind

This question of *behind* brings us to another aspect of the screen, the second principal effect of the screen, that of hiding or protecting. *Behind* is an interesting word in English, an old word, derived not from Greek or Latin sources but from Anglo-Saxon and Germanic roots (*Online Etymological Dictionary,* n.d.). It is a relational word, describing a relative position in space, time, status, wealth, or even in relation to our own bodies.[11] It is a sexually transgressive word (to take someone from behind, to put something in one's behind) as well as a word that can split our beings: if I say "I am behind the screen," the I that is talking is split, radically, from that other I to which it refers (in other words, of course, the behind is relative, and the "I" can only ever be in front). And of course, the behind itself is only produced by its relative marker: the screen produces the behind.

Normally, though, the screen has an ambiguous relationship to its behind. Unlike walls, screens are understood as partial barriers, permeable to sight, air, information; they offer only a tenuous protection, as one can easily go around, over, or through a screen. Confessional screens, image screens, privacy screens, all allow the passage of some selected information or materiality while blocking others. Screens, at best, protect by dissembling, by distracting from the behind, but at the same time carry a projected image of the behind on the face, a registration of the back on the front, the way a building's façade registers its interior organization and functions without disclosing the details of the world inside. This registration is a sort of writing on the surface of an interior condition, like the disposition of windows in a façade, or like tattoos[12] that present to the world an interior reality of desire that may or may not exist, and by registering the reality, bring it into existence. It is reminiscent, too, of the machine writing that sentenced the condemned in Franz Kafka's ([1919] 1988) story "The Penal Colony," or for that matter, the performative writing of gender on the surface of the body as described by Judith Butler in *Gender Trouble* (1990). The registration of the interior on the exterior, of the behind on the front of the screen, makes no claim to the truth, the reality, or even the existence of that interior, at best presenting a filtered, censored, and at worst entirely dissembling vision. Indeed, to some extent, the interior, the behind, is brought into being by its existence as a representation that appears on the surface. And in any case, we should remember that the interior, the behind that the screen shows us, is always partial, distorted as much by our own techniques of observation as by any character of the screen or for that matter the interior itself.

Johnson's Glass House provides a good example of this organization of the behind. As we have already seen, the glass projects an image of the sophisticated domestic interior, which forms the background stage on which Johnson himself lounges, that is, the lawn.

The interior, in this image, provides the *behind* and leaks through the screen of the glass to produce the scene of relaxed sophisticated domesticity on the lawn. Likewise, in the accompanying interior photograph, the bucolic landscape outside the house forms the behind, with the scene now located inside the house. What is not so evident, perhaps, is the way in which this glass screen, with its almost complete transparency, nonetheless selectively hides, distorts, and disciplines the behind. There is a clue, I suppose, in the opaque screens that have been drawn to hide the activities in the kitchen, transforming the glass screen into a filtering device that allows only a consistent Image conforming to this notion of sophistication to come through to the scene. However, I would go further with this argument, to point out that the glass wall, with its elegant detailing and flawlessly composed and proportioned form, already acts to filter the information that can find its way through. Information that supports the ideas of elegance, sophistication, and modernity is supported by the wall, by the screen, while information that opposes such readings of the interior is filtered out. The interior of the house, the *behind*, is provided with an irresistible order by the irresistible order of the façade. Likewise for the interior photo: the landscape beyond, in the *behind*, is demonstrated by the impeccable order of the screen to be itself impeccably ordered, domesticated, by the country gentleman, Johnson. This scene on the other side, the behind, which I will call a meta-scene, is not simply the space on the other side of the wall, indeed, it need not be a space at all: rather, it is an idealized, perfected image of an order to which this scene, the only scene we are able to occupy, must conform.

The transparency of the glass wall at Johnson's Glass House certainly serves to clarify these relationships, including the relationship of absolute symmetry between the scene-in-front and scene-behind. Each scene is projected on the other, transforming the other in the process; scene and meta-scene are connected as elements of a single apparatus. The transparency here, though, only serves to make evident a relationship that always pertains in an architectural setting, even in a prison.[13] Even the stone walls of the prison operate as permeable screens, projecting the scene of the prison onto the scene of everyday life and the scene of everyday life onto the scene in prison. The screen of stone, the screen of the prison wall, filters, distorts, and disciplines the scene on the other side. So the screen both hides and displays, demonstrating that one cannot hide without displaying, in fact to hide and to display are in the end reciprocal elements of the same maneuver. Furthermore, the absolute symmetry between front of scene and rear of scene demonstrates that the architectural idea of inside and outside is fiction: that we are always, speaking in architectural terms, in front of the screen, outside of the skin. Behind the surface is only more surface and more surface and more surface as surface becomes depth.

In addition to these two scenes, always conjoined—the scene that is always immediately present, and the scene which is only available to us as its image, mediated by the screen, the meta-scene—a third scene is brought into being by this mechanism of the screen. This third screen, which we might call the ob-scene, it Is also located behind the screen, but behind, as it were, in some extra dimension, not directly accessible to perception.

Ob-scene

The word *obscene* is of uncertain origin. Its full etymology is unknown, although there are a few educated guesses that have been put forward, as well as a few creative derivations. Most likely, the word has nothing to do, from an etymological point of view, with the scene, deriving not from the Greek *skena* but rather from the Latin *caenum*, or filth, in which case the word means something like "in front of filth"—although there is no evidence for this derivation, and it has been suggested that this would be an impossible formation in Latin (see, for example, the Online Etymological Dictionary, n.d.; *Merriam-Webster Dictionary* for the latter derivation; *The Etymology Nerd* [Aleksic, n.d.], and others for the former). We are aware of the Latin word *obscenus*, meaning ill-omened, inauspicious, offensive, and recognize that all three of these words pertain to the current use of the word *obscene*. Regardless of its etymological legitimacy, or lack thereof, the idea of obscene seems to connect, if not conjoin, a number of issues of concern here: the stage, always understood as ill-omened, inauspicious, offensive; the scene of the world; and a particular understanding of filth as that which is abject, that is, cast out of the world. Obscene also brings in the resonance, at least, of a positionality supplied by the prefix *ob-*. The ob-scene, in this rendering, is the filth that is filth specifically because of its positioning off the stage, outside of the scene of the world.

The ob-scene, as mentioned before, is located in principle behind the screen; it is in other words another behind, hidden in this case by the screen. Like the *behind* discussed in the previous section, the ob-scene comes into being because of the screen. Unlike the behind, the ob-scene is not directly perceptible, but the screen is affected by its presence, tainted by its filth, and this taint leaks through to the scene in front. The presence of the ob-scene can be sensed, an uncanny haunting image. It is the sense of something behind us, lurking, something that remains behind us when we turn our heads, something that remains just outside of our field of vision no matter how quickly we spin or twirl.[14]

The ob-scene is the behind not of the screen in its physical manifestation, but of the image that the screen displays; it is the scene behind the image, the scene the image hides, the impenetrable depth of the image plane.[15] It is a scene that is not of this world, or rather, it is the inaccessible off-scene of the world.[16]

But what precisely is this ob-scene? First, we should note that it is precisely the obscene, that which cannot be allowed to be seen but the presence of which cannot be denied. It is the filth whose very appearance shatters the world, the unbearable and abject underpinnings of the world, the ill-omened, inauspicious, offensive reality the hiding of which, by the mechanism of the screen, is the impulse that forms a world.

A return to Johnson's Glass House can help to elucidate this question. In looking at these photographs from a contemporary standpoint, we cannot help but note the presence-as-absence of Johnson's homosexuality. What we might have seen in 1966 as an image of an eligible if aging bachelor lounging, somewhat voluptuously, outside his elegant and sophisticated bachelor pad—marked indelibly by the absence of spaces to accommodate children—clearly, today, appears as the image of a successful middle-aged gay man. The ob-scene in these photos, as in the Glass House itself, that ubiquitously present and indeed formative element, is simply Johnson's (homo)sexuality.[17] The idea of the Glass House as "gay space" is obviously not new; the house has been analyzed as such by a variety of authors including Aaron Betsky (1997), Alice T. Friedman (1998), and Paul B. Preciado (2019). My intention here is not to discuss the Glass House as an exercise in camp architecture or in self-parody, to comment on the politics of display and concealment, of hiding in plain sight, of the politics of the closet (although all of these are interesting and valuable readings of the house and indeed of Johnson's career), but rather to point to the Glass House as a crystallization and clarified expression of a situation that obtains *not only* in houses designed, owned, and occupied by gay men.[18] My point, briefly, is to claim that while sexuality, *sex*, is a formative part of the meta-scene of the domestic inasmuch as it conforms to the image and norms of sexuality of its day (Johnson as the sophisticated bachelor of his day), sexuality to the extent that is non-conforming always occupies the ob-scene, the formative present-absence that is screened, in other words both staged and denied, by the domestic.

At the Glass House, this ob-scene, this off-stage, has been rendered material by the presence of a second building, carefully located just outside of the photos in the *Daily Mail,* the Guest House (Figure 5.7). This second building actually predates the Glass House, having completed construction a few months earlier; however, the interior renovation that will be important in this discussion was completed later, in 1953. Importantly, too, the two houses were considered from the outset as a couple, a complementary set. The Guest House, also known as the Brick House, is exactly that: a brick rectangle, apparently with no openings aside from the door (in fact, the rear of the Guest House, facing away from the Glass House, has three round windows). The two houses have been designed as a compound, and the material relationship of opposites is matched by a clear compositional relationship, as the few photographs that show the two houses together make clear (in two of the iconic images, included in Johnson's 1950 article about the house in *The Architectural Review*, each house is seen in pure elevation from a distance, with the other house occupying the lower left corner of the image). As much as the Glass House aggressively presents itself, the Guest House is easy to miss, or rather, easy to ignore; it appears, at first glance (or even for that matter at third or fourth glance) to be nothing more than a service building, perhaps an electrical substation or a pump room. Within this service building, however, is a bit of fantasy:

a rather opulent bedroom, in complete contrast to the bedroom in the Glass House, complete with decorative columns and arches and walls covered in Fortuny fabrics (more very expensive wallpaper; Figure 5.8). The room has an over-the-top, camp, luxury to it, a sensuality that cannot exist in the Glass House—but that nonetheless reveals the campiness of the latter. As Betsky, for example, describes the bedroom, "Once again, he went to extremes: he buried the bedroom completely, so that it became a queering of the cave into a vaulted chamber covered with raw silk that turned this ultimate Sadean pleasure palace into a shimmering space of closely matched textures, colors and light" (1997, 115). Friedman likewise stresses this camp aspect of the room: "By exaggerating the feminine, the sensual, the secret and the decorative sides of architecture in the Guest House, Johnson...offered a further parody of the rigid sex roles so beloved by middle-class America...Johnson and his gay friends recognized the Guest House as a camp stage set, remodeled, according to Johnson, because he 'wanted to play'" (1998, 156). The Guest House is the off-stage in which the obscene ob-scene of Johnson's gayness, of Johnson's sexuality, and arguably of sex itself can be contained.[19]

It seems to me, though, that there is another reading of the Guest House, a reading that none of the authors mentioned brings up. The Guest House, with its monolithic, seemingly windowless masonry volume, its perhaps overly clear formal symmetry, its distant location from the main house in the garden, resembles nothing, for me, so much as a family mausoleum. The bedroom, if anything, reinforces this understanding of the house; it is certainly easier to imagine this space as a sepulcher, as a glittering final place of repose for a fantastic, heroic king cut down before his prime, than as the site of an orgy. As Betsky points out, one has the feeling in this space of being buried, of being entombed. The Guest House, then, as much as it provides an absent-present staging for Johnson's sexuality, as much as it renders sex ob-scene, off stage, also stages and simultaneously renders off-stage death.[20]

My hypothesis here, as I stated above, is that Johnson's house works as a crystallization and clarification of the domestic in general (this is, contrary to what some authors may have written, what determines the house as *queer space*). Sex and death comprise, together, the basic ob-scene of the domestic screen.[21]

5.7 Philip Johnson in front of his Guest House, New Canaan, Connecticut, 1966. (Photograph by David McLane / NY Daily News via Getty Images)

5.8 Philip Johnson in his Guest House, New Canaan, Connecticut, 1966. (Photograph by David McLane / NY Daily News via Getty Images)

Screen, scene, meta-scene, ob-scene: this schema describes the essential structure of architecture. The surfaces of architecture become screens that hold images, images projected from the meta-scene, images that in turn produce or at least orient the scene, images that occlude the ob-scene, that move it off-stage, without ever being able to banish it; both scene and meta-scene are always, unavoidably, shaken in turn by the presence of the ob-scene, by the lingering presence of queerness and death.

House of Glass, House of Mirrors[22]

In the September 1950 issue of *Architectural Review*, Johnson published an article describing the Glass House and analyzing its sources. Introducing this article, as an uncaptioned and hence somewhat mysterious image—what we might call a teaser—was a photograph taken from outside the Glass House, showing Johnson inside, seated at his desk (Figure 5.9). Highlighted in this photograph are the reflections on the glass wall of the trees behind the house, and presumably behind the photographer (although the photographer does not appear). This reflected foliage comes across as a screen, enclosing Johnson (or rather, the two Johnsons, as his reflected image in the side wall is also caught by the lens) in a complex, multilayered, and confusing pattern.[23]

Images of this kind, images of reflection, are rare in the architectural archives, but certainly not unheard of. We can think, for example, of Mies's drawings of glass skyscrapers in the journal *G* in the early 1920s, or, in later years, the proliferation of mirrored glass office buildings. Architecture, indeed, could be said to have a bit of an obsession with reflection, an obsession with dematerialization, of expansion of space, an obsession that appears as a side effect of its more famous obsession with transparency. Relative to transparency, reflection remains undertheorized, appearing, as in the photograph in question, as an unanticipated effect, an unexpected visitor that brings an uncontrollable strangeness into the architecture.[24]

Reflection is, after all, quite a queer effect when it comes to architecture. Reflection, first of all, casts doubt on the solidity and *reality* of a building, the two primary attributes that architecture is determined to uphold. Reflection can cause whole buildings to disappear—take, for example, Tomas Osinsk and Chris Hanley's aptly named Invisible House (2019), which disappears almost fully into its desert surroundings. Reflection can cause the architecture of a building to distort, to become unreadable, like the mirrors in a funhouse. In other instances, reflection can produce a hole in a building, a hole that seemingly leads into another universe.[25]

Reflection troubles and disturbs several of the clear-cut boundaries that architecture looks to enforce, such as the image|building dichotomy, which, in the final analysis, is nothing more than surface|structure, one of the most discussed of the architectural binaries. Likewise, reflection blurs the line between real and virtual and, through the technique of doubling or twinning, makes unclear the separation of self and other. Who is it we see in the mirror? Is it ourselves, or others? And private|public: is there someone on the other side of the mirror, looking at me, unobserved? Indeed, reflection can even confound the most fundamental of architectural binaries, inside|outside, an uncanny aspect that can make that which is outside appear to be inside, and vice versa. Reflection turns architecture inside out like a glove, turning our self-images inside out along with it.[26]

5.9 Philip Johnson in his Glass House, New Canaan, Connecticut, 1950. (© Arnold Newman / Liaison Agency)

Coda: Ten Plus One Tactics for Betraying Architecture

We start and end with failure.[1] As Jack Halberstam (2011) reminds us, failure is endemic to queerness, a defining feature of the queer. A queering of architecture must first dispense with the teleological pretensions of architecture. We are not trying to draw realizable buildings, let alone produce a better world: we understand that to achieve these goals would be to give up on the promise of queerness. Queer exists not in the hope of victory, but in the joy of the struggle. As I have said before, not even a queer architect can design a queer house. And yet: we keep trying.[2]

In the preceding chapters of this book, I have developed a set of theorems or theoretical positions that, taken together, produce another set of points, not this time for a new architecture, or for a queer architecture, but for understanding architecture from a queer position (and queerness from an architectural position). In the final section of this concluding chapter, I will nail these theses to the church door: not five points, but more, an indefinite number that I do not claim is complete or coherent. In this text it will be a list of ten, plus or minus one or two. Further, each point in what follows is bifurcated, split into thesis and tactic, into two dimensions of queerness: the queerness that has always been and the queerness that can only exist at the temporal limit, the asymptotic queerness.[3]

ONE.

Put your life on the line. Line is the fundamental starting point of architecture, an essential act of violence, producer of the architectural binary. When you draw a line, the line draws you. The line is a thin wire stretched between two worlds: you walk on it as a tightrope walker, knowing that the line could betray you at any moment, you could fall into the abyss. It is the line that queers you, the line that can easily turn itself into a noose, the line that spells your end.

TWO.

Jam a dildo in the machine. Every building and every image is an erotic machine and should be considered using a machinic analysis. What desires are produced by the machine? What are its inputs, its energy sources, and possibly most importantly, its waste products? We need to shatter gears, disrupt fluid and capital flows, break the architectural apparatus. Detangle the organs of pleasure from the organs of (re) production. Sever the connection between penis and phallus, in a permanent castration of architecture. This is, of course, a moment of the purest comedy, and the saboteurs laugh and dance, drunk on their pleasure.

THREE. Keep a packed suitcase under the bed. You will need to be able to make a quick escape when the police arrive—the architecture police, the straight police. Because they will come for you: architecture has its laws, and there is no tolerance possible for the anti-architect. No one can tell you what to keep in the suitcase, except that you will need to have everything necessary to continue on. If you die, the contents of the suitcase should be able to take over your fight.

FOUR. Learn to love your cell. The modern world starts with the prison cell: this is Foucault's position, and it's hard to deny. The cell is the primary unit, the primary void, that defines in turn its corollary, the individual self, and these two become the basic building blocks of modernity. The cell transforms into the room, agglomerates into the house or the apartment—the unit in contemporary language—and the individual self becomes the primary economic unit that moves capital, the primary political unit that moves democracies, the primary medico-erotic unit of the pharmacopornographic world. Learn to love your cell: escape is impossible, and escape is the only imperative for the queer.

FIVE. Steal whatever you can. Not little things: don't break into your neighbour's house or take money from your lover's wallet. Do those things if you want. But first you must steal yourself. The architectural enclosure is an act of triple violence: violence to those enclosed, imprisoned, domesticated, subjectified, and changed forever and fundamentally by this enclosure; violence to those excluded, who are othered and objectified; and the fundamental violence of appropriation, the fundamental theft, the claim of ownership. To be queer is to be both thief and stolen property: this is the Law of Architecture, and to be queer is to be an outlaw. We are kleptogenetic beings.

SIX. Be an abject object. To follow this agenda, to escape the prison cell of queer and straight, to queer architecture, we have to take on an impossible maneuver: to need to become other to ourselves, to eject ourselves from our selves, to become fully abject. This is an inevitable end state, the final position of the already-abjected queer. We need to push this logic of abjection to its limit, to turn ourselves inside out like a glove, to be neither inside nor outside the line of enclosure but behind the drawing, behind the screen, behind architecture, inhabiting the ob-scene.

SEVEN. Be a porn star (we are all sex workers). Embrace drawing as the most intimate of sex acts. In the contemporary world, architecture can only be pornography; we need to make the great wheel of capital spin faster and faster until it falls off its axle and crashes to the ground. Expose yourself for all to see. Be glorious, seduce, ravish. Choose a porn name. Every drawing you make is a drawing of you fucking or being fucked. Draw your deepest, ugliest fantasies and sell them to the universe.

EIGHT.

Jump into the Void. Draw from inside. Remember the presence of the primary voids of which our lives and our selves are composed: cell, closet, brothel, tomb. There is a void in every image and in every building that can never be seen. The void is a black hole, powering the machine of image with its massive gravity. Remember what is not able to be seen. Design is a matter of designing our (queer) selves. Architecture wants us to forget this, this is why we must betray architecture. Architecture presents a false and impossible exterior view. We queerly draw from inside the void.

NINE.

Penetrate everything: walls, keyholes, concepts, assholes. Architecture presents an illusion of reality, an illusion in which the ob-scene, that which sits behind the image, behind the screen, behind architectural reality, is not exactly invisible, but obfuscated. This is the genesis of the uncanny. There is a behind to every image, even architectural images. The purpose of the image is to both hide and expose this behind, which we call the ob-scene, which cannot fail to make itself known. Architecture is the art of the omnipresent front, and to queer it we must penetrate that façade, dig our way into its body.

TEN.

Masturbate on your drafting board. Architecture is always filled with sex, drawing is fornication. Sex is both the energy that drives the machine, the founding principle of the kleptogenetic world, and the unsettling power that threatens the structure, the power that must be disciplined, screened, relegated to the behind. Sex is the opening, the site of potential penetration, the frontal attack on the fortress that is architecture. Queering architecture means to understand and participate in the erotics of design; imagine the beautiful bodies you are delineating, cutting, dissecting, penetrating. Draw faster, harder, until your drawings start to moan then finally explode in pure pleasure.

BONUS.

Betray the things you love. You don't know the depth of love until you betray it. Betrayal is the most intimate relationship between things.[4]

Notes

Introduction

1 In other words, we need to operate as, or with, a thief.

The thief in this project is Jean Genet (1910–1986), French orphan, vagabond, homosexual, thief, novelist, playwright, activist. The work draws extensively on Genet's life and work, including aspects of his private life and aspects that have been fictionalized or invented, to clarify or to disturb the critical questions of the text. In order to approach this *behind* of architecture, a second narrative is constructed in these endnotes. This is both a nod to Jacques Derrida's great work about Genet and Hegel, *Glas* (and also to the overtly personal, fragmented, and often onanistic writing of Genet) and a way to think outside of the normative structures and strictures of architectural theory. It is a way of glimpsing into the *behind* of the primary text, of presenting the *ob-scene* that the primary text both obscures and displays. In short, this second text offers a queering of the main text.

2 Derrida: "Do I write for *him*? What would I like to do to him? Do to his 'work'? Ruin it by erecting it, perhaps" ([1974] 1986, 200). Genet's biography is well known, at least in its rough outline, and has been extensively studied, most notably (in English) by Edmund White (1993). Genet was born in December 1910 and abandoned by his mother at the age of about eight months. He was placed in the care of a foster family in the French region of the Morvan, where he lived until completing his formal education at the age of thirteen. After running away from a series of apprenticeships, in 1926 Genet was sent to the Colonie Agricole et Pénitentiare de Mettray, where he remained until he joined the army in 1929. Genet stayed in the army until 1936, when he deserted, and embarked upon a period of vagabondage, prostitution, and petty criminality. By the time the Second World War broke out, Genet was in Paris, where he was arrested on several occasions for offences such as stealing (most often books), and at least once for taking a train without a valid ticket. According to Genet's texts, particularly *The Thief's Journal*, at this time he also took up burglary, breaking into bourgeois

apartments, although he appears to have never been caught for these activities (Genet [1949] 1987). Still, Genet spent time in prison on numerous occasions between 1938 and 1944.

By the end of the 1940s, however, Genet had produced his five great novels, four of which are unabashedly, if unreliably, autobiographical, mixing elements of fiction, fact, and fantasy in a completely integrated if fragmented fashion. The first two of his novels were written, or at least begun, during his time in Fresnes prison. In 1947 Genet's first play, *The Maids*, was performed in Paris to critical and popular success, followed by several more important plays in the 1950s: *The Balcony*, *The Blacks*, and *The Screens*, by which time Genet was acknowledged as one of the most important voices in modern theatre, alongside such figures as Samuel Beckett and Eugène Ionesco.

In May 1968 Genet supported the student uprisings in Paris and wrote his first political text, although he did not play an important role in the uprisings. A period of political activity followed, which included covering the 1968 Democratic Convention in Chicago (for *Esquire*), spending a significant period of time with the Black Panthers in 1970 and with the Palestinian fedayeen in 1970–71, and producing a series of magazine articles and other political or philosophical texts, including two texts that explicitly take on questions of architecture. This period of political action, or probably better of political observation, was remembered in Genet's last novel, *Prisoner of Love*, published in 1986, just over a month after his death in Jack's Hotel in Paris.

Such are the basic facts of Genet's life, as best we know them. These dates and records, though, are not sufficient to explain his role within this story about architecture. After all, Genet was not engaged in the world of architecture during his life, publishing only two brief articles that explicitly discuss architecture in any way—"That Strange Word...," originally published in *Tel Quel* in 1967, and "Chartres Cathedral," published in *L'Humanité* in June 1977 (Genet 2003, 103–12; 152–58). What is more, Genet remained a nomad for his entire life, either as a vagabond and runaway as a youth, a deserter from the army, or by living in (cheap) hotels later in his life; Albert Dichy, literary director of Institut Mémoires de l'Édition Contemporaine (IMEC), and a well-known specialist on the work of Genet (and author of a very useful chronology of Genet's life), commented to me during a conversation in 2018 on the marked difference between Genet the wanderer and Alberto Giacometti, who lived most of his life in the same house and studio. On the face of things, Genet certainly seems a strange candidate for a book about architecture.

However, there are several factors, maybe not immediately obvious in the bare facts of his biography, that I will argue make Genet an important figure in thinking about the architecture of the modern world, and particularly, of course, about the question of *queer* in architecture. First, those bare facts of Genet's life place him in direct contact with key moments in the development of the modern world: the formative years of modern utopianism in the 1840s, in the form of the Mettray colony; the facts of his birth and abandonment, which locate him in an eccentric position to what I will claim as one of the key institutions of modernity, the family; Genet's years of vagabondage at the height of the modern movement in architecture in the late 1930s; Genet's time spent as a thief and emerging writer in Nazi-occupied Paris; and Genet's engagement with radical groups in the late 1960s, such as the Black Panthers and the Palestinian fedayeen. As well, his experience was unusually heterotopic, connected to prisons and theatres, Mettray and Fontevraud. And of course, Genet brings a variety of other side characters onto the stage, characters such as Georges Bataille, Jean-Paul Sartre, Michel Foucault, Jacques Derrida, Jacques Lacan, Leo Bersani, Edward Said, Michael Hardt, Alenka Zupançiç, Benjamin Bratton, Angela Davis. Genet takes us back to the initiation of the modern world in 1840 and forward to the concerns of migration, borders, and the future of the human body of today. Furthermore, Genet's trajectory explicitly connects a concern with the body and with the erotic, a concern with sex, to the political and finally to the geopolitical, by implication placing sex firmly at the centre of our thoughts about modernity.

Second, there is the question of the central absence of the house in Genet's work and in his life. The characters in his books inhabit cheap hotels, rooms, flophouses. And yet, we understand that the concepts of *house* and its corollary *family* are central preoccupations in Genet's work and life—both most striking in their absence, on the one hand (for Genet the orphan, for Genet the homosexual, for Genet the vagabond, for Genet the petty thief), but also striking in their transformation, in their erotic transubstantiation by Genet the writer. The key spaces in Genet's work are perhaps best described as non-houses: theatres, prisons, brothels, tombs. These spaces are all houses of mirrors, producing shattered and broken reflections of modern architecture's new-found concern with the house. At the same time, they are also *holes*: insides that are outside, constitutive voids at the centre of our modern psyches. And of course, Genet's writings are filled with intense and repeating architectural images, fragments of buildings charged with meaning: stairs, doors, balconies, walls, mirrors, screens. Genet's work has a shattered, fragmented architecture as its basic setting.

Also striking is the role(s) houses played, or did not play, in Genet's (private) life. On several occasions—at least three and perhaps as many as five—Genet played the part of architect, designing and arranging for the construction or renovation of houses. Between 1947 and 1952, for example, Genet designed and had built a house in Le Cannet, a suburb of Cannes, as a wedding gift for his lover Lucien Sénémaud, on Sénémaud's marriage to Ginette Chaix. As was typical of these houses, Genet set aside a bedroom for himself, but a bedroom that would remain empty, as he preferred to sleep in the hotel—normally with a packed suitcase under the bed in case he needed to make a quick getaway.

Third, Genet's nomadism, his wandering existence mentioned above, is not accidental, but rather part of a consistent anti-architectural position in his work and in his life. Or better yet, an anti-architectural architecture. Genet is against all structure—as Jean-Paul Sartre ([1952] 1963) tells us, Genet is bent on the pure evil of destruction—and expresses this denial of structure through structure. Genet is the master of the gesture (but what is the architectural gesture?), of the construction of appearance in order to destroy appearance and, by implication, to destroy the world in its entirety. He is the master of the contradiction, of the whirligig, of the impossible, of the trap door. All of this makes of Genet a supremely architectural figure.

When Genet enters the scene of this project, as a result, he brings with him unfamiliar ways of seeing and thinking, mechanisms that lie to some degree outside the realm of regular architectural discourse, mechanisms that Sartre ([1952] 1963), again, locates in the masturbatory fantasies of Genet the writer-in-prison. These methods, while often troubling, while they may do violence to other thinkers and designers and even to architecture itself, are, in my intuition, potentially fecund, able to open new lines of consideration for the questions at hand. How better to understand the role of sex within architecture than through the onanistic fantasies of the anti-architect?

3 Materials for the construction of a queer theory of architecture are abundant in the life and works of Genet and in selected critical writings about him. Primary among the sources are Genet's quasi-autobiographical novels written in the 1940s and early 1950s, *Our Lady of the Flowers* ([1943] 1987, *Flowers*), *Miracle of the Rose* ([1946] 1988, *Miracle*), *Funeral Rites* ([1949] 1963, *Funeral*), and *The Thief's Journal* ([1949] 1987, *Journal*), and indeed it is from these novels that fundamental components are developed. For example, *Miracle of the Rose* contains the most vivid descriptions of both Mettray and of prison life—in this case, of Fontevraud—in Genet's oeuvre. The work also makes use of aspects of Genet's two other novels, *Querelle* ([1947] 1987,

Querelle), and *Prisoner of Love* ([1986] 1992, *Prisoner*), as well as his plays, particularly *The Maids* ([1947] 1994, *Maids*), *The Balcony* ([1956] 2008, *Balcony*), and *The Screens* ([1961] 1998, *Screens*), and his film, *Un chant d'amour* (1950); these works are used in more limited ways, in order to develop particular issues and ideas, such as the question of twinning or mirroring in *The Maids* and *Querelle*, or the dissolution of the wall in *Un chant d'amour* or in *The Screens*. Several of his literary or art-critical essays make important provocations to this work, or act as background material, particularly "That Strange Word…" and "Chartres Cathedral" (2003, 103–12, 152–58).

Materials taken from Genet's life have been pieced together from various sources, including his own (unreliable) descriptions in the books. These have been added to and in some cases verified through the work of his biographers, particularly Edmund White, and through personal communications from Albert Dichy and others. Meanwhile, various commentators on Genet have also provided important material. The most substantial of these is Sartre's *Saint Genet: Actor and Martyr* ([1952] 1963), which provides a robust and comprehensive psychoanalytic view of Genet's life and work to the 1950s. Sartre presents a clear framework of psychological development within which to read Genet's work. Although, following Guy Hocquenghem (2006), we can be critical of Sartre's work, and suspicious in particular of his teleological position, of his characterization of *the homosexual* as a quasi-species, and in particular of his assertion that *thief* comes (chronologically and psychologically) before *queer*, various elements of my argument are presented or clarified by Sartre. One particular mechanism developed by Sartre that plays a major role in this discussion is the *whirligig*: the game of impossible mutual contradictions, the *chute en abyss*, that is key to certain aspects of modern architecture.

The second key commentary on Genet is that of Derrida's *Glas* ([1974] 1986), which serves more as a precedent for the present study than as a source. *Glas* operates on several levels to develop a critique of philosophical methods as presented in the work of Hegel—or perhaps rather to offer a supplement to Hegelian dialectical thinking. Hegelian and Genet(ic) developments, especially of the family, are presented in twin columns; the formal structure of the Hegelian column is complemented by the poetic form of Genet's, which could be said to "wind around" Hegel: this is the image from "Le condamné à mort," Genet's early poem, of wisteria climbing around a column, and an image that is reprised in *The House Is (Not) a Prison* in the relationship between primary text and notes. Hegelian dialectics are presented as a staircase, allowing us to climb step by step to a higher level of knowledge, while Genet's column emphasizes falling, the void, the tomb, making use of the French pun, *tombe/tomber*. Other puns figure prominently: in the Genet column, every occurrence of "*être* (to be)" is replaced by "*bander* (to get hard)," which means both to get hard, to get an erection, but also to operate in a roundabout way or, as Hocquenghem states, to operate from the margins (2006, 136). The constant presence of the engorged penis is tempered in the work though, or perhaps complemented, by an annular structure, by the structure of the anus, as each of the two columns circles around, end to beginning. *Glas* thus represents the phallus and anus structure that forms an important machine in portions of *The House Is (Not) a Prison*.

A number of other commentators on Genet furnish less significant but nonetheless important materials for this discussion. Edward Said (1990) and Michael Hardt (1997), for example, provide insight into Genet and the other in the context of his relationships with the Palestinians. Benjamin Bratton (2015), in his piece on the transvestitism of power, provides useful materials around the role of violence in architecture, useful more as baseline theory than as specific Genet(ic) material. Leo Bersani, *in Homos* (1996), portrays Genet as an example of the gay outlaw, but his essay "Is the Rectum a Grave?"

(2010) provides important material for my discussion on the behind, and his work on gay betrayal poses a major question on the role, if any, of betrayal in architecture.

4 Genet's work makes use of a number of heterotopic forms that become primary materials for this work (Foucault 1986). The first of these heterotopias is a pair of linked architectural forms, the prison and the house. In this work, I am considering these forms as a couple, and also as *primary heterotopias.* The heterotopic nature of prisons is straightforward: these are heterotopias of deviation, places in which those who are other, or those who are to be designated other, are held. More importantly, prisons are themselves other, pure interiors that are conceptually exterior, in the sense of being exterior to society. Prisons are rigorously separated spaces, defined indeed by the rigour of their separation, but that both mirror and reveal structural aspects of the regular world. Spatial organizations, regimes of discipline and control, structures, hierarchies, and modes of resistance, all have their counterparts inside and outside of the prison walls.

Prisons are central in the work of Genet, especially (but not only) in his early novels. The most important of the prisons in his work is the Maison Centrale de Fontevraud (Fontevraud Prison), located in the former Abbaye Royale de Fontevraud (Royal Abbey of Fontevraud), although there is no record of Genet being incarcerated there; Fontevraud is the primary setting of *Miracle of the Rose*. Other prisons and jails appear scattered through his work, in *Our Lady of the Flowers* and in *The Thief's Journal*, in his film *Un chant d'amour*, in his poetry and in essays, in his defence of the Black Panthers; and of course, we should not forget that his first novels were written, or at least begun, in prison. Prison is certainly the single building type most closely associated with Genet.

On the other hand, there is a curious absence of houses in Genet. The characters in his books inhabit cheap hotels, rooms, flophouses, even caves; they live in institutional settings—ships, reformatories, and especially prisons—but almost never houses. And Genet himself, as I have noted already, never, after the age of about sixteen, lived in a house. Still, I argue that the question of the house plays a central role in Genet's work, if central in its absence: the absence of the house is as striking as the presence of the prison. Although Foucault does not discuss houses in his work on heterotopias, I argue that the house, like the prison, is heterotopic as a type, an institution in which the Oedipal structures of society are allowed to develop in relative secret, behind closed doors and solid walls. The house, like the prison, mirrors and potentially exposes the structures of society as a whole. We could say that the house is a productive heterotopia, in that the otherness of its spaces produce and reproduce those of society, while the productive nature of the prison heterotopy is less obvious. Following Foucault, we could suggest that the prison, in its development in the early modern world out of the medieval dungeon and jail, serves to define and create the criminal as a class and as a being, defining by corollary the disciplinary force of the law. The couple of prison-house is brought together in Genet in the Mettray colony. Mettray effectively combines the two primary heterotopic forms, operating both productively and disciplinarily, operating on the fields of both criminal and family.

There are other important heterotopias in Genet's work, such as brothels, which operate as houses, un-houses, prisons, or some combination of the two; the brothel in *The Balcony*, for example, explicitly acts as a counterpart, a representation of society as a whole. Two other heterotopic systems in Genet's work that play a role in *The House Is (Not) a Prison* are those of cemetery and theatre, which, like prison and house, operate as a couple for Genet, as he discusses in his essay "That Strange Word..." (2003, 102–12).

5 There is also a collection of elements, mostly architectural components, that appear regularly in Genet's work. These elements are necessarily incomplete in relation to the heterotopias discussed above, but present moments in which the

fundamental characteristics of the heterotopia are expressed, emphasized, or called into question. *Windows*, for example, are locations or presentiments of danger, a reminder of the uncontrollable enemy that always lurks in the outside world: the cemetery outside Divine's window in *Our Lady of the Flowers*, the cemetery in which Divine will reside by the end of the novel; the streets of Paris, dangerous with snipers, the streets where death lurks for the German soldier Erik outside Mme Decarnin's apartment in *Funeral Rites*; the window in Genet's bedroom in Le Cannet, organized to provide a view of anyone—that is, the police—arriving up the hill. Windows are dangerous moments of leakage between otherwise isolated and enclosed spatial organizations. Closely connected to windows are *balconies*, provisional locations outside of the bounds of safety, transitions between inside and outside, locations where danger becomes realized (*Funeral Rites, The Balcony*). *Mirrors*, on the other hand, provide glimpses into otherwise separate realities, allowing us to see ourselves differently (*The Maids*) or more precisely (*Funeral Rites*), to catch a glimpse into other realities (*The Balcony*), or to lose ourselves, to become a play of pure images, as in the House of Mirrors in which Stilitano becomes lost in the last pages of *The Thief's Journal*. Mirrors are an intrusion into our world of a different reality. They are also dangerous, containing (at least) a triple danger: they can allow us to be seen without affording the ability to see, producing an unexpected state of surveillance; they can magically produce that uncanny situation in which we can see behind our heads without turning around; and they can embody, distort, fragment, and dissolve our identities. It is no wonder that Genet (according to Dichy) would never choose a bar or café that had mirrors on its walls.

Windows and mirrors act always as gaps or openings in *walls*. Not surprisingly for a writer concerned with prison, walls comprise a primary figure in Genet's work. Walls of course allow for transgression: they come with doors or other cracks that a smart thief can jimmy open. The wall between two convicts provides the fundamental mechanism for erotic transgression in *Un chant d'amour*, while the lack of walls at Mettray becomes its own *Miracle of the Rose*: "One of the subtleties of the Mettray colony's inventors was that they knew not to put up a wall...It's much more difficult to escape when it's simply a question of crossing through a patch of flowers than if there's a wall for you to climb" (Genet 2004, 191).

Meanwhile, the walls of Fontevraud Prison themselves become insubstantial through a pure act of will on the part of Genet, allowing the condemned murderer Harcamone to simply walk out of the prison—almost. This question of the dematerialization of the wall, the movement from wall to screen and eventually to pure image (see, for example, the use of drawings on screens in early scenes of *The Screens*), is critical in Genet, and also critical to the development of modern architecture. The wall relates to borders (*The Thief's Journal*), to the separation between the living and the dead (*The Screens*), and, I will argue, to the question of what bounds us as humans. Walls are things to be climbed over, walked through, demolished.

Walls are contrasted or complemented by floors, platforms, stages, which I will refer to here as *levels*. The separation and relation between levels is critical in Genet's work, finding its roots probably at Mettray, where the lower levels of the "houses" are radically distinguished (as workshop) from the living spaces above. The same relationship is found at Fontevraud in *The Miracle of the Rose*: in the prison, the cells are on an upper level, the punishment cell (and various other spaces) on a lower. We see it in *Our Lady of the Flowers*, and particularly in the relationship of Divine's room to the cemetery which it overlooks; and in the plays, especially *The Blacks*, in which upper and lower levels imply separate worlds, and most clearly of all, in *The Screens*, which uses levels to develop multiple realities, most strikingly the world of the dead in the lowest level. Levels are often set with inscriptions, such as the circles, the anuses, in the punishment cell at Fontevraud (*Miracle of the Rose*), and in the Barrio in Barcelona (*The Thief's Journal*).

Important components in the play of levels are the means of transportation and communication between them—or the lack of these means. Often, the levels for Genet remain completely isolated: movement from one level to another is not possible, or can only be the result of a powerful event. Divine cannot move to the lower level of the cemetery, except by dying (*Our Lady of the Flowers*). The German soldiers and Riton can only move to their purgatory—the vacant apartment—by climbing down from the roof (*Funeral Rites*), and of course we cannot forget the importance of roofs as grounds of action. Culafroy can only ascend to the position of Divine through the intercession of a miracle (*Our Lady of the Flowers*). In other cases, there are miraculous connections—strange connections—between levels, such as the improvised trapdoor that allowed a vertical escape from Mettray in *Miracle of the Rose*.

The most important mode of transport between levels, though, is the stair. The act of moving up and down a stair is never neutral in Genet; the stair always embodies the act of moving from one realm to another. We see this, for example, in *The Thief's Journal*, in which Stilitano leads Genet up the dark stair by the hand, the stair that is alive to their presence. We feel it in the stair to Divine's apartment in *Our Lady of the Flowers*. Most important of Genet's stairs, though, is the stair at Fontevraud: "The stairway, which goes from the floors on which the workshops and refectories are installed, to the ground floor, where the offices, prison court, medical room and visitors' room are located, is the main meeting-place. It is cut into the stone of the wall and unwinds in shadow. That was where I almost always saw Bulkaen. It was the lovers' trysting-place, particularly ours, and it still vibrates with the sound of the kisses exchanged there" ([1946] 1988, *Miracle*, 45). Stairs for Genet are vertical shafts, erections. They never act alone, but always in conjunction with levels and their inscriptions. They are places of passage and places of emotion. They are the impossible connections between worlds.

6 I call the iconic houses that I discuss in this book *un-houses* because they exist in the world not (or not only) as places where people live, sleep, and fuck, but more importantly as images or ideas. As houses, in the everyday sense of the word, these structures are all failures, abandoned by their owners (Savoye), difficult to live in due to the lack of storage space, plate glass walls, and regular flooding (Farnsworth), or needing supplemental spaces in order to function (Glass House). And of course, if we consider the house as corollary of the modern family—that is, as a site (or machine) for domestic reproduction—all three houses stand as failures: Farnsworth and the Glass House due, arguably, to the nature of their owners, and Savoye due to its reputed inability to safeguard the health of the Savoye's family.

This failure, so to speak, lifts Farnsworth, Savoye, and the Glass House off of the earthly plane that houses must inhabit and places them onto another level, a level in which their houseness fades. Like Heidegger's broken tool, their failure opens up a presence, a rupture in time that delivers new avenues for analytical consideration. In this text, discussions of these houses should not be considered as case studies; that is, the text does not attempt to give an honest analysis of the buildings as a whole. Rather, the intent is to make use precisely of the failures in the houses in order to develop an argument, or a set of arguments, about modern domesticity as a whole, an argument that might run something like this: *The failures of these houses, their oddities and contradictions, are condensations and apparitions of the hidden structures of modern domesticity.* We do not study these un-houses as much as interpret them, in the way that psychotherapy will interpret dreams, jokes, and slips of the tongue.

Un-houses are structures or objects that have some relationship to, or act in some respects as houses, but that somehow possess either a lack or a surplus that excludes them from a consideration as fully or simply a house. There are many examples in Genet's work, some of which are obvious. The prison cell, for example, possesses house-ness in the simple fact that convicts sleep there (there will be much more to be said about cells later) but do not participate in the broader conditions of the house, such as property ownership and familial structure; brothels, at least for Genet, present an image of the house; the Hall of Mirrors at the end of *The Thief's Journal* presents a radically fragmented and unlivable image of a house. All of these are un-houses, as are other less obvious objects: the house of sheets constructed by the young protagonist in *Our Lady of the Flowers*; the outhouse in the same novel; the pissoir in Barcelona from *The Thief's Journal*; the coffin that Genet carries in his pocket (in the form of a matchbox) in *Funeral Rites*; Jean Decarnin's rectum; the destroyed house in *Prisoner of Love*, which I call the Teacup House; the many one-star hotel rooms that Genet slept in over the course of his life. And, of course, the stage.

7 The cell is also revealed as highly problematic from the point of view of sexual discipline; here I recount the argument relayed by Genet regarding a preference for the cell (as the ideal site for masturbation) versus the dormitory (as the ideal site for homosexual relationships) at the Mettray colony. The idea that the prison cell, the epitome of discipline of the (deviant) individual, is also the locus for masturbation par excellence, is an incredible problem at the core of the modern.

8 I'm not aware of any closets in the work of Genet, aside from Madame's closet in *The Maids*, but there are certainly two other primary voids in his thinking: that of the brothel (which has many characteristics in common with the closet) and the tomb. And a third, if one allows it, although in my analysis this third is just another tomb: the anus. In this section I discuss the role of the anus in its relation to death, especially in Genet's novel *Funeral Rites* as well as the strictly heterotopic nature of the brothel in his play *The Balcony*—including a discussion of the chaos that breaks loose when the wall of the void is breached.

The brothel is a space of a split and fractured self, a space in which we can perform fantasy-identities; it is connected to two other important spaces of architectural modernity, the closet and the theatre. The tomb, which is also figured in the interior of the body (and especially, for Genet, in the rectum), is the space of no-self, the space in which we cannot be while remaining ourselves, while also presenting (in the form of the death drive) the energy source that drives the modern (and contemporary) architectural machine.

9 This analysis of the Villa Savoye is conducted in parallel with an analysis of another architectural machine, that of Fontevraud Prison, as described by Genet in his novel *Miracle of the Rose*. The endnote develops a parallel between the two buildings in which each is seen as a transform of the other.

10 There is no demonstrated connection between Genet and any of the iconic works of modern domestic architecture discussed in this book, so I invented one. On coming across a chance reference to Poissy in *Miracle of the Rose*—a reference in which Genet is pointing to the Maison Centrale de Poissy, the state prison located a short walk from the Villa Savoye—I realized that there must be a connection between the prison and the Villa, so I placed a twenty-four-year old vagrant, newly returned to France from his travels around Europe, at the Villa. Later, when reading about the Barcelona pissoir in *The Thief's Journal*, I imagined that the structure being presented was nothing other than Mies's Barcelona Pavilion: after all, Genet would have been in Barcelona at the time of the pavilion. I imagine the parade of pimps and whores and homosexuals in memory of the pavilion when it was dismantled in 1930:

> Those whom one of their number called the Carolinas paraded to the site of a demolished street urinal. During the 1933 [*sic*] riots, the insurgents tore out one of the dirtiest, but most

> beloved pissoirs. It was near the harbor and the barracks, and its sheet-iron had been corroded by the hot urine of thousands of soldiers. When its ultimate death was certified, the Carolinas—not all, but a solemnly chosen delegation—in shawls, mantillas, silk dresses and fitted jackets, went to the site to place a bunch of red roses tied together with a crape veil. The procession started from the Parallelo, crossed the Calle Sao Paolo and went down the Ramblas de Las Flores until it reached the statue of Columbus. The faggots were perhaps thirty in number, at eight o'clock, sunrise. I saw them going by. I accompanied them from a distance. I knew that my place was in their midst, not because I was one of them, but because their shrill voices, their cries, their extravagant gestures had, it seemed to me, no other aim but to try to pierce the shell of the world's contempt. The Carolinas were great. They were the Daughters of Shame. ([1949] 1987, *Journal*, 65)

I love this phrase, the Daughters of Shame...The line of the wandering thief starts to tie together the narrative history of modern architecture. Further along in *The Thief's Journal* he puts in a brief appearance at the house of an industrialist in Brno, Czechia—a house that can only be Mies's Villa Tugendhat. Later I imagine him at the Farnsworth House in 1968, during his trip to Chicago to review the Democratic National Convention for *Esquire* magazine; in my imaginings he camps out near the river, watching the two women in the house perform his play *The Maids*, their actions and their internal thoughts caught on the glass screens of the building like X-rays. I imagine him invited to a dinner party at Philip Johnson's Glass House while he is giving a talk at

Yale University in 1970, a dinner party in which the thief steals first the cutlery, then the plates, then the furniture, then finally walks away with the Glass House, now the size of a matchbox, in his pocket.

11 *Ob-scene* here is a word taken from Genet, where he takes it to mean "the off-scene of the world" ([1943] 1987, *Flowers*, 301). For Genet, though, this *ob-scene* is nothing less than the world of death; the note provides a brief discussion of the location of death behind the screens in *The Screens*. One could, of course, walk around the screens to be behind them, but to get to the world of the dead it is necessary to go *through* the screens. Death, in other words, is the *ob-scene* of life.

12 I propose a series of tactics that make use of both the technical process of architectural design and the liberatory potential of queer sexuality: *Be a pornstar. Start and end with failure. Fall off the line. Jump into the void. Masturbate on your drawing board. Always wear a mask. Learn to love your cell. Penetrate everything. Draw what is behind your head. Jam a dildo in the machine. Every design is for a porn set. Draw the ob-scene. Steal whatever you can. Draw until you get hard, draw until you cum. Raise new monsters. Work harder, faster, deeper. Work harder. Harder. Harder. Don't stop. Don't stop...*

13 As Bersani puts it, this figure, which Genet likens to the prow of a ship, is a "fucking of the world instead of each other" (1996, 166).

14 In an interview with Hubert Fichte in 1975, when asked what sort of revolution he would prefer, Genet responded that he had no desire for any revolution: "The current situation, the current regimes allow me to revolt, but a revolution would probably not allow me to revolt, that is, to revolt individually...My point of view is very egotistic. I would like for the world—now pay close attention to the way I say this—I would like for the world not to change so that I can be against the world" (2004, 132).

Chapter 1

1 Of course, several varieties of line make their presence known in Genet. First, there is the pure line of separation, the line that divides A from B, the line that the whirligig is designed to make vanish. There are occasions though when these lines take on real effects, become meaningful lines on the map, become borders. Borders are a common theme for Genet, most notably in *The Thief's Journal*, where he crosses a number of borders, but also in *Prisoner of Love*. The crossing of a border for Genet the vagabond and thief is always dangerous, but also full of magic: everything changes at the border. Below are just a few examples, from *The Thief's Journal*:

> Almost always alone, though aided by an ideal companion, I crossed other borders. Yet I was not going through Europe but through the world of objects and circumstances, and with ever fresher ingenuousness. ([1949] 1987, 113)
>
> I got caught in the barbed wire of a fort where I heard the sentinels walking and whispering. Crouching in the shadow, my heart beating, I hoped that before shooting me they would fondle me and love me. (113)
>
> Later on I left Italy for Austria. I crossed fields of snow at night. The moon cast my shadow. (113)
>
> When the police and then the customs officers made me cross the Italian border, by the mountain road and on a freezing night, I headed for Trieste. (116)
>
> During my expeditions (my thefts, my reconnoiterings, my flights) objects were animated. The stones and pebbles on the roads had a sense through which I was to make myself known. The trees were surprised to see me. (127)

And we could add that Genet continues to cross borders, both literal geopolitical frontiers and metaphysical divisions, throughout his life. Remember the crossing of the border of death in *The Screens*, of crashing through the paper screens on the lowest level of the stage. Remember his travels to the United States, which he entered without a visa. Remember his crossing of the border of Mettray, of crossing from the world of prostitute to thief, to novelist, to playwright, to...? The border always represents a moment of danger and exhilaration, a moment of caution mixed with abandon, a moment of heightened awareness in which the trees are surprised to see us: "A border is where human personality expresses itself most fully, whether in harmony or in contradiction with itself... Whatever they may say, anyone approaching a frontier stops being a Jacobin and becomes a Machiavelli. It might be a good thing to extend border areas indefinitely—without, of course, destroying the centres, since its they that make the borders possible" ([1986] 1992, *Prisoner*, 147).

The ideal would be, one imagines, to live one's life at the border, to let the others live in the safety and dullness of the centre (although just as the border cannot live without the centre, so the centre cannot exist without the border). To live on the border, permanently in the space between A and B, neither Slovenian nor Italian, neither nature or culture, neither male or female—this is the ultimate revolutionary act, stronger and more abject, because more permanent and requiring more conviction, than the whirligig. This is the heroism of Divine, but even more so of transsexuals: "Changing sex doesn't consist merely in subjecting one's body to a few surgical adjustments: it means teaching the whole world, forcing upon it, a change of syntax...Transsexuals are heroines" ([1986] 1992, *Prisoner*, 150).

Maybe this is why Genet fell so deeply in love with Abdullah, the high-wire artist, and why he was so crushed by Abdullah's death. Genet understands, I think, that to inhabit the border demonstrates that the binary does not exist, that there is always in any binary a third term (at least), a space of overlap, a both-and and neither-nor, the thickness of a wall, a strip of land planted with mines, the Name-of-the-Father. Architecture.

2 Bratton's (2015) article takes as its analytical starting point Genet's great play *The Balcony*, in which transvestitism does not concern a gender binary as such, but rather a different sort of crossing of the line, the line of power.

It's useful, I think, to present a brief synopsis of this play, as it is in fact all about the crossing of lines. Although Genet produced several versions of the play, the most commonly read version both in French and English is today the second version, completed in 1960. The plot of this second version of *The Balcony* takes place largely within the walls of Le Grand Balcon, a high-end brothel, or house of illusions, overseen in meticulous detail by the Madame, Irma. This brothel is comprised of numerous studios that have been designed and constructed in such a manner as to allow the brothel's clients to play out whatever particular fantasies they desire. In the first three scenes of the play, we are shown three of these studios, where we see The Bishop forgiving the sins (which may or may not have been invented) of a prostitute; The Judge, sentencing and overseeing the punishment of another prostitute, guilty of theft; and The General, who rides his horse, a third prostitute. All three characters are dressed in exaggerated fashion in abstracted regalia suitable to the office, with exaggerated broad shoulders and high *cothurni*. Periodically, machine-gun bursts are heard in the distance.

Meanwhile, we are told, a revolution is being waged in the city outside of the brothel; one of Irma's girls, Chantal, has left the brothel to become the figurehead of the revolution. The Bishop, The Judge, and The General, or rather, the clients that have taken on those roles, hesitate to leave the brothel to go home, afraid that the streets are too dangerous. Irma and her second-in-command, Carmen, pass time doing the accounts and discussing the nature of the house of illusions, while they wait impatiently for the arrival of the Chief of Police, under whose protection the brothel can remain open. An Envoy arrives from the Queen (why would a Royal Envoy visit a brothel?) to inform Irma and the Chief of Police that matters are getting more desperate, that the Archbishop's Palace, the Law Court, and the Military Headquarters have all been taken; The Generalissimo has gone mad, the Attorney-General has died of fright, and The Bishop is...missing. A large explosion is heard and felt, which is taken to be the destruction of the Royal Palace (the Queen, meanwhile, may or may not be embroidering). The Chief of Police has a brilliant idea, a scheme that he hopes will restore order: The Bishop, The Judge, and The General, who are still loitering in the brothel afraid to venture outside ("they're standing around looking at themselves in the mirrors" [[1956] 2008, *Balcony*, 68]), and who already have the costumes, will present themselves as the real personages of power. The plan succeeds: the three figures present themselves on the balcony of the brothel, along with Irma in the costume of the Queen, the Chief of Police (in the rear, dressed as himself), and Chantal. The revolution is quelled by the reappearance of the figures of order. Chantal is shot dead. Order is restored.

The final scene focuses on the Chief of Police and more precisely on his image, his regalia. We have been told already that the Chief of Police is obsessed with one question: has anyone come to the brothel to dress up as him? Of course, the answer is always no, nobody has come to dress up as the Chief of Police. Still, Irma has been busily constructing a new studio for the Chief of Police, the mausoleum studio (as all strong men desire as their final image a magnificent tomb). The Chief of Police reveals his latest idea for his regalia, for the costume that will be worn by whomever does come to act the part of the Chief of Police: he will be dressed as a giant phallus, a "prick of great stature" (one imagines that the Chief of Police has been called, simply, a giant prick). Shortly after, a client does indeed arrive at the brothel asking to play the part of the Chief of Police—but the client is none other than Roger, the plumber, who had been Chantal's lover and the head of the revolution.

Roger is brought to the mausoleum studio, where he is dressed not as a giant phallus, but in the everyday clothes of the Chief of Police, including the Chief of Police's toupee. Roger is shown the mausoleum studio by Carmen, and when his time is up refuses to leave, becoming more and more agitated, until finally he castrates himself. The Chief of Police recognizes that his image is now secure (the vestibule is filled with clients), and walks into the mausoleum studio, to his own death, where he will stay for two thousand years.

Irma closes the brothel down for the night and tells the audience to go home and prepare their own roles. A machine-gun burst is heard.

3 With apologies to Bratton, we could perhaps put his argument (or something related somehow to his argument) succinctly as follows:

- Power is violence clothed in images. Naked power is violence dressed in a costume of nakedness. Architecture suspends violence through the violence of its construction (although, of course, the suspension of violence is itself just imaginary. Real violence continues). This is architecture as image.
- Power does not exist apart from or prior to its images. Power is entirely *vested* in its images. The lesson of *The Balcony* is that the clothing of power can be repurposed: that image produces power as much as power produces image. This is architecture as structure.
- Structure is a substrate for the projection of further images legitimating further violence. *Architecture allows power to change its clothing*. In the process, architecture itself can change its clothes. This is architecture as the wolf in sheep's clothing.
- The plot precedes its execution: from the viewpoint of the after, the image is the repetition-in-advance of the

event. The architectural design and the terrorist plot both represent the willing into form of a new world. This is architecture as desire.

In the end we have a sort of rock-paper-scissors game: structure freezes violence. Image covers structure. Violence shatters image. The building of the great city transforms the violence of colonial exploitation to the power of capital. The imagery of the soaring tower against the blue sky covers the brutality of capital with the confidence and clarity of technological modernity. The violence of the plane crashing into the tower shatters the image of confidence producing, in the process, new images of disarray.

The subtle and not-so-subtle shifts and twists and flips and flops of image-making in relation to power in this story are astonishing, the ways in which power—multiple forms and loci of power—dress themselves in multiply shifting clothing depending on the audience and the precise nature of the situation. Perhaps this is what Bratton means by "the transvestitism of power," that power is constantly putting on new clothes to present itself as other than what it really is—because one could contend that it is really nothing other than those very clothes. And this constant shimmering and shifting of images, of feather boas and morning suits, produces, in relation to the field of desire (desire of power, desire for power), a sort of jouissance, an excess, a need to play the game of power for its own sake.

4 *Roger* is an archaic English slang term for a penis.

5 Furthermore, what does it mean in any case to talk about the transvestitism not of a person but of an abstract concept such as power? What is the line, the divide that is being *transed* by power in its games of dressing-up? How does power engage in the erotic and performative aspects of transvestitism? Can we talk about these things without falling into the use of metaphor?

6 As Genet put this, speaking not of architecture but of the violent power of criminals, "Yet, what is their violence compared to mine, which was to accept theirs, to make it mine, to wish

it for myself, to intercept it, to utilize it, to force it upon myself, to know it, to premeditate it, to discern and assume its perils?" ([1949] 1987, *Journal*, 16).

7 Cutting things off is an important animator in the work of Genet: think, for example, of Stilitano's severed arm, the onstage castration of the plumber-cum-police chief in *The Balcony*, or the execution on the Guillotine of Harcamone in *Miracle of the Rose* or of Our Lady in *Our Lady of the Flowers*: "Forty days later, on a spring evening, the machine was set up in the prison yard. At dawn it was ready to cut. *Our Lady of the Flowers* had his head cut off by a real knife. And nothing happened" ([1943] 1987, *Flowers*, 291).

Derrida: "Language cuts, decollates, unglues, decapitates" ([1974] 1986, 74). But how can we avoid the *coup*? Derrida suggests a doubling, a belt-and-suspenders approach, two columns in case one is cut off, buckles, snaps, two lines of argument in case one collapses: "If I write two texts at once, you will not be able to castrate me. If I delinearize, I erect. But at the same time I divide my act and my desire. I—mark(s) the division, and always escaping you, I simulate unceasingly and take my pleasure nowhere. I castrate myself—I remain(s) myself thus and I 'play at coming' [je 'joue à jouir']" (65).

To be named is already to be cut off: Genet, Genet-ic, *gêner*, generous, generate, gene(t)ology, genital, genius. To be named a thief (homosexual) is to have a wall built between yourself and the world of the non-thieves (straights), the right-thinking people, in Sartre's terms. In the courtroom scene in Our *Lady of the Flowers*, Genet describes carefully the violence and humiliation of the name: "[the court] uttered for the first time, following the name Baillon, the words 'Known as Our Lady of the Flowers.' Our Lady was given the death penalty" ([1943] 1987, 291). To have two names is not necessarily a protection from the cut. The blade moves back once more to Derrida: "Return to natural denomination, that is, to the first classificatory violence, inversion of sex, reintroduction of the first name that comes, in all taxonomic rigor, second" ([1974] 1986, 99).

8 Genet's method, at least one part of his method, is to reject wherever possible (and perhaps wherever not possible) the fundamental binary structuring operation of the wall, insisting instead on inhabiting both sides of the wall, both positions of the binary, simultaneously. As Sartre describes the method,

> He refers to two opposing systems of values and refuses to choose one or the other...He does not write [the contradictory sentence] *in spite* of the contradiction it contains but *because* of it. Far from dreaming of concealing this contradiction, of transcending it towards some synthesis or other, he experiences keen satisfaction in making it sparkle in the false unity of the Word. ([1952] 1963, 330)
>
> I have called these devices *whirligigs*: Genet constructs them by the hundred. They become his favorite mode of thinking. (333) Or again, "His will will pose the incompatibility of the two theses and will decide in sovereign fashion that they constitute a fundamental unity" (332).

While for Genet this denial of the binary is spatial, it is a matter of denying front and back, of spinning so fast that one can see both sides of an impossible coin, both sides of the wall, simultaneously:

> As he watched himself moving, he thought: "He spun about," and the word "spun," immediately caught on the wing, made him about-face smartly. ([1943] 1987, *Flowers*, 199)
>
> Was it true that philosophers doubted the existence of things in back of them? How is one to detect the secret of the disappearance of things? By turning around very fast? No. But even faster? Faster than anything? I shot a look behind me.

> I spied, I turned my eyes and head, ready to... No, it was no use. These things are never caught napping. You would have to wheel about with the speed of an airplane. You would then realize that the things have disappeared and yourself with them. ([1949] 1963, *Funeral*, 48)

Sartre names this method whirligigs, after the child's toy in which a rapid circular motion of a disk or propeller creates an illusion, dissolving difference. It is this dissolution of difference, the merging of opposites *without synthesis* that is important here. The whirligig is a quantum effect, an effect of pure motion, a question of undecidability, of never resting on either side of the divide long enough to be trapped. The whirligig is not a method for analysis, not a staircase that leads us to some final understanding, but a pure negation of difference, a pure refusal of meaning. Sartre, like Derrida after him, confronts Genet's whirligig with Hegel's dialectics: "In Genet, the movement of thinking can only be *circular*. In Hegel, the thesis moves into the antithesis...Genet arranges his oppositions in such a way that each term, without ceasing to exclude the other, remains in the background when the other is present" (Sartre [1952] 1963, 332). As Derrida points out, the whirligig does not result in the removal of the wall, the removal of the cut, just the removal of its possibility, a deferral of its effects by spinning too fast: "That does not mean (to say) that there is no castration, but that this *there* is does not take place. There is that one cannot cut through to a decision between the two contrary and recognized functions of the fetish, any more than between the thing itself and its supplement. Any more than between the sexes" ([1974] 1986, 229).

The whirligig rejects the need to confront difference—since it destroys difference—but also eliminates the need to decide, to locate oneself on one side of the wall or the other, to be inside or outside, good or evil, male or female. In fact, the result of the whirligig is to dissolve the wall, to simply not accept the reality of the binary. The whirligig rejects the line, rejects structure itself. The whirligig is the epitome of *queer*.

The whirligig is perhaps the most important mechanism in this discussion of architecture. We could develop an extensive list of architectural binaries that are able to be dissolved by the whirligig, a few of which might be up|down, inside|outside, structure|skin, ground|structure, prison|house. The whirligig provides one, although not the only, mechanism for dealing with the wall separating the terms of the binary; all we need to do is to move quickly enough to be on both sides of the divide simultaneously.

9 For Sartre, the whirligig is a trap, a "circular prison" ([1952] 1963, 339); "the mind that enters one of these vicious circles goes round and round, unable to stop" (333). Genet presents this vicious circle, this impossibility of structure, in a scene at the end of *The Thief's Journal* in which Stilitano is trapped in a house of mirrors, unable to find the structure that would allow escape:

> As I approached the booth, the only one on the fairground, there was such a big crowd watching it that I knew something unusual was going on. The people were laughing. I recognized Roger in the crowd. He was staring at the involved mirror system; his face was tragically tense. Before seeing him I knew that Stilitano, and he alone, was trapped, visibly at a loss, in the glass corridors. No one could hear him, but by his gestures and his mouth one could tell he was screaming with anger. He was looking at the crowd in a rage, and they were looking at him and laughing. ([1949] 1987, 265)

And we can find it as well in the endless circulation of the Villa Savoye, in the confusion and disorientation of its ramp, of the women in *Architecture d'aujourd'hui*, forever trapped in the undecidable position of the ramp.

10 Opposing, in Genet, the line of the border, is a second type of line: the wandering line of the vagabond. The wandering line is, of course, fundamental to the structure of *The Thief's Journal*, but is equally evident in all aspects of Genet's life and work. We can see this line in his constant travels, his sojourns with the Palestinians and the Panthers, his habit of lodging in hotels (even when there was a house nearby ready to receive him, with a room set up for him). The wandering line shows up in his fantasies at Mettray of pirate voyages, in his romanticizing of deportation to the penal colonies in the Guianas, even, arguably, in his fascination with Jacky Maglia's racing career.

Genet's vectors though are designed to deny architecture, to refuse domestication. The wandering line is never able to be described fully, to be mathematized, predicted, mapped. The wandering line does not so much oppose architecture, as it takes little notice of it: the vagabond can just as easily spend a night in a prison as in a coast guard hut, in a park, or simply on the ground. The wandering line simply ignores architecture, does not recognize the structures it puts in place. And this is perhaps the most threatening of all attacks on architecture, to take away or refuse its ability to create a world, to refuse the domestication of the world.

11 Think, for example, of the tie with which Our Lady of the Flowers strangles the old man, the tie that appears at Our Lady's trial as a symbol of his destiny.

12 We could start perhaps by looking a bit more closely at the architecture of *The Balcony*. What exactly is hidden in plain sight in this play? There are, of course, several aspects of the situation that we have already discussed, but which merit a recap—and in some cases a further elaboration—here. First, we have the clear presentation of the most architectural of all devices, the separation of inside and outside; as Lacan (2017a) and Badiou (2020) tell us, the inside is a space of perfect order (although a perfect order of absolute disorder, so to speak, a disorder held in rigid order by the central and unquestioned control of Mme

Irma), held separate and isolated (by the brothel wall) from an outside of absolute disorder, manifested in the play primarily by the sound of machine-gun fire and the occasional explosion. The essential diagram of the play is therefore absolutely clear and fundamentally architectural in its nature. Furthermore, the action of the play mirrors (literally, through a process of doubling) this architectural diagram, as we have seen, with both characters and events coupled across the boundary between regimes, like particles and anti-particles mirrored across the horizon of a black hole, in a sort of theatrical Hawking radiation. Not only the setting, but also the plot and, I would suggest, the thematics of the play are therefore profoundly architectural. This architecture describes, we could say, the real of the play, the mechanism that underlies, supports, and is in turn produced by the various events and actions, the various scenes and scenarios that take place.

The interior portion of this architectural schematic takes on the form of a closet, a complex, labyrinthine storage room in which not only costumes but also identities are stored, organized, and indeed produced. This interior takes on rigorously the form of a heterotopia as described by Foucault, the particular form in which any location can stand in for any other location, and as such it acts as a productive engine, as an organizing node for society as a whole. The brothel is therefore not simply a site of order opposed to the disordered exterior, but rather is a sort of factory in which order is produced along with its raw materials of fetishes, perversions, and fantasies. The brothel choreographs, organizes, arranges, categorizes, indexes, develops, anticipates, produces the entire realm of desires, producing as a side effect two supplements: the jouissance of the clients and the income of the brothel. In the end, though, these are insignificant extras; the real value of the brothel, of this interior architecture, lies in its role as guarantor of the possibility of order.

The exterior situation is in many ways the exact opposite of the highly ordered interior of the brothel, as is mentioned by most of the commentators. However, they seem to glide over what seems to be the most significant difference: while the interior is presented to us directly, we are only ever (with the exception of one scene, cut in later versions of the play) told about the events on the exterior. At most, we are allowed to hear the sound of machine guns coming, presumably, from the exterior; otherwise, we hear reports of what is happening in this other realm. The exterior is thus, in common language, an imaginary world, a world that may or may not exist. As the leader of the rebellion, the plumber Roger, puts it almost at the end of the play, "Outside, in what you call life, everything has crashed...no truth was possible" ([1956] 2008, *Balcony*, 93). Outside, in what *you call* life: the exterior is not the real. The exterior is the realm of shadows, of untruths, of rumours and possibilities.

13 The key element to recognizing the architectural story of *The Balcony* is precisely that: the balcony. As Lacan says of the letter in Poe's "The Purloined Letter," the balcony is "the true subject" of the tale (1972, 59). *The balcony* is of course an ambiguous term within the confines of the play, referring simultaneously to the title of the play, the name of the brothel, and the location of the pivotal scene in the play (a location that is itself doubled by Chantal's mention of the balcony of the Palace, and doubled again by the status of the balcony as stage set).

Of all the elements of architectural construction, a balcony is one of the most *odd*, ambiguously situated neither properly outside nor properly inside—or rather, to be more precise, it is at the same time, like the embroidering queen, both inside and outside. A balcony acts therefore to stitch together inside and outside, to trouble or question the interior|exterior distinction, to suspend the normal relations of the architectural diagram. To take this further, a balcony can act as a hinge to the architectural schema, to turn it inside out "like a glove," to use a term employed both by Genet and Lacan. The appearance of the balcony, its arrival onto the stage, is an immediate clue, if we know what we are looking for, of this introversion of the architectural diagram.

14 My argument here is that the balcony in *The Balcony* performs a function equivalent to that of the letter in Edgar Allen Poe's

([1844] 1988) "The Purloined Letter," equivalent not only in terms of dramatic structure but also in terms of the structure of signification. If this is the case, then we should be able to understand the balcony in relation to Lacan's famous dictum that "a letter always arrives at its destination" (1972, 72). How could we rewrite this phrase with reference to the balcony? What is the destination of a balcony, how does it arrive? In order to pursue these questions, I would like to examine the role of the balcony in relation to the three registers of the interior|exterior, that is, of the architectural diagram, introduced above. In order to do this, in turn, I will make use of Slavoj Žižek's analysis of the arrival or non-arrival of a letter in relation to the symbolic, imaginary, and real registers, as found in his article "Why Does a Letter Always Arrive at its Destination?" (2016, 13).

The literal balcony—that is, the architectural component of the façade of the brothel—appears on two brief occasions in the play (that is, in the second version, which is the most readily available currently; in the first version, the balcony only shows up once). First, the balcony shows up in the background of the street scene between Roger (the revolutionary plumber) and Chantal (in the first version of the play, this scene is set in a café). This is the critical scene for the conception of the exterior in the play, the locus of a somewhat ambiguous externality, and also the moment of confusion between brothel and Palace (Chantal is here designated the role of singing on the balcony of the Palace, with the balcony of the brothel in the background). The balcony appears again, more substantively, two scenes later, in the shortest and arguably most pivotal scene in the play (there is only one spoken line).

In the symbolic register, this scene describes the "coming out" of the images of power, their appearance before the revolutionary masses as part of the counter-revolutionary plot. In Žižek's analysis of "The Purloined Letter," in the symbolic mode "a letter always arrives at its destination" means that the true destination of the letter is indeed the sender; as Lacan puts it, the sender always receives his message back from the receiver, in inverted form. Likewise, in the play, the characters do not appear or come out, however, as something new; rather, these characters describe a return to visibility and a return to order. Likewise, Mme Irma takes up the role of Queen: or, stated differently, the Queen becomes again the Queen. Here, the balcony is literally acting as a letter, sending a message from the (highly structured) interior, from the interior of power to the disordered exterior of revolution, a message that indeed comes back to the interior. We could say that, architecturally, this is always one role of a balcony, to enable a message, a communication, between the isolated worlds of interior and exterior, a message that in the end, coming back to the interior, reconfirms the boundary line.

The imaginary register, understood here as a scenario in which there is no absolute exterior, but in which both the revolution and counter-revolution are scenes within a studio in the brothel, is not quite as straightforward to analyze from an architectural standpoint. For Žižek, in this case, we would say that "a letter always arrives at its destination" because the letter's final location determines itself after the fact as the (preordained) destination, establishing a misrecognition of a teleological trajectory. In *The Balcony*, then, it is the emergence onto the balcony that creates the destinies of Bishop, General, Judge, and Queen—and of course Hero. If the balcony in the symbolic mode represents and enables a reciprocal communication across the interior|exterior boundary, in the imaginary register it describes a sort of bubble, a herniatic enfolding of that same boundary, allowing a fictive and usually temporary emergence into an imaginary exterior. If the balcony in the symbolic register is redolent of communication, here in the mode of the imaginary it is the locus of exposition and display.

Finally, in the register of the real, the balcony punctuates a moment of crisis within the lives of all who participate. As Žižek tells us, "A letter always arrives at its destination" means simply that the letter, as a "death warrant," is always with us, an indication of the death drive, of the circumlocution that we go through on our drive. What only matters in this last register is the long and convoluted path that the letter takes, and that we take with it. So it is with the balcony in scene 8 of *The Balcony*: It is here that the Chief of Police becomes the Hero, leading inevitably to his death in the Mausoleum; the Judge, Bishop, and General become Judge, Bishop, and General, condemned to a life of power and service; Mme Irma becomes, as she perhaps always was, the Queen of all; and of course, Chantal is assassinated. The balcony here is the locus of judgement.

The balcony, then, is a critical component of the architectural diagram, at least in *The Balcony*. The balcony is both flaw and lynchpin, the element that both troubles the diagram and allows it to function. This most queer of architectural elements, by virtue of its ambiguous position with relation to the diagram (the balcony is neither in nor out, yet not of the boundary itself; it is both in *and* out, and neither in *nor* out), the balcony enables communication, display, and judgement across the boundary and throughout the diagram. The balcony, the exception to the rule, the (necessary) supplement that completes the structure, is, in the end, the centrepiece, the true subject, of the story.

This should come as no surprise. After all, we knew from the beginning that the architecture of the brothel, of Le Grand Balcon, would be the main theme of the play: Genet tells us as much in the title, emphasizes the point in the opening scenes, and reiterates it in his commentary on the first productions. The other elements of the play, the revolution, the scenes in the studios, the costumes, the assassination, the appearance of the phallus, these are all games (as the Chief of Police admits to us apropos of the revolution), all distractions, allowing us to miss the essential story: that the brothel, that is architecture, the architectural diagram, always remains in place. Architecture here is the final incarnation of power, holding to its diagram, despite the masks and costumes that it might put on.

Chapter 2

1 Genet, in *Our Lady of the Flowers*:

> Prisons have their silent stories, and so do the guards, and even the lead soldiers, which are hollow. Hollow! The foot of one of the lead soldiers broke, and the stump revealed a hole. This certainty of their inner emptiness delighted and distressed me. At home, there used to be a plaster bust of Queen Marie-Antoinette. I lived right next to it for five or six years without noticing it, until the day when its chignon miraculously broke, and I saw the bust was hollow. I had to leap into the void in order to see it. ([1943] 1987, 169)

2 There are voids everywhere in the work of Genet. The void comes in many guises, many forms: the void inside the bust of Marie Antoinette, the void of the tomb, the void of the cell, the matchbox, the closet, the anus, the heart of the murderer, the empty suitcase in the first scene of *The Screens*, the packed suitcase Genet kept under his bed. The void is always there, central to the action, a massive gravitational weight around which the characters of the stories revolve. The void, in Genet's cosmology, is where we come from and where we end up and is with us always, pulling us towards its massive emptiness, a palpable uncanny presence that only occasionally is recognized, like in the beautiful passage from Genet's first novel, *Our Lady of the Flowers*, cited in the previous note. If, for Foucault, our lives are constructed through a series of encounters with disciplinary institutions (family, school, barracks, prison, hospital), for Genet that role is taken by a series of voids, not necessarily separate from those institutions.

3 The cell, of course, is a primary space in the work of Genet. This typology plays a major role in his first novels, central to both Our *Lady of the Flowers* and *Miracle of the Rose*, central not only as

the scenes of much of the action of these novels, but also as the scene of their writing. What's more, Genet's first novel, Our *Lady of the Flowers*, opens in the cell, as a sort of introductory scene: Before we are introduced to the main characters or to the scenes of the action, we find ourselves in cell 427 of Santé Prison, in Paris. And of course, it appears elsewhere, outside of these two novels: in his first play, *Deathwatch*; as the scene of action of his first and only film, *Un chant d'amour*. The cell is not only a critical central location for his production, but also the place of firsts: literally, the site of origin of his literary production, the architectural setting for its genesis. It is amazing that Sartre, for whom Genet was motivated primarily by a search for his missing mother, did not notice or did not call attention to this womb-like character of the cell, to its ability to give birth to a world. In the context of Genet, we can consider the cell as a productive void, a void because of the way in which the cell, like the prison itself, is cut out of the fabric of the world, removed from society, a missing piece. Indeed, the cell is doubly void, a void in the prison as well as a void in society, a void whose interior is, to those on the outside (in the world), invisible, *because to them it cannot exist*. This is the nature of a void: it is a space removed from the normal world, a space that operates under the rules of a different universe, a space that is, by nature of its absence, invisible to those outside it. It is, as Genet puts it, an impossible nothingness: "This book, *The Thief's Journal*, pursuit of the Impossible Nothingness" ([1949] 1987, *Journal*, 94).

4 Fontevraud is located only about sixty kilometres from Mettray, and the identification, the linkage between Mettray and the adult prison, is critical to *Miracle of the Rose*. The novel opens with the following astonishing paragraph, which contains within it already all the themes of this work—the prison and the house, the thief and the homosexual, the wall and its dark heart:

> Of all the state prisons of France, Fontevrault is the most disquieting. It was Fontevrault that gave me the strongest impression of anguish

and affliction, and I know that convicts who have been in other prisons have, at the mere mention of its name, felt an emotion, a pang, comparable to mine. I shall not try to define the essence of its power over us: whether this power be due to its past, its abbesses of royal blood, its aspect, its walls, its ivy, to the transient presence of convicts bound for the penal colony at Cayenne, to its prisoners, who are more vicious than those elsewhere, to its name—none of this matters. But to all these reasons was added, for me, another: that it was, during my stay at the Mettray Reformatory Colony, the sanctuary to which our childhood dreams aspired. I felt that its walls preserved—the custodial preserving the bread—the very shape of the future. While the boy I was at fifteen twined in his hammock around a friend (if the rigours of life make us seek out a friendly presence, I think it is the rigours of prison that drive us toward each other in bursts of love without which we could not live; unhappiness is the enchanted potion), he knew that his final form dwelt behind them and that the convict with his thirty-year sentence was the fulfillment of himself, the last transformation, which death would make permanent. And Fontevrault still gleams (though with a very soft, a faded brilliance) with the lights emitted in its darkest heart, the dungeon, by Harcamone, who was sentenced to death. ([1946] 1988, *Miracle*, 5)

5 Despite the fact that cells were not the dominant structural system at Fontevraud, *Miracle of the Rose* concentrates on the cell as the primary site of incarceration in the prison: the site

of Genet's fantasies and phantasies, the world in which the prisoner is invariably enclosed and contained. More than that: the cell is the prisoner. Genet's Fontevraud is not exactly a true image of the prison, which is perhaps no surprise since Genet never actually stayed there as a prisoner.

The cell is the heart of the novel, literally: the cell that the murderer Harcamone is held in, the energetic beating heart of the prison, the cell from which Genet engineers a phantastic escape, the cell that is mirrored by another heart, the heart of the murderer himself.

6 As Genet points out in another beginning, on page seven of *Miracle of the Rose* ([1946] 1988), "I cannot tell how it looked from the outside—I can tell this about few prisons, since those which I know, I know only from the inside."

7 Despite the absolute impossibility of movement across the boundary of the cell (or, for that matter, of the self), there remains, as Genet reminds us, the possibility of an uncanny transference of information across the barrier. The barrier of the cell as a result is always a porous membrane: "Another was mentioned, almost sung, by the prisoners—their song became fantastic and funereal (a *De Profundis*), as much so as the plaints which they sing in the evening, as the voice which crosses the cells and leaves me blurred, hopeless, infected" (Genet [1943] 1987, Flowers, 52). *The sound* moving across the barrier is uncanny, an appearance of that which cannot be, an appearance here on the inside of that which can only exist (if it exists at all) on the outside. It is a viral reminder of another world. It is a reminder as such of the possibility of the impossible, a variety of Hawking radiation flowing, in this case, from the black hole of the cell. The flow of energy, of information, operates in both directions and, critically, the events that take place inside the cell, the production of the cellular machinery, can produce real effects on the exterior.

Genet's entire literary career, inaugurated by texts written in cell 427 of Santé Prison, is evidence to that productive character of the cellular void. So, too, is the miracle of the rose, the escape sequence for Harcamone invented by Genet in his cell at Fontevraud Prison in *Miracle of the Rose*. So, too, are the masturbatory fantasies of every prisoner, whether in a cell, in a modern bedroom, or in a self.

8 The void inside this boundary, this void which stands as a platonic model for many other architectural spaces (to give just two examples, Divine's apartment in *Our Lady of the Flowers* and the modern bedroom) is an idealized space. For Genet, it is an ideal geometric form: "My cell is an exactly cubic box" ([1943] 1987, *Flowers*, 249). Within this ideal space of the cell is absolute security: "Prison offers the same sense of security to the convict as does a royal palace to a king's guest. They are the two buildings constructed with the most faith...The masonry, the materials, the proportions and the architecture are in harmony with a moral unity which makes these dwellings indestructible so long as the social form of which they are the symbol endures. The prison surrounds me with a perfect guarantee" ([1949] 1987, *Journal*, 87). Which becomes, regardless of the actuality of the cell, a place of happiness and joy, or to be more accurate, a place of rightness, the right place, the correct place, a place with which one falls hopelessly in love:

> The sweet prison cells! After the foul monstrousness of my arrest, of my various arrests, each of which is always the first, which appeared to me in all its irremediable aspects in an inner vision of blazing and fatal speed and brilliance the moment my hands were imprisoned in the steel handcuffs, gleaming as a jewel or a theorem, the prison cell, which I now love as one loves a vice, consoled me, by its being, for my own being. ([1943] 1987, *Flowers*, 103)
>
> My good, my gentle friend, my cell! My sweet retreat, mine alone, I love you so! If I had to live in all freedom in another city, I would first go to prison to acknowledge my own, those of my race, and also to find you there. (129)

Or again: "I have made myself a soul to fit my dwelling. My cell is so sweet" (305). The void of the cell is the void of the self, isolated from all other worlds, inescapable, idealized by its occupant and loved regardless of its misery. At the very least, we can say that for Genet there is a clear relation, even if not a metaphorical intent, between cell and self; as he tells us in *The Thief's Journal*, "the prison remains sure of itself, and you in the midst of it sure of yourself" ([1949] 1987, 88). The argument operates in both directions, making clear once again the architectural construction of the self: "we" exist, inasmuch as "we" are, not so much in a cell, but as a cell, radically separated from all exterior and indeed never fully certain that there is an exterior (this is something that we cannot in fact know): the cell is the primary topology of consciousness.

9 In September 1926, the fifteen-year-old Jean Genet arrived at Mettray, having been consigned to the colony "until his legal majority" (White 1993, 59); in fact, Genet remained in the colony until 1929. Mettray in the 1920s was no longer the radical liberal proposition that Demetz had founded in 1840; after the death of Demetz in 1873, the colony suffered a systematic qualitative decline, which has been described by Toth (2019) through his review of the colony's archives. By the 1920s, Mettray was known as a place of harsh discipline; in his biography of Genet, Edmund White (1993) cites several records of punishments at Mettray from this period, which are starkly different in their intensity from those noted by earlier observers. Indeed, public opinion with respect to the colony had also shifted; reports in newspapers now tended to be highly critical. Mettray was closed, partly because of this criticism, in 1936. Following Foucault (1986), one might suggest that, by the 1930s, Mettray's heterotopic function had become obsolete in two senses: its productive cycle was complete, having given rise to the classic modern disciplinary state and, as a consequence, because everyday reality had become a mirror of the ordered existence of Mettray, the

colony was no longer able to offer a contested or inverted representation of that reality. In other words, just as Mettray in 1926 was not the Mettray of 1840, so France of the 1920s was not the France of the July Monarchy.

10 Genet, like most colonists, was an orphan who had spent most of his young life in and out of foster care and juvenile prisons (see White 1993, for a thorough account of Genet's youth). By the time he wrote his account of Mettray in 1943, he had joined (and deserted from) the army, travelled throughout Europe as a vagabond and thief, and spent several short periods in prison on minor offences (including the theft of a volume of Proust from a Paris bookshop). In 1943 he was in danger of being given a life sentence as a habitual offender (which meant likely transferal to a concentration camp); this was avoided by the intervention of Jean Cocteau, who had arranged for the publication of Genet's first novel. Cocteau, with the support of other members of the Paris intelligentsia, presented Genet to the judge as "the greatest writer of the modern era" (as cited in Dichy 1993, xxviii). Thus, Genet's writing *literally* allowed him to escape from prison. Although Cocteau's presentation of Genet is debatable, Genet's novels and plays represent—and the attention paid to his work by other thinkers (Sartre, Bataille, Sontag, and Derrida) identifies it as—one of the most significant bodies of literature of the past century, a constitutive irritant within the modern world.

11 At first blush, Genet's depiction of the Mettray colony in *Miracle of the Rose* corresponds very closely to both the physical evidence of the site and to descriptions made by earlier visitors to the colony. His descriptions of the colonists' clothing, the hammocks in the dormitories, and the ship in the main square all concur with other descriptions. Still, the overall effect is not really one of a description of the colony as much as a *redrawing* of Mettray, as one might do on a sheet of tracing paper laid over it. Each element appears, but changed. The colonists' clothing is described in terms of the extra (illicit) pockets that were sewn into the pants or the sharpening of

the sabots into weapons (Genet [1946] 1988, *Miracle*, 146); the hammocks become tents for illicit lovemaking beneath (188). The primary technique by which these twists and pulls are made is one of *tactical reappropriation*: At every step, the colonists find a tactical response to the colony's strategic discipline, appropriating—stealing, one might say—the mechanisms of that discipline for a contrary, resistive, and ultimately creative and imaginative purpose. As Genet put it, "Each object in your world has a meaning different for me from the one it has for you. I refer everything to my system, in which things have an internal signification, and even when I read a novel, the facts, without being distorted, lose the meaning which has been given them by the author and which they have for you, and take on another so as to enter smoothly the other worldly universe in which I live" (78).

Genet the writer makes use of this same technique, learned, one imagines, at Mettray; for example, the ship in the square becomes a pirate ship, on which Genet, in his erotic fantasies, serves as cabin boy (77).

12 The collision between the deviancy and criminality of Genet and the order and discipline of Mettray, Foucault's signpost for the institution of the modern carceral regime, can be expected to result in revised views not only of Genet and Mettray but also of the modern world itself. I do not use the term *modern* world loosely; rather, I would point out that embedded in Genet's work are three distinct moments in the history of modernism. The first is the formative period of the founding of Mettray in 1840; through Mettray, Genet's work offers us a distant view into the fundamental conditions of a mechanistic, positivist modernism. The second moment that Genet brings to light is that of the mid to late 1920s, the moment of Genet's stay at Mettray and his subsequent vagabondage across Europe and also the moment of the first full bloom of European modernism (at least in architectural terms). This is the moment of Le Corbusier's radical schemes for the transformation of our urban environments,

as well as of his early, masterly villas, culminating (at least in the standard chronology of architectural history) with the Villa Savoye and with Le Corbusier's famous dictum—perhaps the ultimate expression of positivistic modernism—of the house as the machine for living in ([1923] 2009, 279). The third moment, of course, is that of 1943, hardly an inconsequential year for the world, for Europe, or for France. It seems incredible that in the charged environment of Paris of 1943, intellectual society was able to rally itself to save the still little-known Genet; Sartre clearly had other things to worry about (1943 was also the year of publication of *Being and Nothingness*). One could speculate that a society which found itself a prisoner under Nazi control may have felt a resonance with Genet's prison societies, with its shadows, its structures and strictures, and perhaps most important, its underlying core of resistance.

13 Each of these small dislocations has the effect of pulling at the conceptual surface of Mettray, lifting it "up" into a new, altered, heightened state, locally separated from the old. The cumulative result of many such transformations is a conceptual delamination of the two realities. Like the tracing paper mentioned earlier, Genet's Mettray floats in this sense above other versions of Mettray. These other, older versions are not destroyed, removed, or replaced by Genet's revisions but superceded. Through the tactical reappropriation, which pits imagination and creativity against disciplinary structure, a new Mettray—perhaps a new world—is formed. This new world is primarily an erotic one; the disciplinary structures of the colony have been subverted, transformed, and ultimately rendered powerless by a surreptitious kiss, a grope on the stairs (Genet [1946] 1988, *Miracle*, 149), or the marriage of two boys in the garden, under the moonlight (72–73).

14 The marriage of two Mettray colonists is not presented by Genet as a metaphor. It is not a sham marriage, not *like* a marriage, not conducted in jest: it is, simply, a marriage. Furthermore, this central scene in the novel, this moment when Genet is

transformed from thief to bride, is again a reappropriation of an element of the colony. For after all, if the central structuring concept of the colony is that of the family, then what is marriage but the logical result and expression of that family structure? In this critical scene, Genet steals not a minor component of the colony but its central grounding concept.

Genet has found an opening, a lock to be picked. He inserts himself in the gap between family as metaphor and, simply, family. This amounts, strangely enough, to a refusal of metaphor: a determination that metaphors be taken literally, that houses be houses, families, families. Metaphor must not be used to structure reality—although this last statement is probably reading too much into the text. At the least, the marriage scene points out the chief weakness of a metaphoric structure: metaphors always bring with them unintended elements and meanings, open to misuse, abuse, and exploitation. This reappropriation of the concept of *family* also reminds us that Mettray is itself structured on the *metaphor* of family. The families at Mettray are distorted abstractions of real-world families, which repress the erotic aspects of families in favour of the domestic. This is true of most of the important elements of Mettray. The houses the colonists live in, the hammocks they sleep in, the clothes they wear, the ship on which they learn to be sailors—these are all images, tracings, of objects in the outside world, but shifted, twisted, pulled. In founding Mettray, Demetz and Blouet used precisely the same process of reappropriation as Genet did in redrawing it, with one exception: although Genet carried out his reappropriations by making use of the reality of the colonists' bodies, Demetz and Blouet reappropriated the structure of the outside world through metaphor. Structure and meaning are conflated, at best; at worst, structure is taken to stand for meaning. The structure of the family, the imposition of names, is assumed to be sufficient for the effective use of the family-machine, even when the reality of the family, the meaning of the family, is missing. The colony, as a result, bears the same delaminated relationship to the world outside its boundaries as Genet's description does to the colony. Mettray floats above the old world, a separate plane, isolated and insulated from the premodern world of disorder, provisionality, criminality, and messiness. Mettray proposes, creates, a new world above that old one. It is for this reason that Mettray needs no wall: escaping Mettray would not be a matter of leaving its boundaries, of moving horizontally but of moving vertically, of going back, down, to an older world. It would mean escaping the world of discipline, leaving the structure of the family.

15 And yet the colonists managed to make of this world of discipline a second world, an erotic world—or it might be better described as a world of *the body*. The colonists pit their bodies—their last line of resistance—against the concept and structure of the world they are presented with. The colonists' bodies become sources of friction, impeding the workings of the machine of the colony, stealing energy out of the system.

Chapter 3

1 Some years ago, while working on a study of the Villa Savoye and rereading Genet's great novel *Miracle of the Rose*, my eye caught the following passage: "There are things one could say about destinies, but note the strangeness of that of monasteries and abbeys (which prisoners call the bee): jails and preferably state prisons! Fontevraud, Clairvaux, Poissy!" ([1946] 1988, 64–65). For a student of modern architecture, the name Poissy can mean only one thing: the Villa Savoye. More perhaps than any other house, this enigmatic, mysterious building rests in the consciousness—and in the unconscious—of the world of architecture. It is the *House of Architecture*. We cannot escape it.

2 Coincidentally, in 1937 Genet arrived back in France after a year of wandering around Europe. Genet deserted the army at almost the same moment that the Savoyes deserted their Villa.

3 This house is a prison: not literally, of course, but in my imagination, spurred on by Genet. I begin to invent a fantasy: the young Genet escapes from Mettray and makes his way to Poissy. He breaks into the Villa Savoye and hides out on the roof terrace, watching the scenes of family life playing out below. Or the year is 1943, and Genet is being held at Poissy—not in the real prison, the Maison Centrale, but at Savoye—and it is here that he writes his masterworks. Or both: in 1943, the vagabond and thief returns to Poissy, now deserted by the Savoyes, largely in ruins, and occupied by soldiers. He returns to his prison to write.

None of this is true—at least, I have no proof that it is—but the fantasy does hold, for me at least, a truth of sorts. A queer truth. I begin to look for evidence. I see it everywhere: in the roses at Savoye, planted, without a doubt, to remember the author of *Miracle of the Rose*. In the sheer formal strangeness of the house: a rigorously square box, raised up off the ground (according to Le Corbusier, to avoid dampness—contamination), in the centre of an open field, separated in both plan and section from the world.

In the windows placed all the way around the building on all sides—long, narrow windows, perfect for seeing out; for surveying, controlling, this open field; for stopping a thief from reaching the house. I see it in the gardener's cottage, with its formal relation to the Villa, floating above the wall, and in the cottage's even more uncanny formal relation to the guardhouse at the real prison, the Maison Centrale in Poissy, just down the street.

4 It is at Fontevraud Prison that the main events of *Miracle of the Rose* take place, about a decade after the construction of the Villa Savoye. We thus have a double constructive absence: if the prison is strangely missing, missing but present in the houses of Le Corbusier, we could say that the house is equally strangely missing from the prisons of Genet. Furthermore, if the Villa can be considered a machine for living in, Fontevraud Prison can be thought of also as a machine. Like Savoye, with its circulatory system, ramp, stair, and plumbing, Fontevraud has its own mechanism. Genet in fact makes this reading entirely clear: "I am caught in the mechanism of a cycle" ([1946] 1988, *Miracle*, 52).

Physically, the prison (in Genet's description) is dominated by two places, two scenes, two mechanisms: the punishment cell and the stairway—the site of forbidden interaction, of love. The first of these, the punishment cell, is a kind of big shed, the floor of which has a high polish—I don't know whether it's polished by brushes and floor-wax or by the canvas slippers of generations of punished men who walk in a circle and are so spaced as to occupy the entire perimeter of the hall without anyone being first or last, and who walk in circles the way punished colonists at Mettray walked round and round the yard...

> At regular intervals, two yards from and parallel to the walls, is a series of masoned blocks with rounded tops, like the bitts of boats and wharves, on which the punished men sit for five minutes every hour...At the centre of the circle is the can into which the men shit, a recipient three feet high

> in the form of a truncated cone. It has two ears, one on each side, on which you place your feet after sitting down, and a very low back-rest, like that of an Arab saddle, so that when you drop a load you have the majesty of a barbaric king on a metal throne. When you have to go, you raise your hand, without saying anything; the assistant makes a sign, and you leave the line, unbuttoning your trousers, which stay up without a belt. You sit on the top of the cone with your feet on the ears and your balls hanging. The others continue their silent round, perhaps without noticing you. They hear your shit drop into the urine, which splashes your bare behind. You piss and get off. The odour rises up. When I entered the room, what struck me most was the silence of the thirty inmates and, immediately, the solitary, imperial can, centre of the moving circle. (38–39)

Photos of the punishment cell at Fontevraud show that Genet's text is itself a dislocation of the actual space in the prison. The stools on which the men would rest are not in a single ring parallel to the walls, but organized in a grid, and scuff marks visible on the floor suggest that the punished men did not walk in a single circle, but rather each man circled separately around his stool (according to published accounts, prisoners would walk twenty-five kilometres per day). Furthermore, the can is not visible in the photo, or its presence even suggested. Rather than a single orbit around the "solitary, imperial can," the photo implies instead an entire constellation of solitary walkers, operating in a complex choreography of clockwork. Genet has reconfigured the punishment cell not only to match the traditional representation as seen in images such as that painted by Van Gogh (*Prisoners' Round*, 1890), but also to match Genet's own recollection of the punishment cell at Mettray. Perhaps more importantly, Genet has reconfigured the space to put the anus at the centre of the system with the prisoners revolving around that dark sun like planets.

The second primary scene in the novel, the stairway, is the site of clandestine meetings between prisoners, between Genet and his would-be lover, the beautiful tattooed angel Bulkaen, the site where cigarettes and caresses are exchanged, where masculine and feminine are defined by sectional position: who is above or below, on his way up, or going down?

> The stairway, which goes from the floors on which the workshops and refectories are installed, to the ground floor, where the offices, prison court, medical room and visitors' room are located, is the main meeting-place. It is cut into the stone of the wall and unwinds in shadow. That was where I almost always saw Bulkaen. It was the lovers' trysting-place, particularly ours, and it still vibrates with the sound of the kisses exchanged there. (45)

> I shall never sing sufficiently the pleated stairway, and its shadow. The fellows used to meet there. (61)

I want to imagine the stair as a sort of drive shaft, a screw, driving the prison-machine, developing its cycles, engaging its productive mechanisms. In addition to these two physical elements, the prison is animated for Genet by the presence, seldom seen, but always felt, of the condemned murderer, Harcamone: the energy source that drives the system. A schematic diagram of the prison-machine starts to reveal itself in four primary elements: the plane of circulation in the punishment cell and the shaft of the stair as its two geometric axes; the black hole of the can—the circulation of shit—and the invisible rose-heart of the murderer as its twin driving forces. The punishment cell and the anus are below, the murderer is above, and the stair links the two storeys.

The punishment cell is planar, horizontal, and annular. The stairway is linear, erect, shaft-like. The punishment cell is about shitting. The stairway is about love. The punishment cell is an anus, the stairway is a penis. By implication, the prison is a manifestation of Genet's body. It is a specifically male body, and a specifically queer body. This is hypothesis one: the prison is the body of the thief (like the house is the body of the heteronormative family).

5 The Carnot cycle apparatus is made up of a heat source at a temperature T1 (body H), a heat sink at a temperature T2 (body K, where T1>T2), and a fluid (Φ) which circulates between the two. The cycle itself is made up of four reversible stages, during which the state of the circulating fluid Φ is altered:

1. Compression at constant heat content
2. Expansion at constant temperature (in contact with body H)
3. Expansion at constant heat content
4. Compression at constant temperature (in contact with body K).

Work must be put into the system in stage one (typically using a pump or compressor), while work is obtained from the system in stage three (as the expansion of the gas drives a turbine). The efficiency of this system is defined in terms of the ratio of the work inserted to that extracted (Qin/Qout), and is found to be roughly proportional to the ratio T1/T2. The Carnot cycle in an ideal state is the most efficient possible heat engine operating between temperatures T1 and T2, but it has a number of limitations that are of interest to this discussion, not least of which is the impossibility of ever achieving this ideal state. The Carnot cycle requires absolute reversibility of its processes, which means that any irreversible unexpected effects, such as heat loss from pipes or friction or turbulence in the liquid, or, in a more generalized sense, political resistance or sexual deviancy, would result in a loss of efficiency. The ideal process is thus utopic in nature: in order to eliminate all friction and turbulence, the process in a perfect Carnot cycle would have to move infinitely slowly. And of course, since power (in thermodynamic terms) is just work/time, the ideal Carnot cycle, as a result of this infinite stasis, provides zero power.

6 Despite the impotence of the utopic form of the ideal Carnot cycle, which we might extrapolate to the impotence of the utopic in general, the Carnot cycle in its less-than-perfect materializations proved to have immense power not only to move people and things, but also to produce new worlds—new societal structures, new modes of being.

7 The role of the Carnot cycle was not lost on the world of artistic production, especially in the years leading up to and after the First World War. In *Marchand du sel*, Marcel Duchamp describes his *Large Glass* as a "steam engine with masonry foundations on [a] brick base" (1975, 52). Indeed, the *Large Glass* bears a strong pictorial resemblance to the illustrations of steam engines, especially that of Perkins, in Carnot's work; it would not be an absurd guess to imagine that Duchamp came across these illustrations while employed at the Bibliothèque Sainte-Geneviève, from 1913 to 1915 (Peyré and Toussaint 2014), a position that Duchamp parlayed into a significant period of research in the library's holdings, especially in the sciences. In passing, I would note here that the Bibliothèque Sainte-Geneviève is another very important building in the canon of modern architecture, with a reading room designed by Henri Labrouste between 1838 and 1851—that is, at precisely the same moment as Blouet, one of Labrouste's classmates and, as we have seen, the foremost expert on prison design in nineteenth-century France, was designing Mettray. Labrouste's reading room for the bibliothèque is best known today for its innovative use of iron structure, providing an unheard-of lightness to the space. Less often discussed in the history of architecture is the sectional mechanism of the building, with the storerooms of books below and the reading room above, connected by a lift that would allow the books to circulate to the readers (although the lift was not installed until the 1890s). The building as a result presents a section that is remarkably similar to both the Perkins steam engine and Duchamp's *Large Glass*.

8 In his 2011 article "Material Deviance: Theorizing Queer Objecthood," as well as in his subsequent book *The Hoarders*, Scott Herring examines the notion of the queer object. Herring's concern is primarily for the "normative" in "heteronormative"; although clearly sympathetic to the sexually non-normative, his positions in relation to queer objects take a wider view. Like Ahmed, Herring understands the ways in which normativity is produced by careful selections and organizations of objects, and quotes Daniel Miller to this effect: "It was these practical taxonomies, these orders of everyday life, that stored up the power of social reproduction, since they in effect educated people into the normative orders and expectations of their society. What we now attempt to inculcate in children through explicit pedagogic teaching...had previously been inculcated largely through material culture" (quoted in Herring 2011, 7). Queer objects, then, might be thought of as objects that fail to play the role of "educating people into the normative orders," whether intentionally, accidentally, or through some failure, objects that "cause trouble, act inappropriately, break down or become incoherent" (Herring 2011, 11). There are, of course, many ways in which objects can fail in their pedagogic or orienting function. Herring discusses, in his piece about hoarding, objects that become strange, deviant, or queer through breaking down, through reaching the end of their normative useful life: a decomposed pumpkin that its owner cannot bear to part with (dissociated from its normative role as source material for baking), broken-down appliances covering the lawn of a suburban scrap metal dealer. These objects have become objects in the wrong place, or in the wrong time, objects that tell a different story than the normative, objects that, by holding place in the house or on the lawn send a message of the value of uselessness, of decay, of non-production that counter the "normative orders and expectations of society."

It is important to note that for Herring (although as far as I am aware he does not make this point explicitly) what makes an object queer is not so much its form or materiality (although of course there are objects that we can think of as being stereotypically "queer"), but rather its position out of place or out of time, disconnected from the carefully organized setting of a space and time and disturbing to its pedagogies. An object that is perfectly normal in one setting becomes strange and disorienting when it appears unexpectedly in another milieu. I have vivid memories of everyday objects that appeared unexpectedly in my life in childhood episodes, objects and episodes that helped to disorient my life, objects and episodes that encouraged my path to deviate. I could produce a list:

A box of broken tools in the basement
My older brother's jockstrap, appearing in my underwear drawer
My sister's perfume, left behind in my bedroom
A novel with a few racy pages left where I could read it
A copy of Playgirl *discovered under my sister's bed*

And so on. The objects in question, like the decayed pumpkins or obsolete refrigerators of Herring's hoarders, are displaced from their normative constellations of meaning, their standard operative functions, dislocated, broken. These objects are, in this sense, failures: They "cause trouble, act inappropriately, break down or become incoherent." What understanding could a four-year-old make of a jockstrap mysteriously appearing, prefiguring perhaps the sudden and mystifying appearance of puberty some years later? Transported from its customary world of teenage athleticism, of maleness and virility, the jockstrap becomes an object of mystery, of unknowingness. This is a sort of failure: the jockstrap is "out of place" in my underwear drawer, "out of time" for a four-year-old boy, failing in both cases in its designated function, failing to orient me towards a heteronormative future. It is not so much that the object is a queer object, but the way the object, in its dislocation, queers the field of play, rearranging meanings and organizations, reorienting both space and subjects, creating a new world.

9 The *Large Glass* is described by Duchamp as having a four-part mechanism that precisely mirrors that of the Carnot cycle:

1. The Bride (La Mariée)
2. The Mechanism (Les Rouages)
3. The Desire Engine (Le Moteur Désire)
4. The Cooling Device with Wings (Le Refroidisseur à Ailettes (1959, 53, author's translation)

In other words, the *Large Glass* is a representation of an engine of the type of the steam engine. The *Large Glass* can be thought of as depicting an energy cycle, in which the difference in temperature between a body at high heat, the bride, who reacts to the bachelors "hotly (and not chastely)," and a body at low heat (the bachelors) is exploited in order to obtain work which can be put to some external purpose.

10 A sketch description of Fontevraud Prison as Bachelor Machine would look something like the following: Bulkaen, who Genet meets on the stairs (that is, in the upper portion of the system) is that object of desire with which consummation is never possible. Bulkaen and Harcamone are related: Bulkaen dies because of Genet's desire, Harcamone is desired because of his impending death.

Bulkaen, in this sketch, plays the part of the bride. The bachelors are, of course, the prisoners in general, the prisoners in the punishment cell more specifically, and Genet most of all; the purely formal similarity between the punishment cell and Duchamp's *moules mâlic* is striking. This similarity is not just coincidence, but is due to a structural similarity between the *moules* and the punished prisoners. Both are stuck, caught, moving in endless circles as part of a machine that they do not understand, and which is intended to kill them. Fontevraud prison is hence a Bachelor Machine, but a complex and difficult Bachelor Machine. The sexual divisions of the classical Bachelor Machine are more ambiguous here, as characters oscillate between bride and bachelor (even the prison itself—even Genet's body, even Genet himself—is both bride and bachelor). The prison operates on a contingent, changeable, uncertain model of difference, a model that is not exactly binary, that doesn't exactly separate or divide, that refuses the structural cut. Indeed, it is never clear in which direction the cycle at Fontevraud operates: whether it is Genet's desire that drives the cycle, leading it to Harcamone/Bulkaen's death; or whether it is the impending death of Harcamone/Bulkaen that drives Genet's desire.

11 But what is the role of the prison in this economy? What work is being done by these hapless, emaciated prisoners? I am reminded, here, of the useless labour of the treadwheel in Victorian prisons. This is, of course, where Genet has his biggest insight: energy at Fontevraud is diverted away from work that is of value to the state or to hetero society. Instead, it is a work of transformation, of queering. To put it simply, Fontevraud queers the Bachelor Machine—by which I mean the prison appropriates, questions, and twists the underlying principles of the Bachelor Machine, producing a (distorted) mirror image.

12 This, then, is our second hypothesis: for Genet (and not only for Genet), *to be a homosexual is always-already to be a thief*. Genet makes this very clear in *The Thief's Journal*: "Betrayal, theft and homosexuality are the basic subjects of this book. There is a relationship among them which, though not always apparent, at least, it seems to me, recognizes a kind of vascular exchange between my taste for betrayal and theft and my loves" ([1949] 1987, *Journal*, 171). Or again—and here we see the connection to family, to house, made explicit: "Abandoned by my family, I already felt it was natural to aggravate this condition by a preference for boys, and this preference by theft, and theft by crime or by a complacent attitude in regard to crime. I thus resolutely rejected a world which had rejected me" (87).

13 This brings us to our third, and perhaps the most obvious hypothesis: *The prison is a house*, or rather, a house-machine. Fontevraud, of course, does have the functional dispositional

qualities of a simple house: work space (the workshops, but also the real place of production, the punishment cell) below, bedrooms (sexual spaces, most particularly the stairway) above. Certainly, this recapitulates the structure of the dormitories at Mettray. And in a Foucauldian disciplinary structure, houses and prisons bear a certain structural similarity (along with schools, hospitals, barracks, factories) as places of confinement. However, this third hypothesis intends to move beyond the recognition of a similarity or homology; the prison is not like a house; the prison is, in this telling, a house. Genet is obsessed by the prison as that to which he aspired as a youngster, while an equal obsession with the house—often the absent, impossible house—is also clearly evident. In *The Thief's Journal*, for example, we hear that "when [Genet] walked miserably along in the rain and wind, the tiniest crag, the most meagre shelter became habitable. [He] would sometimes adorn it with an artful comfort drawn from what is particular to it: a box in the theatre, the chapel of a cemetery, a cave, an abandoned quarry, a freight car and so on. Obsessed by the idea of a home, [he] would embellish, in thought, and in keeping with its own architecture, the one [he] had just chosen" ([1949] 1987, 169).

And this is not the only example: one thinks for example of the abandoned prison, the Bagne de Brest, in which the young murderer Gil in Genet's *Querelle de Brest* takes refuge, the apartment in which the soldiers hide in *Funeral Rites*. All of these spaces fall short of being houses, except in imagination, however, because they lack the *correctness* of the prison, that is, of the ability to correct. Which means only that Genet is, first and foremost, a thief; and that a thief lives in a prison. The prison is the only house the thief can have. In *Saint Genet*, it is in a house that Sartre has Genet first identified as a thief; and not just any house, but his own house. In other words, Genet is a thief even in his own house, which means his only proper house can only be a prison.

In Genet's writing, all these interpretations work simultaneously in the same text. It is therefore only by looking at such interpretations in parallel, rather than taking each one as an isolated theme, that we can begin to understand Genet and, by extension, to understand architecture. This is to say that, for Genet, each of these interpretations of the relationship between Fontevraud and Savoye is the same thing: to say that Fontevraud Prison is a queer body is already to say it is Genet's house, because house and body are just separate manifestations of a generalized desire. And to say that both of these and the prison are Bachelor Machines is just another wording of the same idea, as a Bachelor Machine is simultaneously a house and a body.

14 Strange objects are pervasive in the work of Genet: a necktie that is a noose in *Our Lady of the Flowers*, a matchbox that is a casket in *Funeral Rites*, a tube of Vaseline, a dismembered arm, an artificial flower worn in the pants in *The Thief's Journal*. The waste products of an on-stage castration. And others. Like Stilitano's arm, these are all *abject objects*: objects cast out from ourselves, objects that are part of us, that represent who we are. These objects glow with a kind of reminiscence of the self: they glow from a hollow interior, like the bust of Marie Antoinette in *Our Lady of the Flowers*. Genet reminds us that all objects are indeed abject objects, that Ahmed, in a way, has the situation turned inside out (like a glove): that the objects that orient us are already parts of us that we have cast outside ourselves. And that all objects, all abject parts of ourselves, are indeed both out of place and out of time. Abject objects are entities that both thrown out and thrown against, that confront us in our status as waste; they are doubly abject, in that they have been abjected and that they are abjecting.

15 A curious coincidence: in her classic *Purity and Danger* ([1966] 2003), Mary Douglas describes waste as matter out of place. In his 2014 book, *Waste: A Philosophy of Things*, William Viney extends this definition to include matter out of time. For Herring, queer

objects (does this include queer human bodies?) are objects that are out of place or out of time. It's hard here to avoid assigning a functional equivalence to the terms waste and queer.

16 This then becomes our fourth hypothesis: the prison is the primary site of containment for the waste products of bourgeois society: thieves, murderers, homosexuals. Or, simply, thieves.

17 Thus, in *Miracle of the Rose*, the absent house—already the object of unattainable desire—is transformed twice: first into the prison, the site of punishment; and then into the body of the prisoner—the homosexual. It is the house, when understood in its role of familial dwelling, that points out the inadequacy of the queer body, and therefore that defines Genet as a thief. But if Genet steals energy from the official circuit of the Bachelor Machine, we must recognize that Genet does not squander this energy. Instead, Genet uses this energy within the machine of the prison to construct—what? What is the product of Genet's prison-machine? In a masterful use of tactics (and we should remember that every tactical action is by nature a theft), by inventing other machines, provisional machines, abject assemblages, Genet takes the humiliation, disapprobation, and ugliness that is his natural position in life and turns it to glory and beauty.

Michel Carrouges: "The bachelor machine...transforms love into a technique of death" (1975, 21). Fontevraud Prison in *Miracle of the Rose* does precisely the opposite: the prison turns death into a technique of love.

18 To be queer is to be shit: surely this explains why images of excrement appear so readily in Genet's books.

19 Certain views of Montmartre Cemetery, such perhaps as the view from the window of Divine's apartment, give a view of rows of tombs side by side lining the curving pathways. One could be forgiven for having the impression that one is looking down on a picturesque village filled with small but sturdy stone houses. The land of the dead replicates the land of the living; the tomb-as-house gives form to the formless-

ness of the tomb, scale to its infinite enormity. The tomb is rendered not as an incomprehensible void, not as that which is unknowable, but simply as the house of the dead, like any other house. The infinite void that lies outside of existence is domesticated, tamed. This is the role of architecture, or one of its roles.

The more interesting question, though, is not how the tomb takes on the form of the house, but rather its inverse: how does the house take on the form of the tomb? Where can we locate traces of the infinite void of the non-existent in the domestic? We can see easily how the house partakes of the nature of the cell as the site of both disciplinary subjectification and erotic self-construction, and we can see how the wall of the house, like the boundary of the cell is both inviolate and permeable. The cell appears in the individual bedroom (go to your room!) as well as in the individual unit of contemporary housing, in the inviolable unity of the Levittown house. Likewise, we can see the house as a closet/brothel in which we hide our secrets that tether us to this domestic disciplinary site. But what about the tomb? How does this third void figure in the domestic?

To put the matter succinctly, I would argue that there is a void at the centre of every house, just as there is a so-called supermassive black hole at the centre of every galaxy: a supermassive attractive force of the unknowable that puts the mechanism of the house into motion. The house, the family home, the childhood home, the ancestral home, to grandmother's house we go: the house is built over the pit of death, separating us from the void of non-existence, and prevents us, always on the edge, from falling in, leaping instead from one generation to the next. The house is the permanence that obfuscates our mortality. Or to put it another way, the mechanism of the house is driven by the energy of the void of death, that is, by the death drive: death here (and it seems to me that this is in fact what Freud was trying to get across) is not the final end towards which we are driven, but the propulsive force, the engine, the drive, that pushes us through life. We are not driven to death but driven by death. In other words, the source of the energy that drives the machine of the house relentlessly around and around is the inaccessible void at its heart.

Chapter 4

1 Jean-Paul Sartre, in *Saint Genet*, has this to say about Genet's first novel: "No wonder *Our Lady [of the Flowers]* horrifies people: it is the epic of masturbation" ([1952] 1963, 367).

2 The last scenes of *The Balcony* take place in or near the mausoleum studio, a new space that has been constructed in the brothel. The mausoleum studio, a cylindrical space, is described in strikingly Ledoux-esque terms:

> DESCRIPTION OF THE MAUSOLEUM STUDIO: The stones of the wall, which is circular, are visible. At the rear, a stairway that descends. In the centre of this well there seems to be another, in which the steps of a stairway are visible. On the walls, four laurel wreaths, adorned with crêpe. When the panels separate, ROGER is at the middle of the stairway, which he is descending. CARMEN seems to be guiding him. ROGER is dressed like THE CHIEF OF POLICE, though, mounted on the same cothurni as the Three Figures, he looks taller. His shoulders have also been broadened. He descends the stairs to the rhythm of a drum. (87)

Maybe it's just because I have been so embedded in this work for so long, but I can't help feeling that somehow Genet has placed this scene in the Oikéma, especial in the strange oval room in the head of the phallus.

3 The appearance of the phallus threatens to open up the fundamental wound of signification. In other words, and with apologies to Lacan and to all Lacanian scholars, the mechanism works something like this.

- For Lacan, at a certain point a child experiences a *no*. The paradigmatic example is a no in relation to the desire of the mother, a no dictated by the father, but it is important to understand that this is just an example, there are other forms of no.

- The child experiences this as an imagined or imaginary castration, a loss of both power and desire, connected to but not equivalent to the real of the penis; this is the loss of the imaginary phallus. A void is thus experienced. Note that, because of the imaginary nature of this castration, it is not restricted to male children.
- In order to cover over this void, the child substitutes a symbolic phallus for the (lost) imaginary phallus. This is the first act of signification. This symbolic phallus must be experienced as real for it to be an effective cover.

4 The most important brothel in Genet's work is no doubt Le Grand Balcon, the brothel that provides the setting (and the title) for *The Balcony*. This brothel, meticulously overseen by its Madame, Irma, is comprised of numerous studios that have been designed and constructed in such as manner as to allow the brothel's clients to play out whatever particular fantasies they desire. In the first three scenes of the play, we are shown into three of these studios, where we see The Bishop forgiving the sins (which may or may not have been invented) of a prostitute; The Judge, sentencing and overseeing the punishment of another prostitute, guilty of theft; and The General, who rides his horse, a third prostitute. Meanwhile, a revolution is taking place outside the brothel. When the Generalissimo goes mad, the Attorney General dies of fright, and the Bishop goes missing, the three brothel clients are convinced to take their place—after all, they already have the costumes. The three appear on the eponymous balcony of the brothel, and order is restored.

5 Like the closet and the cell, the brothel (at least in *The Balcony*) is a place apart, a void in the structure of the world, a heterotopia in which the ordinary rules of existence are suspended.

For Genet, the brothel is a condensed mirror image of the outside world, a true house of illusions: not simply a house in which illusions appear to come to life, but a house that is in fact founded on the principle of illusion. The brothel is also a container, not only of the various props and costumes needed to bring the miscellaneous erotic fantasies of its customers to life, but also of those erotic fantasies themselves, and of course also of the multiple erotic subjectivities that the brothel itself helps to bring into existence (which reminds us of the productive aspect of the closet, of its ability to not just warehouse but indeed produce multiple subjectivities). The brothel, in other words, like the closet, is the locus of split, multiple, secret, and hidden (self)-identities. It is a place of secret knowledge, of things that are known but cannot be revealed, and its boundary must remain sacrosanct. Genet's play reminds us of the dangers that ensue when this boundary is breached, when what should be inside the brothel (or closet) appears on the outside, and does so, fittingly, with the architectural element that itself is neither inside nor outside, but both at once: the balcony.

6 In a critical scene of Genet's unpublished screenplay *Le langage de la muraille*, the designers of the new reformatory at Mettray are faced with a dilemma: What sort of sleeping arrangements should they construct for the colonists? Open dormitories, of course, would risk the development of clandestine sexual relationships, that is, sodomy, among the boys; on the other hand, closed cells would run the risk of encouraging masturbation. Which was the bigger danger? The King, Royal Patron of the Colony, doesn't really care one way or the other—after all, either way they will be prepared for their future lives as sailors:

LE ROI (sévère): Assez! Le royaume de France survivra à cela. Vices de princes, d'ailleurs. Mettez des cloisons ou des lampes, Messieurs, laissez que

	ces enfants se branlent ou s'enculent, mais faites-en des soldats et des marins. Habituez-les à la Marine Royale. Et notre théologie, que pense-t-elle de tant de perversions? (113)
THE KING (severely):	Enough! The Kingdom of France will survive this. And these are the vices of Princes. Put in partitions or lamps, let the children masturbate or screw, but make of them soldiers or sailors! Get them used to being in the Royal Navy. And our theology—what do you think of these perversions?

While the advice of the religious advisors is no clearer:

LE JESUITE	(*s'inclinant et souriant*): C'est à la fois un péché et une faute, d'ailleurs ma phrase n'était pas finie. C'est un péché devant Dieu. C'est une faute grave quand on le commet...en public. Aux architectures de dire s'il y aura péché de chair plus faute, selon qu'on établira des cloisons ou non, entre les lits.
DOMINICAIN:	Mais c'est spécieux. C'est un péché devant les hommes quand on le commet en public, qu'on le publie. C'est un faute devant Dieu, mon Révérend. Que ce soit onanisme ou sodomie. Je penche pour l'abolition des cloisons. Mais c'est à l'architecture de décider.
FRANCISCAIN:	S'il est vrai qu'un sentiment d'amour peut naitre de l'amitié, in ne faut pas s'égarer. Saint François d'Assise aimait l'amour la pluie et les corbeaux. Il importe de ne rien briser de l'amour mais de l'obtenir, et d'obtenir un sentiment sans mettre souillure.
LE ROI (*amuse)*:	Vous êtes pour la cloison?
FRANCISCAIN (*debout*):	Sire, oui. Mais idéale et non matérielle. (115–16)

THE JESUIT (*leaning back and smiling*): It's both a sin and a misdemeanor—and I have more to say. It's a sin before God. It's a bad misdemeanor when one does it in public. It's for the architects to say whether there will be both a sin of the flesh plus a misdemeanor, depending on whether we put partitions between the beds or not.

THE DOMINICAN: But that's specious. It's a sin before men when one commits it in public, when one publicizes it. It's a misdemeanor before god, Reverend. Whether it's onanism or sodomy. I lean towards the abolition of partitions—but it's for the architecture to decide.

THE FRANCISCAN: If it's true that a feeling of love can be born out of friendship, we should not lose it. Saint Francis of Assisi liked love, the rain, and the crows. It's a matter not of breaking love, but of obtaining it, and obtaining it without a stain.

THE KING (*amused*): You are for the partitions?

THE FRANCISCAN (*standing*): Yes, Sire. But ideal and not material. (Author's translations)

It's for the architecture to decide... Thus, we have the appearance of the problem of masturbation right at the moment of founding of that institution that Foucault describes as the beginning of the carceral regime. Masturbation is revealed as the evil remainder at the core of the carceral, or perhaps as the grain of sand in the oyster of the carceral. And even more: the idea that the prison cell, the epitome of discipline of the (deviant) individual, is also the locus for masturbation par excellence, is an incredible problem at the core of the modern.

7 Sartre, of course, is on the mark in *Saint Genet* when he calls *Our Lady of the Flowers* the epic of masturbation. Genet tells us this himself, in the introductory scene of *Our Lady*; the book is a story concocted with the help of his imaginary lovers,

those with whom he spends the nights under his sheet, alone in his cell. The book, like his later novel *Miracle of the Rose*, is comprised of masturbatory fantasy, is itself an ejaculation, a product of his solitary activities.

8 The pages of this book are stained sheets.

9 As an onanistic fantasy, however, the novel is a bit peculiar. To begin with, it would be rather difficult to call *Our Lady of the Flowers* pornographic: the writing, even the most florid descriptions of sexual activity (of which there are very few in the novel) do not seem intended to titillate or cause excitement; the reader is not invited to masturbate along with the narrator. Quite the opposite: the book is designed in fact to elicit horror, pity, sadness, perhaps empathy for the abject lives of the characters (those that Sartre calls creatures); the pleasure that the narrator takes in the actions of these characters only serves to both move us (to pity perhaps, but not to eros) and simultaneously repel us. If the book is obscene, it is so in the very specific sense of being off-stage, behind the scene, the demonstration of a normally hidden (and monstrous) world: "I was, through my monstrous horror, exiled to the confines of the obscene (which is the off-scene of the world), facing the graceful pupils of the school of light-fingered theft" ([1943] 1987, *Flowers*, 301). As readers, we are never brought into the action; rather, we remain observers, watching the scene of misery play out in front of us, unable and undesiring to touch the scenes in question, observers who are shown an almost unbearably intimate picture; the veils are pulled away, and we are given access to the most private of acts. We are placed literally *ob-scaenum*, "in front of filth," but always radically separated from it: the filth is other, the filth is Genet.

Sartre devotes a few pages in *Saint Genet* to an analysis of masturbation. Masturbation is not itself the problem, for Sartre; masturbation is simply an ordinary, everyday activity. The problem, rather, is what use Genet makes of masturbation. As Sartre tells us, "All prisoners engage in onanism. But usually it is for the lack of something better. They would prefer the most lamentable whore to these solitary revels. In short, they put the imaginary to good use: they are honest onanists...But Genet wants to make bad use of onanism. To decide to prefer appearances is to place onanism, in principle, above all intercourse" ([1952] 1963, 367). In other words, Sartre tells us that masturbation is fine, as long as one masturbates while thinking about real sex with a real partner, as a substitute for sex with a real partner at times when that real sex is not available. For Genet, though, there is no reality behind the fantasies: Divine and Darling do not stand in for actually existing or potential lovers but exist only as creatures of Genet's imagination. By preferring and glorifying masturbation, Genet validates the creatures of his imagination over the inhabitants of the real world, hence denigrating and abnegating the real, physical world. Masturbation in this sense, masturbation that is not anchored to an imagined object that actually or at least potentially exists, has as its goal the disappearance and derealization of both the world and of Genet himself: "At the moment of orgasm, Genet's two conflicting components coincide, he is the criminal who rapes and the Saint who lets herself be raped. On his body a hand is stroking Divine. Or else this hand which is stroking him is Darling's hand. The one who is being masturbated is derealized...Genet has disappeared: Darling is making love to Divine" (Sartre [1952] 1963, 367).

Indeed, it seems that for Sartre this aspect of derealization of the world is an essential aspect of masturbation: "Onanism, which is a pure demoniacal act, maintains an appearance of appearance in the heart of consciousness: masturbation is the derealization of the world and of the person masturbated as well" ([1952] 1963, 368). But this derealization of the world, and especially of the subject, this raising of image above reality, or, as Sartre puts it, this subordination of being to value is for Sartre nothing less than pure Evil, a determined an intentional move away from being and towards nothingness.

Masturbation, although it takes place largely in the world of fantasy, of images, of nothingness, nonetheless has real, physical effects. Here Sartre is not so much concerned with the effects on the masturbator (which we will discuss in the following paragraphs) but the effects on the world external to the subject: "And yet, by a reversal which will bring the ecstasy to its climax, this limpid nothingness will cause real events in the real world: the erection, the ejaculation, the damp spots on the covers, are caused by the imaginary" ([1952] 1963, 368).

In the case of Genet, this external effect of the internal process is more severe. We are not speaking here of damp spots on the covers, but of the dis-semination of his ejaculatory visions to the public: in short, the problem is that Genet writes about his onanism. Genet is making public that which should be private (or causing the appearance on the exterior of that which should remain in the interior). This is an uncanny haunting; the wall is torn down between the fantasy world of the interior and the real world of the exterior; the essential disciplinary architecture of the self is breached. Genet makes use of masturbation in order to tear down the walls of the world (we note in passing that this is literally the case, as it was his novels, in the end, that allowed him to leave the walls of prison). He makes use of his masturbatory fantasies in order to infest us with the world of appearances: "He is already a virus by virtue of his very existence; since he lives without working, others must feed him...Genet jerks off at the taxpayer's expense, that increases his pleasure" (Sartre [1952] 1963, 369).

But one thing, I think, is unclear: Is *Our Lady of the Flowers* an infestation, a contagion, or an inoculation?

10 Reviewers of this book have mentioned that Masters and Johnson asked volunteers to masturbate on camera as part of their experimental apparatus. However, I would argue that such films still do not fit the category of time-and-motion studies, as they are not intended to help develop a model for more efficient masturbation.

11 If the relationship between architecture and masturbation is itself invisible, if indeed invisibility is at the core of the relationship, if the maintenance of invisibility of masturbation by architecture is fundamental to it, then masturbation holds within it a potential for resistance, a potential revolutionary force, that operates, as Sartre tells us of Genet, beyond fantasy. And if privacy is indeed the primary technique used by architecture to discipline masturbation (and sex in general), indeed if a making-private is a fundamental role of architecture, then Sartre is right in his analysis: the problem in *Our Lady of the Flowers* is not that Genet masturbates, but that Genet tells us he masturbates. By breaking the taboo of privacy, Genet liberates masturbation, and hence the masturbator (which is of course all of us) from its prison.

12 The cell is thus comprised of a double mechanism, two machines that operate against but largely in spite of each other: the official mechanism of the administrative, disciplinary regime, designed in Foucauldian terms to produce a subject disciplined to the spatial and temporal expectations and requirements of the modern bourgeois capitalist state; and the masturbatory machine, productive of pleasure, but also productive of redesigned worlds that move specifically against these spatial and temporal expectations. The masturbatory machine transforms convicts into pirates, murderers into lovers, and even transforms the cell (the self) itself: "In the evening, as soon as Darling stretches out in bed, the window carries the cell off toward the west, detaches it from the masoned block and flies off with it, hauling it like the basket of a balloon" ([1943] 1987, *Flowers*, 249). This double mechanism, which, since the cell is the model for all architectural voids, exists in all architectural spaces (the disciplinary mechanism of architecture operating against the ejaculatory mechanism of sexuality), is perhaps most clearly identified by Genet still early in his first novel: "Still, I managed to get about twenty photographs, and with bits of chewed bread I pasted them on

the back of the cardboard sheet of regulations that hangs on the wall. Some are pinned up with bits of brass wire" ([1943] 1987, *Flowers*, 54). The two mechanisms could not be clearer in their relationship: each invisible to the other, each hidden out of any possible view, literally the obverse and reverse of the same condition.

13 If the cell can be read as the basic prototype for the modern world, our contemporary world of late capitalism (Badiou's pornographic age, Preciado's pharmacopornographic era) finds its most potent architectural image in the brothel. Not surprisingly, perhaps, *The Balcony* has been the topic of a series of insightful essays in the early twenty-first century, essays that use Genet's play as a way to understand the contemporary condition: Alain Badiou (2020) on democracy as the phallus of the contemporary age, the untouchable concept (the phallus, in Lacanian terms) that guarantees our political inequalities; Benjamin Bratton (2015) on the relationships between violence, the image, and architecture; Alenka Zupančič (2016) on comedy, appearance and power; and Aaron Schuster (2020), most recently, again on power, appearance, and Trumpism. Schuster in particular makes the claim that Genet's brothel, which he characterizes as "a versatile and protean organization that is at once a fantasy factory, a media empire, a political rally, a sexual orgy, a modern church, a glorified tomb, a profitable business, and a theater," should be understood as a key (architectural) paradigm for our contemporary world (2020, 167).

There are, in this reading, two particular aspects of the brothel that tie it to the contemporary condition; both of these rely on the particular role taken up by desire. First, the heterotopic function of the brothel is to provide a locus that is other, in which desires can be taken up that could not be realized in the ordinary world. The brothel is a place in which fantastic desires of any sort, and not only sexual desires, can be acted on, can be made flesh. The desires presented by Genet, it must be noted, are not explicitly sexual, the desire is never, simply, for an orgasm, but lie rather on the plane of identity: it amounts to a desire to be a Bishop, to be a General, to be a Judge, to be in effect other than that which one is.

If, though, we understand the desires taken up in the brothel as desires of being, we are immediately confronted with the truth that, in the brothel, the taking up of the desire amounts to a question of *having*, that is, of having, for a short time and in limited terms, the costume, the paraphernalia, and the power of the desired being. The brothel, in other words, is a place in which desire can indeed be taken up and acted on, but only in its images. Isn't this, though, a description of our contemporary condition, and especially of our political condition, in which we are able to fulfill any desire we may have as long as that desire remains nothing more than the image of its desire? In the contemporary market, isn't any desire satisfiable, as long as its satisfaction in the end amounts to nothing more than having? And aren't recent political events further evidence of the chaos that ensues when the boundary between image and ordinary reality is breached?

Second, the brothel, as a business, provides a mechanism for making money from desire, and without ever depleting the supply of desire. If anything, it is clear that the fantasies that take place in the brothel, fantasies that we must remember only take place on the level of the image, only serve to increase the desire, to increase the need for more and more fantasy. Desire, and especially erotic desire, provides an inexhaustible resource, a perpetual motion machine, for the pornographic age. And is it not the case that this description works not just for the brothel, but for the world of late, image-based, desire-driven capitalism in which we live?

Chapter 5

1 Genet, in an interview with Antoine Bourseiller: "One of the subtleties of the Mettray colony's inventors was that they knew not to put up a wall...It's much more difficult to escape when it's simply a question of crossing through a patch of *flowers* than if there's a wall for you to climb" (2004, 191).

2 For Genet, who was a colonist at Mettray at about the time of the Hilberseimer project, this absence of walls made escape impossible; one cannot climb a wall that doesn't exist. However far a colonist ran—in space or in time—he would remain in Mettray. In *Miracle of the Rose* Genet puts it like this: "I am brash enough to be of the opinion that prisons and children's homes do not depart sufficiently from the unusual. Their walls are too thin and not impervious enough. Mettray alone profited from a prodigious achievement: there were no walls, but only laurels and flower borders; yet nobody, to my knowledge, succeeded in escaping from the Colony itself, for the facility of doing so seemed to us very weird, protected by watchful spirits" ([1946] 1988, Miracle, 115).

3 In *Le langage de la muraille* (possibly written in response to Foucault's work), we read the following dialogue:

COURTEILLES: Adieu. Ah! Auguste, une autre : comme on demandait à un colon pourquoi il ne s'évadait pas, il répondit :« Il y a une bonne raison à cela, c'est qu'il n'y a pas de murs à Mettray ! » (113)

COURTEILLES: Farewell. Oh, Auguste, one other thing: when we asked a colonist why he didn't run away, he said, "There's a good reason for that, it's because there are no walls at Mettray!" (Author's translation)

Murs indeed have been superceded by *moeurs*, the confining wall replaced by internalized practices and mores, isolation substituted by techniques of normalization. There are thus two languages of the walls at Mettray: the language of restraint—the language of "Dieu te voit," but also of morals, the *moeurs*, of normalization, and the language of resistance of the colonists. The story of the colony, as Genet tells it, is one of constant struggle, of tug of war between these two languages.

4 *Murs, mœurs, miroirs*.

5 The closet is, of course, a primary notion and important concept in queer thinking and one of the most critical original connections between queer and architectural theories, as formulated and developed by Eve Sedgwick (1990), Henry Urbach (1996), and Aaron Betsky (1997), among others. It is not my intention here to trace the metaphor of the closet in queer thinking, however. Instead, following the discussion of the cell, my interest is in the closet as a second fundamental form of architectural void. While, as I have claimed, the cell stands as the essential model of the architectural space of self-creation, in which the twin mechanisms of discipline and (onanistic) fantasy work their tension, the closet acts as a space in which pieces of the self, alternate selves, can be set aside for safekeeping or easy access. This relationship of the closet to the self is easily seen in the relationship of Claire and Solange to Madame's clothing, the way that putting on the clothing produces the real identity of Madame, in Genet's play *The Maids* (centred as this play is on Madame's wardrobe) or, even more explicitly, in *The Balcony*. The closet is in some senses the inverse of the cell: while the cell contains our bodies while allowing our fantasy selves freedom to roam, the closet holds safe our fantasy selves while our bodies remain free to access the wider world outside. The cell is an (illusory) image of a unified self, while the closet is the mechanism of a split and fractured self. The closet is the price that must be paid for the ability to leave the cell and to enter into society.

The closet, as Urbach (1996) has pointed out, is a product of the rise of the bourgeoisie. A quick review of historical house plans shows that closets were rare before the nineteenth century (the storage functions of the closet having been taken up by furnishings such as chests and wardrobes) and ubiquitous by the classic modern era after the Second World War, as epitomized by the Levittown houses. Both Mies's Villa Tugendhat and Le Corbusier's Villa Savoye show built-in wardrobes, rather than closets as such; but by the time of the 1947 Cape Cod House in Levittown the closet had become codified in the form we take for granted today (although, of course, smaller than a contemporary bedroom closet). As Preciado (2019) has pointed out, the lack of closets was a major irritant for Edith Farnsworth at her Mies-designed country house. The contemporary closet, as befits the location dominated by secrecy (the location in which the "real" self was kept hidden) had itself become hidden, literally swallowed up in a thickening of the house's wall—becoming, in the process, quite literally a void, neither structure nor occupiable space but outside of both. The closet becomes, quite literally, the centre of the house, taking over the position held in previous centuries by the fireplace. The closet, as a result, is the clearest possible representation of the *domestication* of the modern subject, as the split self, in other eras contained in movable objects—wardrobes, chests, and perhaps most critically suitcases—becomes now literally part of the house, not so much *in* the house as *of* the house, part of its very structure. The closet is thus perhaps the clearest mechanism by which we become incorporated into the modern disciplinary regime in a permanent and structural way: we become one with our houses. From this point of view, the suitcase—such as the suitcase that falls open and is revealed as empty in the opening scene of *The Screens*, or the suitcase which Genet has been said to have kept always packed under his bed (but packed with what? If we opened this suitcase, would we find it too was empty?)—has to be understood as a tactic of resistance to the subsumption of the modern house.

6 I'm thinking here of the prison of Fontevraud, the cell in which the first of Genet's great novels opens.

7 And I'm thinking here, of course, of the last great architectural image in Genet's novels of the 1940s, the scene in which Stilitano, the pimp, is lost in his own reflections in a fairground hall of mirrors in Antwerp.

8 The characters in Genet's play *The Screens* are caught in a world of planes: horizontal planes, levels of the stage, disconnected from each other, with the world of the colonialists on the uppermost level, and the world of the dead on the lowest; and vertical planes, the screens of the title, screens that hide (What is behind the screen?), screens that hold images that become real (What is behind the image?), screens through which the characters burst onto the stage in the moment of death (What is left behind?).

9 Genet, in his stage directions in *The Screens*, is very clear in each scene about the requirements for the screens, for example: "The screen—five panels—depicts a field of palmettos. A round, yellow, tissue-paper sun painted on a very blue sky. In front of the parapet, a wheelbarrow (red)" (1988, scene 4, 29). Another example: "In the foreground, that is, on the foot of the stage, two screens: three panels at the right, three at the left. At the foot of each of the screens, which represent the prison, is a black stool chained to the screen" (scene 11, 77). At the beginning of the play, in a section titled "Some Directions," Genet twice points out that at least one role of the screens is to problematize the relationship between real objects and constructed images. As he puts it, "Near the screen there must always be at least one real object (wheelbarrow, bucket, bicycle, etc.), the function of which is to establish a contrast between its own reality and the objects that are drawn" (10). But what exactly does this mean—its own reality—and what is the corresponding status of the drawn objects, that is to say, of drawing?

10 This production of the scene by virtue of the screen and its image is played out in *The Screens*, not only in the obvious

sense that the image painted on the screen (the image of a sun shining down on the desert, for example) determines the parameters of the scene, but also the productive attribute: When, in scene 9, Leila draws a clock in charcoal on the screen, the clock is taken by all the characters to be a real clock , and even produces a chime.

11 Behinds behind: garbage and waste, the toilet room. Shit piles up in Genet's work.

12 Also like the tattoos worn by prisoners in Genet's novels (and in particular, the tattoos applied by colonists at Mettray, or the tattoo worn by Bulkaen in *Miracle of the Rose*).

13 As Genet tells us, in speaking of Fontevraud Prison, "Behind the walls, the commissary, the offices. We had to speak very low. Also behind, the Warden, the countryside, the free people, the towns, the world, the seas, the stars, everything was close to us though we were far away...Behind the walls I could sense the presence of our past life, of our days in prison, our sorrowful childhood" ([1946] 1988, *Miracle*, 47).

14 Genet on the behind:

> Was it true that philosophers doubted the existence of things that were in back of them? How could one detect the secret of the disappearance of things? By turning around very fast? No. But faster? Faster than anything? I glanced behind me. I was on the watch. I turned my eyes and head, ready to...No, it was pointless. Things can never be caught napping. You would have to spin about with the speed of a propeller. You would then see that things had disappeared, and you with them. ([1949] 1963, *Funeral*, 48)

As he watched himself moving, he thought: "He spun about," and the word "spun," immediately caught on the wing, made him about-face smartly. ([1943] 1987, *Flowers*, 199)

15 And again: "The crossing of borders and the excitement it arouses in me were to enable me to apprehend directly the essence of the nation I was entering. I would penetrate less into a country than to the interior of an image" ([1949] 1987, *Journal*, 49). Or, at the end of scene 1 of *The Balcony*, the stage directions read, "(The stage moves from left to right, as if it were plunging into the wings. The following set then appears)" ([1956] 2008, 13).

Plunging into the wings: In the original French, the phrase was "s'efonçait dans la coulisse," possibly better translated as to sink into the backstage. Not only does this provide an image of the scene disappearing like a shipwreck, but it also suggests that the backstage is a mysterious, perhaps unknowable depth, ultimately separate from the world of illusion on the stage. Again, this is not simply a pragmatic means of handling the quick changes of set; when Peter Brook solved this problem in Paris with a revolving stage, Genet was incensed. It is the notion of sinking, like sinking below the surface of consciousness, that matters.

16 And yet again: "It was at that moment that I understood the room. I realized—for a fraction of a second—its essence. It remained a room, though a prison of the world. I was, through my monstrous horror, exiled to the confines of the obscene (which is the off-scene of the world), facing the graceful pupils of the school of light-fingered theft" ([1943] 1987, *Flowers*, 301).

17 Behind, and especially taking from behind, is an important concern in the kleptogenetics of architecture. First, the idea of taking from behind has clear and inescapable connections to queer, and especially gay male, culture through the practice of anal intercourse. Especially, but not only: Preciado bases his *Countersexual Manifesto* in the liberatory potential of anal sex, since everyone—men, women, and those who refuse this binary—has an asshole (2018, 30). Taking from behind also has resonances of cowardice (shooting in the back) and of betrayal, and we will need to take both of these into account.

Aside from its connotations of anal sex, taking from behind also has a useful history in philosophy. I'm referring here to Deleuze's comments on his own process:

> I suppose the main way I coped with it at the time was to see the history of philosophy as a sort of buggery or (it comes to the same thing) immaculate conception. I saw myself as taking an author from behind and giving him a child that would be his own offspring, yet monstrous. It was really important for it to be his own child, because the author had to actually say all that I had him saying. But the child was bound to be monstrous too, because it resulted from all sorts of shifting, slipping, dislocations, and hidden emissions that I really enjoyed. (1995, 6)

I'm referring also to Žižek's appropriation of the same concept in his discussion of Deleuze in *Organs Without Bodies*. For Žižek, we should understand Deleuze's philosophical buggery not as an attempt to shock, we should not approach it with "an obscene, condescending and dismissive sneer," but with "completely naïve seriousness" (Žižek 2015, 42). And despite the understated but clearly present tone of skepticism or even of moral disapproval of this technique of buggery legible in Žižek's text (the necessity that Žižek feels, for example, to point out our need to take this approach with "naïve seriousness," or even to insist that this seriousness must be naïve, that is, not exactly mature or considered), Žižek is also clear to point out that taking from behind remains a matter of producing an intimate relationship: "While Derrida proceeds in the mode of critical deconstruction, of undermining the interpreted text or author, Deleuze, in his buggery, imputes to the interpreted philosopher his own innermost position and endeavors to extract it from him. So, while Derrida engages in a 'hermeneutics of suspicion,' Deleuze practices an excessive benevolence toward the interpreted philosopher" (42).

18 So, while Deleuze's buggery remains, as Žižek tells us, "much more violent and subversive" than Derrida's deconstruction, and while it "produces true monsters" (2015, 42), it remains, even in Žižek's description, an act of love and intimacy. One might ask, of course, why it is that taking from behind, anal intercourse, buggery, needs to be violent, subversive, and productive of monsters? Might we focus instead on the pleasure that is produced in this activity, pleasure of course for both the buggerer and the buggered, and consider the offspring of this union not so much as monsters (although they may be beautiful monsters), but as hitherto unrecognized and unseen pleasures? Could we say that taking from behind involves a pure pleasure, a pleasure unencumbered by productive outputs, pleasure with no strings attached, a pleasure that does not entwine us into the machine of the law?

And behind, of course, has an inescapable relationship to architecture, to that art form that only and always shows us a front, even if that front is now a three-dimensional surface. What more complete betrayal of architecture could there be than to demand to see what architecture hides from us, to see what is behind the architecture image, to uncover and let loose the ob-scene, that which Genet calls "the off-scene of the world" ([1943] 1987, *Flowers*, 301)?

19 In *Funeral Rites*, Genet narrates his experience of mourning the death of his teenage lover, Jean Decarnin, who was killed during the Liberation of Paris in August 1944. The novel makes use of Genet's common technique of doubling to construct an elaborate network in which to examine questions of death, grief, and, ultimately, betrayal. Tombs and burials, of course, play a central role in the book, as the burial of Decarnin is twinned by the burial of his stillborn child, the mother raped and sealed up in a mausoleum (from which she escapes, in time, seemingly without incident). The novel seems to be an extended questioning of what happens

in the tomb, of what it means to die, or rather of what it can mean to be that which we can never know. This is a space that Genet can never quite penetrate: He can carry it with him, in his pocket, the coffin miraculously transformed into a matchbox, but he can never understand its emptiness. The only way to talk about the silence of the tomb, it seems, is to invent fantastic stories about the endless and sordid noise of life.

Funeral Rites is also probably Genet's most explicitly sexual work, the book in which sex is perhaps most frequently and most vividly described: Paolo (Jean Decarnin's half-brother) sodomizing Hitler, Riton (Jean Decarnin's teenage killer) raped by German soldiers, a fantastic sequence of Genet rimming Decarnin. It is always about the anus: indeed, the book can be said to be a powerful meditation not only on the tomb, but also on the anus. Genet writes this incredible sentence about anuses: "The veneration I feel for that part of the body and the great tenderness that I have bestowed on the children who have allowed me to enter it, the grace and sweetness of their gift, oblige me to speak of all this with respect" ([1949] 1963, *Funeral*, 21).

Or a few pages later, describing Decarnin: "I loved the violence of his prick, its quivering, its size, the curls of his hairs, the child's eyes, and the back of his neck, and the dark, ultimate treasure, the 'bronze eye,' which he did not grant me until very late, about a month before his death" (24). And these two voids, anus and tomb are connected, explicitly, in the description of the funeral itself:

> On the day of his funeral, the church door opened at four in the afternoon on a black hole into which I made my way solemnly...
>
> "It's as dark up here as up a [black man's] asshole." It was that dark there, and I entered the place with the same slow solemnity. At the far end

> twinkled the tobacco-colored iris of the "oeil de Gabès." And, in the middle of it, haloed, savage, silent, awfully pale, was that buggered tank-driver. (22)

I note as an aside here the relationship between anuses and doorways, a relationship that recurs in the novel and that serves once again to architecturalize the body. So we have, at the very end of the book, the following description of Genet's desire to enter the void beyond Decarnin's anus, to live there:

> Without wanting to speak too long in this tone about the eye of Gabès and create a confusion close to punning, I wish to say that Jean's eye became funereal to me. When I stretched out on his back, when I went farther down, I sharpened my tongue to a very fine point so as to burrow neatly into that crack which was as narrow as the eye of a needle. I felt myself being (I've got him by the ass!)...I felt myself being there. Then I tried hard to do as good a job as a drill. As the workman in the quarry leans on his machine that jolts him amidst splinters of mica and sparks from his drill, a merciless sun beats down on the back of his neck, and a sudden dizziness blurs everything and sets out the usual palm trees and springs of a mirage, in like manner a dizziness shook my prick harder, my tongue grew soft, forgetting to dig harder, my head sank deeper into the damp hairs, and I saw the eye of Gabès become adorned with flowers, with foliage, become a cool bower which I crawled to and entered with my entire body, to sleep on the moss there, in the shade, to die there. (253)

20 The third form of architectural void, that which we can never enter without ceasing to be ourselves but yet which draws us towards us like a magnet, finds its clearest architectural representation in the tomb. Tombs, and in a more general sense death, show up frequently in the work of Genet, coming to play right at the beginning of his opus, immediately after the introduction to the cell: "The garret in which Divine lived for such a long time is at the top of one of these houses. Its large window propels the eyes (and delights them) toward the little Montmartre Cemetery. The stairway leading up to it plays an important role today. It is the antechamber, sinuous as the hallways of the Pyramids, of Divine's temporary tomb" ([1943] 1987, *Flowers*, 57).

Already, the cell, the tomb, and indeed the closet are linked, superimposed, entwined in the void of Divine's apartment. The tomb is the final studio, the culmination of the action, in *The Balcony*; the action of *The Blacks* takes place around a catafalque; *The Screens* ends in the world of death; *Querelle* and *Miracle of the Rose* both revolve around a murderer. The most sustained investigation and analysis of death, of mourning, of the tomb, however, is to be found in Genet's novel *Funeral Rites*.

The tomb is in some obvious and topological way the opposite of the cell. We have already discussed one particular difference: The tomb is the place we can never be, while the cell is a place we must always be. There are other differences: while the cell takes an ideal form—for Genet, the cube—the tomb is *informe*, without specific or knowable form, indeed in some important manner without form at all (I am speaking here of the tomb as void, not the external housing of that void: the pyramids, for example, take on strict geometric form, but they are only the external appearance of the tomb, which, in itself, is sometimes not even to be found). Further, the cell is defined by its boundary, physically impassable although porous to the fantastic, while the boundary of the tomb is diffuse, physically irrelevant, but absolutely closed to creation:

one can't fantasize into or out of death. While the cell holds us in place (as does the closet, rooting us to the fabric of the house), the tomb envelopes us, is all around us: we carry the tomb with us everywhere we go. The tomb is as gigantic as the universe and as small as a matchbox in our pocket:

> The procession left the church.
>
> The matchbox in my pocket, the tiny coffin, imposed its presence more and more, obsessed me:
>
> "Jean's coffin could be just as small."
>
> I was carrying his coffin in my pocket. There was no need for the small-scale bier to be a true one. The coffin of the formal funeral had imposed its potency on that little object. I was performing in my pocket, on the box that my hand was stroking, a diminutive funeral ceremony as efficacious and reasonable as the Masses that are said for the souls of the departed, behind the altar, in a remote chapel, over a fake coffin draped in black. My box was sacred. It did not contain a particle merely of Jean's body but Jean in his entirety. His bones were the size of matches, of tiny pebbles imprisoned in penny whistles. His body was somewhat like the cloth-wrapped wax dolls with which sorcerers cast their spells. The whole gravity of the ceremony was gathered in my pocket, to which the transfer had just taken place. ([1949] 1963, *Funeral*, 33)

The tomb is opposed, as well, to the closet: while the closet is the space of jouissance, the tomb is the space in which enjoyment is no longer possible. While the cell and the closet/brothel both speak to the erotic nature of the self and the split self, the tomb is the location of the impossible non-self, the ultimate location of all eroticism. In addition, the tomb operates as a void in the fabric of knowledge, as a space of which no knowledge is in principle possible. This relationship to knowledge differs from that of the cell, which is unknown but in principle knowable, or the closet, which is the realm of secret or hidden knowledge; the tomb is the realm of that which is not merely unknown, but indeed unknowable, unthinkable. The tomb is the void to which we go when we cease to be human; it is also, by extension, the void from which we come as humans. The tomb, in other words, is the immense void that is for us as human everything outside of the human, everything indeed outside of existence as such.

21 The relation between the screen and death is clear as well in the work of Genet. In *The Screens*, the ob-scene behind the screens is nothing less than the scene of death. Death, in the play, is a matter of crashing through the screens. There are two *behinds* to the screen: there is the behind that can be reached by walking around the screen, what I have called previously the meta-scene, and the behind that one reaches by rupturing the screen, by entering into the image. Death, here, is a matter of entering into the image, of *becoming Image*. As Genet describes in his essay "The Tightrope Walker," becoming image is already a sort of death:

> Dance alone, then. Pale, livid, anxious to please or displease your image: but it is your image that will dance for you...
>
> Death—the Death of which I speak to you—is not the one that will follow your fall, but the one that precedes your appearance on the wire. It is before climbing onto it that you die. (2003, 71)

The tightrope walker must die before mounting the tightrope, die by transforming himself into an image of himself, or rather an image of the tightrope walker. Similarly, in Genet's play *Elle*, the pope-as-man dies, ceases to exist, in becoming Pope-as-image ([1955) 2010).

22 *Funeral Rites* revolves around a universe of death, anuses, and shattered mirrors.

23 It is certainly nothing new to point out that mirrors play an important part in the work of Genet. As Albert Dichy points out, mirrors held a particular fascination, or perhaps anxiety would be a better word, for Genet, who, so the story goes, would not enter a café or bar whose walls were covered with mirrors. This is of course the thief's fear, the fear of having his reflection seen by the police, but it seems to me that there is more to it than that. Mirrors play critical roles in several of Genet's works, most notably his 1948 ballet *'Adame Miroir*, with music by Darius Milhaud, danced in its premier by Roland Petit, but also in *The Balcony, The Maids, Funeral Rites*, and *The Thief's Journal*. Mirrors, though, are ubiquitous in Genet's work; they show up in almost every one of his novels and most of his plays and are a feature of the majority of his descriptions of rooms, apartments, and houses, and particularly those which will play some important part in the action. For example, in *Our Lady of the Flowers*, we read the following excerpts:

> With a kind of smooth sliding, the room descended so that it blended with a luxurious apartment, adorned with gold. The walls were hung with garnet-red velvet; the furniture was in a heavy style, toned down with red faille curtains; here and there were large beveled mirrors, ornamented with candelabra and their crystal pendants. ([1943] 1987, 64)
>
> At the other end of the kid's studio flat, the mantle-piece was topped by a huge mirror framed in rocaille crystal, with complicated facets; a few chairs padded with yellow silk were scattered about. (261)
>
> You first had to study the lay-out of the mirrors and their bevels, and also the oblique ones hooked to the ceiling, which reflect you in an

> upside-down world, but which the detectives, by a stage-trick that functions in their brain, quickly turn right side up and orient correctly. (245)

The mirror seems to appear at a time and a place of danger, as a sort of premonition or sign of the arrival of a critical moment in the story. This is the case in all of the examples I've just cited, not only in those in which, like the last, which describes the impending arrest of Darling Daintyfoot on shoplifting charges, the mirror plays at least a potentially active role in furthering the plot. In the first example, the arrival of the mirror presages the murder of Divine by her mother, Ernestine; in the second, the unexpected confession by Our Lady to the murder for which he is, eventually, executed. Indeed, the mere mention of mirrors, or rather the mere mention of the absence of mirrors, is enough to produce a sense of danger in this scene, in which Genet is describing the stone house in which Ernestine lives with her son, Culafroy: "She could have lived in luxury, could have been waited on by several servants and have moved about amidst huge mirrors that rose from the carpets to the gilded ceiling" (142).

Mirrors are always, for Genet, a destabilizing presence. They bring another, alien world into being, intruding on the scene; they bring about confusion; they announce the presence of death:

> Our Lady had a foreboding that the whole session would be faked and that at the end of the performance his head would be cut off by a mirror trick. ([1943] 1987, *Flowers*, 274)
>
> Revolutionaries are in danger of getting lost in a hall of mirrors. ([1986] 1992, *Prisoner*, 259)
>
> Have you ever wondered what your reflection thinks of you when your back's turned? ([1986] 1992, *Prisoner*, 152)

Mirrors shake the foundations of the world (the room descended), fixing us and our world as images, splitting us and producing an uncanny, ob-scene twin.

24 Mirrors are a more explicit part of the action in *The Balcony*. In the directions to scene 1, we find that the scene on stage is to include a large mirror, which indeed remains a key part of the scenery for the famous first three scenes, in which we are introduced to the Bishop, the Judge and the General: "On the right wall, a mirror, with a carved gilt frame, reflects an unmade bed which, if the room were arranged logically, would be in the first rows of the orchestra" ([1956] 2008, 7). The destabilizing effect of the mirror is evident from the outset of the play. A geometric confusion is brought into play: a second, virtual space, superimposed on the space of the audience. A reversal—literally a reflection—takes place, in which the off-stage is brought to the front of the house, or alternatively the audience is repositioned behind.

As these first scenes progress, The Bishop, The Judge, and The General address their images in the mirror, while being spied on by Madame Irma and her observation-machine (the mirrors are also, as it turns out, surveillance devices). For all three characters, it seems that their image in the mirror is somehow more real, more accurate than the man wearing the costume: the man in the bishop's costume remains a local tradesman, while the image in the mirror is that of the Bishop. This is the power of the mirror: it splits the world and us in it, fixing one part of us as image. It is also, of course, the central theme of *The Balcony*: the question of becoming-image.

Mirrors are commonplace in brothels, at least in the opulent French brothels from the early part of the twentieth century. Photographs of opulent Parisian brothels show an amazing mirror-world in which mirrors cover virtually all surfaces (although not all Parisian brothels were so reflective). We see it in Genet's novel *Querelle*, in the description of the brothel La Féria and its madame, Lysiane: "She moved slowly among her girls without so much as touching them, she climbed the stairs, walked along corridors hung with gilt leather, through astounding halls and salons we shall attempt to describe, sparkling with lights and mirrors, upholstered, decorated with artificial flowers in cut-glass vases and with erotic etchings on the walls" ([1947] 1987, 27).

Mirrors in the brothel heighten the fantastic—it would be easy enough to get lost in this infinite world of reflections. The mirror in the bedroom, the mirror on the ceiling, the mirror in which we see ourselves fucking, has a more specific effect. First, we become the object of our own fascinated gaze. Separated from our mirrored selves, we watch our motions that cannot (and must not) be seen, we are shown "the secret of the disappearance of things." We become other: Our gestures and actions are not fully our own (but isn't that the nature of sex in any case?); we would not be surprised to see our reflected selves moving independently of our material bodies. We become our own pornographic feedback loops, our own objects of desire. We start to dematerialize, inhabiting not just the physical body on the bed but also (perhaps more strongly) the spectral bodies in the mirrors. We become pure image.

25 In a remarkable passage towards the end of *Funeral Rites*, Erik, the German tank driver, is billeted, along with five fellow soldiers, in a château in Loiret. The entrance hall to this château is covered in mirrors. One evening, on returning to the château, drunk, Erik encounters himself—his image in the mirrors—in the entry.

> When the soldiers went out in the evening with their friends in the town, they got drunk, and when they returned to the château, the mirrors in the entrance hall reflected sparkling images of warriors lit up by wine. The first evening, Erik, drunk with wine, drunk with being in his own presence, looked at himself in the hall with curiosity...His red face in the mirror became tragic and so handsome that

> Erik doubted that it was his own...The gesture begun by Erik was continued by the image with set eyes. Its left hand opened the holster and took out the revolver, aimed it at Erik, and fired. A burst of laughter burst with the shot. It came from the five others who were returning. A salvo resounded. All five shot at their images. The same orgy was repeated every evening, but whereas they aimed at the heart, Erik fired at his sex and sometimes at that of the others. ([1949] 1963, 222)

This scene develops all the characteristics of the mirror for Genet: it produces confusion, presages (and indeed is the cause of) death, fixes Erik as an image, an uncanny, ob-scene twin inhabiting an alien duplicate world. In this sense, this scene is a microcosm of the novel, dominated as it is by the coupled concepts of murder and the twin. *Funeral Rites* is structured around a dense but loosely constructed network of twins, of mirrored characters: Jean Genet (Jean G.) and his dead teenage lover, Jean Decarnin (Jean D.); Jean D. and his brother, Paulo; Jean G. and Hitler; Paulo (or Jean D.) and Riton, Jean D.'s killer.

In each case, death follows the production of twins, death flows from the mirror: the doubling, the splitting of the subject, is an impossibility; it is unstable, and one aspect or the other must cease to exist. This is not a new theme for Genet; it features in *Querelle* and in *The Maids*, and even in *The Balcony*: one term of the mirror-couple must be annihilated, death must resolve the confusion produced by the mirror, death specifically resulting from a betrayal. The splitting and doubling of the mirror require a murder, a murder of the image-other which is, at the same time, a murder of the self.

We can see this very clearly in the scene in the château, which we can understand as a triple murder. First, of course, it is a murder of the spectral twin, of the other-that-is-self. The uncanny, ob-scene image, produced by the mirror (that is, by architecture), which is already dead, must be killed again, be made doubly dead. Rather, it must be made mute and inconsequential: Erik's bullets aim not at the heart, but at the genitals, at the master signifier, eliminating all possibility of signification; it is signification itself that is being killed. Of course, as I've already noted, the mirror image, as an image, is already dead. It must die again, become doubly dead, but to murder the mirror image is the mirror image of murdering its mirror image: Erik's second murder here is of himself. The third murder, of course, is the killing of that which both produces the split between Erik and his image and links the two together, that which produces both the image and Erik himself, as image of image: that is, the murder of the mirror itself. It is not a choice, here, among these three murders, but rather a triple murder-suicide: of self, of uncanny, ob-scene other, and of the mechanism that produces both.

26 If the scene in the château presents us with the confusion of a hall of mirrors, a pivotal scene in Genet's next novel, *The Thief's Journal*, expands explicitly on this architectural configuration:

> The fairground attraction known as the Palace of Mirrors is a labyrinth partitioned with plates of glass, some silvered and some transparent. You pay and enter; the problem is to get out. You go about desperately bumping into your own image or into a visitor cut off from you by a glass...Before seeing him I knew that Stilitano, and he alone, was trapped, visibly distraught in glass corridors. No one could hear him, but by his gestures and his mouth one could tell he was yelling with anger. He was looking at the crowd in a rage, and they were looking at him and laughing. The manager of the booth was indifferent...The universe became strangely overcast. The shadow which suddenly covered things and people was the shadow of my solitude

> in the face of this despair, for Stilitano, exhausted with yelling and bumping into the glasses, had resigned himself to being the laughingstock of the onlookers and simply squatted on the floor, indicating thereby that he refused to go on. I hesitated, not knowing whether to leave or to fight for him and demolish his crystal prison. (265)

Here we see the ultimate confusion wrought by the mirror, a scene in which our self-image is irretrievably splintered beyond repair, in which our self is not merely duplicated, but fractured and multiplied over and over, dissipated, and distributed onto every surface. In the house of mirrors, we lose track not merely of where we are, but of who we are: are we the ob-scene image or the material body? Are we alive or dead? Or both?

The scene is familiar: We could imagine this as an only slightly odd description of Johnson's Glass House. More to the point, though, it seems to me that the Palace of Mirrors, in its explicit and perhaps unique framing within Genet's work, stands for architecture in general, or, to go one step further, stands, like the Glass House, the Guest House, the Villa Savoye, the Farnsworth House, the Barcelona Pavilion, and a few others as uncanny and ob-scene images of the *house*. Like the Glass House, the Palace of Mirrors functions by exaggerating and clarifying a generic situation of the house that is normally hidden behind the screen, of which we are not normally aware: that is, that *all screens are mirrors*. In other words, all screens, all walls, all buildings, meet our gaze by reflecting back to us a changed and distorted image of ourselves: indeed, our self-image is nothing but the aggregate of these reflections. We are all trapped in the house of mirrors that produces us, uncanny and ob-scene products of our architectural maze, unexpected queer visitors on the glass walls of our selves.

Coda

1 Is this a conclusion? How can I conclude a project that has no end?

2 This project, the project from which this book has been birthed, is first of all a design project, masquerading (in drag) as a work of architectural history or theory. Like a fifth column, working with a little band of malcontents, I have tried to make use of the traditional processes of architectural design—drawing, model-making, and their extensions in the twenty-first century—in order to produce not buildings as such, but knowledge, to break into the house of architecture using its own techniques, to uncover hidden agendas and mechanisms. This is a perversion of what we have been taught to think of as architecture, a subversion of architecture from within. With all respect for Audre Lorde, we recognize that all tools are in the end the master's tools, and especially so in the world of architecture. We use instead the tactics of the prisoner: the tactical reappropriation of the strategies of the master. We sharpen our sabots, cut extra pockets into our trousers. We use architecture to betray architecture.
In other words, we take architecture from behind.

3 Architecture cannot be queered because queer is already an architectural effect: queerness is the outside that is inside, architecture's abjected substance. To queer architecture is to produce an architecture that is an anti-architecture, an architecture that works from the outside to make an impossible inside, an architecture that—to quote once more that famous saying—turns architecture inside out like a glove.

4 Perhaps the greatest quote from all of Genet's work: "Betrayal, theft and homosexuality are the basic subjects of this book. There is a relationship among them which, though not always apparent, at least, it seems to me, recognizes a kind of vascular exchange between my taste for betrayal and theft and my loves" ([1949] 1987, *Journal*, 171).

As Bersani puts it in his analysis of *Funeral Rites* in his 1996 book *Homos*, "This difficult and repugnant truth [Betrayal is an ethical necessity] is bound to be the major stumbling block for anyone interested in Jean Genet...Genet the thief, Genet the jailbird, Genet the flamboyantly horny homosexual: all this is acceptable, almost respectable, compared with Genet's dirty little confession that he handed over to the police his 'most tormented friend'" (151). It's not a new concept; betrayal has been lodged in my head, like a virus, or in my head like the salty bitter taste of some medicines, or blood, or semen, for months or more, since I started to write this text. Like a virus, or like an unwelcome fellow traveller that I'm unwilling or unable to look in the eyes (and taking from behind means, among other things, not looking one's lover in the eyes). I've been avoiding it, putting off a discussion of this topic until the very end of this text. After all, theft and homosexuality are easy enough to confront face on, although of course they present their own tricks and curves; but betrayal is rather more slippery and, perhaps, more threatening. What are the betrayals manifested by this text that I am writing? Who, or what, betrays me, and whom do I betray in this writing? How does architecture betray (does architecture betray?) and how do I betray architecture? What is the role of betrayal within our architectural thinking?

Or even since I first read *The Thief's Journal* a quarter century ago, or even before that (maybe reading *The Thief's Journal* was already, and knowingly, an act of betrayal, a betrayal of my suburban upbringing, of my family, of my education, of myself as I understood it)...

Avishai Margalit (2017), in his discussion of betrayal, focuses on the damage that an act of betrayal does to a relationship, particularly to what he calls a thick relationship; the essential metaphor of betrayal for Margalit is an ungluing of such thick bonds. Michael Marder (2020), on the other hand, seems more concerned with the mechanism of betrayal, with betrayal as a handing over (to an enemy), or with betrayal as an unwanted disclosure of something that should remain hidden; Marder is concerned with the scars that are caused by the cut of the betrayal, by the tissue of betrayal that in the end becomes the fabric of human relationships. We can see how both models might relate to architecture. After all, architecture not only maintains and reifies the hot glue (hot semen) of thick relationships (which to Marder already implies a betrayal), but also helps to orient us towards some relationships and away from others; this is one of the primary roles of architecture. Perhaps from this point of view, to betray architecture is to seek out and pursue relationships that are not valorized by architecture. On the other hand, as we have also seen, mostly in our discussions of masturbation, of the screen and the ob-scene, of the void, architecture is intimately bound up in the question of what can be disclosed and what should remain hidden. To betray architecture might then be to penetrate its voids, to open them up to view.

How might we imagine a non-relational, or indeed anti-relational model of betrayal? That is, betrayal in itself? I'm fascinated here by Bersani's analysis of the end of *Funeral Rites:* "a new possibility emerges: evil...not as a crime against socially defined good, but as a turning away from the entire theatre of the good, that is, as a kind of meta-transgressive *dépassement* of the field of transgressive possibility itself" (1996, 163). For Bersani, this non-relationality is made evident in the concluding scene of the novel, in which Riton is buggered by the German soldier Erik on a Parisian rooftop:

> If the two standing males had looked at each other, the quality of the pleasure would not have been the same. Mouth to mouth, chest to chest, with their knees tangled, they would have been entwined in a rapture that would have confined them in a kind of oval that excluded all light, but the bodies in the figurehead which they formed looked into the darkness, as one looks into the

> future, the weak sheltered by the stronger, the four eyes staring in front of them. They were projecting the frightful ray of their love to infinity. ([1949] 1987, Journal, 249)

As Bersani argues, this passage presents sexual pleasure over sexual intimacy, a "fucking of the world instead of each other" (1996, 165, 166).

The bodies look into the future, a dark future, but they do so separately, not sheltering each other from the abyss, not constructing a ground to span over the upcoming blackness. This, then, is the betrayal of relationality as such, rather than the betraying of any particular relation, a betrayal made possible by the exploitation of the *behind*, literally, by anal sex. In Bersani's reading, this is a betrayal that is inherent to homosexuality (marking, in the process, queerness as anarchitectural). In a similar vein, Preciado's (2018) call for a reorientation of the erotic from penis-and-vagina to a primary focus on the anus marks a complete annihilation of the male|female binary (and perhaps of the binary as such), fatally undermining the Law of Architecture. Or, for the simple reason that the anus provides pure pleasure, disconnected from the world of reproduction, the anus does not produce a new world: it is an irresponsible beauty.

The behind is architecture's weak spot, and it has made its presence felt on a number of occasions in this book. The behind is the necessary externalization, the friction, the waste without which the architectural machine could not function. If architecture is the art of the front, the technique of producing the scene of human activity, then the behind is a necessary component: the front and the behind come into being simultaneously, and neither can exist without the other. The behind, as we have seen, is the ob-scene, that which is off-stage (without which there cannot be a stage), that which is kept outside our public performances, but it is also the obscene, the perverse, the undisclosable erotic, the onanistic, and most particularly, the behind, the rear, the rectum, the anus, the *oeil de Gabès*.

The key point here is that the architectural behind is inevitable. Architecture always has an ob-scene, architecture always contains the obscene. That is simply what architecture is: the containment of the obscene. We can move the leather harness and the dildos from the prop room to the stage, but the backstage remains, and even if we open the curtains and tear down the backdrops *there is still a backstage*, still a behind. The same is true for all the typical strategies of resistance: inversion, subversion, diversion, perversion, abversion, conversion. All the versions in the end remain the same: We can turn the whole system inside out, like a glove, transpose front and behind, but the system remains. All we have done is refitted it for the left hand.

Maybe we can follow the thief once again: Instead of trying to change the scene, instead of looking to change an inalterable system, maybe we can enter the architectural behind, learn to savour the louse under our tongues, discover the pure pleasures and irresponsible beauties of the ob-scene.

References

Ahmed, Sara. 2006. *Queer Phenomenology: Orientations, Objects, Others*. Duke University Press.

Aleksic, Adam. n.d. “Filthy Stages.” *The Etymology Nerd*. Accessed October 12, 2024. https://www.etymologynerd.com/blog/filthy-stages.

Araki, Greg, dir. 2005. *Mysterious Skin*. Alliance Atlantis Vivafilm.

Aureli, Pier Vittorio, and Maria Shéhérazade Giudici. 2016. “Familiar Horror: Toward a Critique of Domestic Space.” *Log*, no. 38, 105–29. https://www.jstor.org/stable/26323792.

Badiou, Alain. 2020. *The Pornographic Age*. Translated by A.J. Bartlett and Justin Clemens. Bloomsbury Academic.

Banham, Reyner. 1965. “A Home Is Not A House.” Illustration by François Dallegret. *Art in America* 53 (2): 70–79.

Barber, Stephen. 2004. *Jean Genet*. Reaktion Books.

Barry, Joseph. 1953. “Report on the American Battle Between Good and Bad Modern.” *House Beautiful*, May, 172–73, 266–72.

Beaumont, Gustave de, and Alexis de Tocqueville. 1833. *On the Penitentiary System in the United States and Its Application in France: With an Appendix on Penal Colonies, and Also, Statistical Notes*. Translated by François Lieber. Philadelphia: Carey, Lea, & Blanchard.

Benjamin, Walter. 1978. *Illuminations: Essays and Reflections*. Edited with Introduction by Hannah Arendt. Translated by Harry Zohn. Schocken Books.

Bergdoll, Barry. 2000. *European Architecture 1750–1890*. Oxford University Press.

Bersani, Leo. 1996. *Homos*. Harvard University Press.

Bersani, Leo. 2010. *Is the Rectum a Grave? And Other Essays*. University of Chicago Press.

Bertreux, Julien. 2016. “Fontevraud, une histoire pénitentiaire aujourd'hui assumée.” *Revue histoire pénitentiaire*, no. 11: Patrimoine et architecture carcérale. Last updated October 16, 2020. https://criminocorpus.hypotheses.org/19358.

Betsky, Aaron. 1995. *Building Sex: Men, Women, Architecture, and the Construction of Sexuality*. William Morrow and Company.

Betsky, Aaron. 1997. *Queer Space: Architecture and Same-Sex Desire*. William Morrow and Company.

Bloomer, Jennifer. 1992a. “D'or.” In *Sexuality & Space*, edited by Beatriz Colomina, 163–83. Princeton Architectural Press.

Bloomer, Jennifer. 1992b. “A Lay a Stone a Patch a Post a Pen the Ruddyrun: Minor Architectural Possibilities.” In *Strategies in Architectural Thinking*, edited by Jeffrey Kipnis, John Whiteman, and Robert Burdett, 48–66. MIT Press.

Blouet, Guillaume-Abel. 1843. *Projet de prison cellulaire pour 585 condamnés précédé d'observations sur le Système pénitentiaire*. Paris: Firmin-Didot.

Blouet, Guillaume-Abel, and Frédéric-Auguste Demetz. 1837. *Rapports à M. le comte de Montalivet [...] sur les pénitenciers des États-Unis*. Paris: Imprimerie royale.

Blouet, Guillaume-Abel, Harou-Romain, and Hector Horeau. 1841. *Instruction et programme pour la construction des maisons d'arrêt et de justice: atlas de plans de prisons cellulaires*. Paris: Ministère de l'Intérieur.

Blouet, Guillaume-Abel, and Jean-Baptiste Rondelet. 1847. *Traité théorique et pratique de l'art de bâtir. Supplement: Planches*. Paris: Firmin-Didot.

Bonnevier, Katarina. 2005. “A Queer Analysis of Eileen Gray's E.1027.” In *Negotiating Domesticity: Spatial Productions of Gender in Modern Architecture*, edited by Hilde Heynen and Gülsüm Baydar, 162–80. Taylor & Francis Group.

Bonnevier, Katarina. 2007. *Behind Straight Curtains: Towards a Queer Feminist Theory of Architecture*. Axl Books.

Boone, Veronique. 2017. “Le Corbusier et le cinéma, la communication d'une œuvre.” PhD diss., Ecole nationale supérieure d'architecture et de paysage de Lille, laboratoire de recherche LATCH / Université de Lille. https://pepite-depot.univ-lille.fr/LIBRE/EDSHS/2017/BOONE_Veronique_Texte.pdf.

Bratton, Benjamin H. 2015. *Dispute Plan to Prevent Future Luxury Constitution*. Sternberg Press.

Butler, Judith. 1990. *Gender Trouble: Feminism and the Subversion of Identity*. Routledge.

Cambridge Dictionary. n.d. "Machine." Accessed March 12, 2025. https://dictionary.cambridge.org/dictionary/english/machine.

Carnot, Sadi. (1824) 1960. "Reflections on the Motive Power of Fire, and on Machines Fitted to Develop that Power." Translated by R.H. Thurston. *In Reflections of the Motive Power of Fire and Other Papers on the Second Law of Thermodynamics*, edited by E. Mendoza. New York: Dover.

Carrouges, Michel. 1975. "Directions for Use." In *The Bachelor Machines*, edited by Harald Szeemann, 21–45. Alfieri.

Chenal, Pierre, dir., and Le Corbusier, writer. 1930. *Architecture d'aujourd'hui*. France.

Colomina, Beatriz, ed. 1992a. *Sexuality & Space*. Princeton Architectural Press.

Colomina, Beatriz. 1992b. "The Split Wall: Domestic Voyeurism." In *Sexuality & Space*, edited by Beatriz Colomina, 73–130. Princeton Architectural Press.

Colomina, Beatriz. 1993. "War on Architecture: E.1027." *Assemblage*, no. 20, 28–29. https://www.jstor.org/stable/3181684.

Colomina, Beatriz. 2019. *X-Ray Architecture*. Lars Müller Publishers.

Colomina, Beatriz, Dennis Dollens, Eve Kosofsky Sedgwick, Cindi Patton, Henry Urbach and Mark Wigley, curators. 1994. *Queer Space*. Storefront for Art and Architecture, New York. Exhibition.

Conner, Susan P. 2017. "The Paradoxes and Contradictions of Prostitution in Paris." In *Selling Sex in the City: A Global History of Prostitution, 1600s–2000s*, edited by Magaly Rodríguez García, Lex Heerma van Voss, and Elise van Nederveen Meerkerk, 171–200. Brill.

Crary, Jonathan. 1990. *Techniques of the Observer: On Vision and Modernity in the Nineteenth Century*. MIT Press.

Crawford, Lucas. 2015. *Transgender Architectonics: The Shape of Change in Modernist Space*. Ashgate.

Dekker, Jeroen H., and Daniel M. Lechner. 1999. "Discipline and Pedagogics in History: Foucault, Aries, and the History of Panoptical Education." *The European Legacy* 4 (5): 37–49. https://doi.org/10.1080/10848779908579993.

Deleuze, Gilles. 1992. "Postscript on the Societies of Control." *October* 59 (Winter): 3–7. https://www.jstor.org/stable/778828.

Deleuze, Gilles. 1995. *Negotiations, 1972–1990*. Translated by Martin Joughin. Columbia University Press.

Deleuze, Gilles, and Félix Guattari. 1983. *Anti-Oedipus: Capitalism and Schizophrenia*. Translated by Robert Hurley, Mark Seem, and Helen R. Lane. University of Minnesota Press.

Deleuze, Gilles, and Félix Guattari. 1986. *Kafka: Toward a Minor Literature*. 1st ed. Translated by Dana Polan. University of Minnesota Press.

Deleuze, Gilles, and Félix Guattari. 1987. *A Thousand Plateaus: Capitalism and Schizophrenia*. Translated by Brian Massumi. University of Minnesota Press.

Derrida, Jacques. (1974) 1986. *Glas*. Translated by John P. Leavey Jr. and Richard Rand. University of Nebraska Press.

Derrida, Jacques. (1976) 2016. *Of Grammatology*. 40th anniversary ed. Translated by Gayatri Chakravorty Spivak. Johns Hopkins University Press.

Dichy, Albert. 1993. "Chronology." In *Genet: A Biography*, by Edmund White, xxi–xlii. Knopf.

Donzelot, Jacques. 1979. *The Policing of Families*. Translated by Robert Hurley. Random House.

Douglas, Mary. (1966) 2003. *Purity and Danger: An Analysis of Concepts of Pollution and Taboo*. Routledge.

Dreyfuss, Henry. 1960. *Measure of Man : Human Factors in Design*. Whitney Library of Design.

Duchamp, Marcel. 1959. *Marchand du sel*. Edited by Michel Sanouillet. Le Terrain Vague.

Duchamp, Marcel. 1975. *The Essential Writings of Marcel Duchamp: Salt Seller = marchand du sel*. Edited by Michel Sanouillet and Elmer Peterson. Thames and Hudson.

Durand, Jean-Nicolas-Louis. 2000. *Précis of the Lectures on Architecture: With Graphic Portion of the Lectures on Architecture*. Translated by David Britt. Introduction by Antoine Picon.

Getty Research Institute.

Edelman, Lee. 2004. *No Future: Queer Theory and the Death Drive*. Duke University Press.

Evans, Robin. 1982. *The Fabrication of Virtue: English Prison Architecture, 1750–1840*. Cambridge University Press.

Flandrin, Jean-Louis. 1979. *Families in Former Times: Kinship, Household, and Sexuality*. Translated by Richard Southern. Cambridge University Press.

Forensic Architecture and Amnesty International. 2016. *Torture in Saydnaya Prison*. https://forensic-architecture.org/investigation/saydnaya.

Foucault, Michel. (1976) 1990. *The History of Sexuality*. Vol. 1, *An Introduction*. Translated by Robert Hurley. Penguin.

Foucault, Michel. 1979. *Discipline and Punish: The Birth of the Prison*. Translated by Alan Sheridan. Vintage Books.

Foucault, Michel. 1986. "Of Other Spaces." Translated by Jay Miskowiec. *Diacritics* 16 (1): 22–27. https://www.jstor.org/stable/464648.

Freud, Sigmund. (1905) 1962. *Three Essays on the Theory of Sexuality*. Basic Books.

Friedman, Alice T. 1998. *Women and the Making of the Modern House: A Social and Architectural History*. Harry N. Abrams.

Furman, Adam Nathaniel, and Joshua Mardell, eds. 2022. *Queer Spaces: An Atlas of LGBTQIA+ Places and Stories*. RIBA Publishing.

Genet, Jean. n.d. *Le langage de la muraille: Cent ans jour apres jour*. Unpublished screenplay. Boite 8, Fonds Genet, Institut Mémoires de l'Edition Contemporaine.

Genet, Jean. (1943) 1987. *Our Lady of the Flowers*. Translated by Bernard Frechtman. Introduction by Jean-Paul Sartre. Grove Press.

Genet, Jean. (1946) 1988. *Miracle of the Rose*. Translated by Bernard Frechtman. Grove Press.

Genet, Jean. (1947, 1949) 1994. *The Maids and Deathwatch: Two Plays*. Translated by Bernard Frechtman. Preface by Jean-Paul Sartre. Grove Press.

Genet, Jean. (1947) 1987. *Querelle*. Translated by Anselm Hollo. Grove Weidenfeld.

Genet, Jean. (1949) 1963. *Funeral Rites*. Translated by Bernard Frechtman. Grove Press.

Genet, Jean. (1949) 1987. *The Thief's Journal*. Translated by Bernard Frechtman. Introduction by Jean-Paul Sartre. Grove Press.

Genet, Jean. 1950. *Un chant d'amour*. Directed by Nikos Papatakis. Cinematography by Jean Cocteau. France.

Genet, Jean. (1955) 2010. *Splendid's: Suivi de "Elle."* Gallimard.

Genet, Jean. (1956) 2008. *The Balcony*. Translated by Bernard Frechtman. Grove Press.

Genet, Jean. (1958) 1988. *The Blacks: A Clown Show*. Translated by Bernard Frechtman. Grove Press.

Genet, Jean. (1961) 1998. *The Screens: A Play in Seventeen Scenes*. Translated by Bernard Frechtman. Grove Press.

Genet, Jean. (1986) 1992. *Prisoner of Love*. Translated by Barbara Bray. Introduction by Edmund White. Wesleyan University Press.

Genet, Jean. 2003. *Fragments of the Artwork*. Edited by Werner Hamacher. Translated by Charlotte Mandell. Stanford University Press.

Genet, Jean. 2004. *The Declared Enemy: Texts and Interviews*. Edited by Albert Dichy. Translated by Jeff Fort. Stanford University Press.

Gorman-Murray, Andrew, and Matt Cook, eds. 2020. *Queering the Interior*. Routledge.

Gorny, Robert, and Dirk Van den Heuvel, eds. 2018. "Trans-Bodies / Queering Spaces." Special issue, *Footprint*, no. 21. https://doi.org/10.7480/footprint.11.2.

Graaf, Reinier de. 2015. "Architecture Is Now a Tool of Capital, Complicit in a Purpose Antithetical to Its Social Mission." *The Architectural Review*, April 24. https://www.architectural-review.com/essays/architecture-is-now-a-tool-of-capital-complicit-in-a-purpose-antithetical-to-its-social-mission.

Griffin, Marion Mahony, and Debora Wood. 2005. *Marion Mahony Griffin: Drawing the Form of Nature*. Mary and Leigh Block Museum of Art.

Grosz, Elizabeth. 2001. *Architecture from the Outside: Essays on Virtual and Real Space*. MIT Press.

Guattari, Félix. 1984. *Molecular Revolution:*

Psychiatry and Politics. Translated by Rosemary Sheed. Penguin.

Halberstam, Jack. 2011. *The Queer Art of Failure.* Duke University Press.

Halberstam, Jack. 2018. "Foreword: We Are the Revolution! Or, the Power of the Prothesis." In *Countersexual Manifesto*, by Paul B. Preciado, ix–xvi. Columbia University Press.

Hardt, Michael. 1997. "Prison Time." In "Genet: In the Language of the Enemy." Special issue, *Yale French Studies*, no. 91, 64–79. https://www.jstor.org/stable/2930374.

Haynes, Todd, dir. 2003. *Far from Heaven*. Universal Studios.

Haynes, Todd, dir. 2019. *Poison*. Zeitgeist Films.

Hays, K. Michael, Catherine Ingraham, and Alicia Kennedy, eds. 1994. "House Rules." Special issue, *Assemblage*, no. 24 (August).

Herring, Scott. 2011. "Material Deviance: Theorizing Queer Objecthood." *Postmodern Culture* 21 (2). https://www.pomoculture.org/2013/09/03/material-deviance-theorizing-queer-objecthood/.

Herring, Scott. 2014. *The Hoarders: Material Deviance in Modern American Culture*. University of Chicago Press.

Hocquenghem, Guy. 2006. *Homosexual Desire*. Translated by Daniella Dangoor. Duke University Press.

Holder, Andrew. 2017. "Five Points Toward a Queer Architecture; Or, Notes on *Mario Banana No 1.*" *Log*, no. 41, 155–60. https://www.jstor.org/stable/26323731.

Holmquist, Paul. 2016. "'More Powerful than Love': Imagination and Language in the Oikéma of Claude-Nicolas Ledoux." In *Chora 7: Intervals in the Philosophy of Architecture*, edited by Alberto Perez-Gomez and Stephen Parcell, 95–116. McGill-Queen's University Press. https://www.jstor.org/stable/j.ctt19jch8m.8.

Jobst, Mark, and Naomi Stead, eds. 2023. *Queering Architecture: Methods, Practices, Spaces, Pedagogies*. Bloomsbury Publishing.

Johnson, Philip. 1950. "House at New Canaan, Connecticut." *The Architectural Review* (London), no. 108, 152–59.

Kafka, Franz. (1919) 1988. *The Metamorphosis, the Penal Colony, and Other Stories*. Schocken Books.

Kaufmann, Emil. 1952. *Three Revolutionary Architects: Boullée, Ledoux, and Lequeu*. American Philosophical Society.

Klein, Yves, and Werner Ruhnau. 2004. "Project of an Air Architecture." In *Air Architecture: Yves Klein*, edited by Peter Noever and Francois Perrin, 77–84. Hatje Cantz.

Kolb, Jaffer, ed. 2017. "Working Queer." Special issue, *Log*, no. 41. Anyone Corp.

Kunzel, Regina G. 2008. *Criminal Intimacy: Prison and the Uneven History of Modern American Sexuality*. University of Chicago Press.

Lacan, Jacques. 1972. "Seminar on 'The Purloined Letter.'" *Yale French Studies*, no. 48, 39–72. Translated by Jeffrey Mehlman. https://doi.org/10.2307/2929623.

Lacan, Jacques. 2017a. *Formations of the Unconscious: The Seminar of Jacques Lacan, Book V.* Edited by Jacques-Alain Miller. Translated by Russell Grigg. Polity Press.

Lacan, Jacques. 2017b. *Talking to Brick Walls: A Series of Presentations in the Chapel at Sainte-Anne Hospital*. Translated by Adrian Price. Polity Press.

Laplanche, Jean. 2002. "Sexuality and Attachment in Metapsychology." In *Infantile Sexuality and Attachment*, edited by Daniel Widlöcher, 35–54. Routledge.

Laporte, Dominique. 2000. *History of Shit*. Translated by Rodolphe el-Khoury and Nadia Benabid. MIT Press.

Laqueur, Thomas W. 2004. *Solitary Sex: A Cultural History of Masturbation*. Zone Books.

Latour, Bruno (aka Jim Johnson). 1988. "Mixing Humans and Nonhumans Together: The Sociology of a Door-Closer." *Social Problems* 35 (3): 298–310. https://www.jstor.org/stable/800624.

Leatherbarrow, David, and Mohsen Mostafavi. 1993. *On Weathering: The Life of Buildings in Time*. MIT Press.

Le Corbusier. (1930) 1991. *Precisions on the Present State of Architecture and City Planning*. Translated by Edith Schreiber Aujame. MIT Press.

Le Corbusier. (1923) 2009. *Toward an Architecture*. Translated by John Goodman. Introduction by Jean-Louis Cohen. Getty Research Institute.

Le Corbusier, and Pierre Jeanneret. 1948. *Le Corbusier: Oeuvres complète*. 5th ed. Les Éditions d'Architecture.

Ledoux, Claude-Nicolas. 1804. *L'architecture considérée sous le rapport de l'art, des moeurs et de la législation*, tome 1. Accessed September 21, 2023. https://gallica.bnf.fr/ark:/12148/bpt6k1047050b/f11.item.langFR.

Lefebvre, Henri. 2004. *The Production of Space*. Translated by Donald Nicholson-Smith. Blackwell.

Loos, Adolf, and Joseph Masheck. 2019. *Ornament and Crime: Thoughts on Design and Materials*. Translated by Shaun Whiteside. Penguin Books.

McQuaid, Matilda, and Magdalena Droste. 1996. *Lilly Reich: Designer and Architect*. Museum of Modern Art.

Marder, Michael. 2020. "Betrayal: A Philosophy." *Research in Phenomenology* 50 (1): 79–98. https://www.jstor.org/stable/27117224.

Margalit, Avishai. 2017. *On Betrayal*. Harvard University Press.

Mathurin, Clémentine, and Florian Stalder. 2016. "La maison centrale de Fontevraud, un patrimoine!" *Revue histoire pénitentiaire*, no. 11: Patrimoine et architecture carcérale. August 23. Updated October 16, 2020. https://criminocorpus.hypotheses.org/19604.

Middleton, Robin. 1993. "Sickness, Madness and Crime as the Grounds of Form." *AA Files*, no. 25, 14–19. https://www.jstor.org/stable/29543832.

Mitchell, W.J.T. 1984. "What Is an Image?" *New Literary History* 15 (3): 503–37. https://www.jstor.org/stable/468718.

Montesse, Alain. 1975. "Lovely Rita, Meter Maid." In *The Bachelor Machines*, edited by Harald Szeemann, 110–14. Alfieri.

Morton, Timothy. 2018. *Dark Ecology: For a Logic of Future Coexistence*. Columbia University Press.

Muñoz, José Esteban. 2009. *Cruising Utopia: The Then and There of Queer Futurity*. New York University Press.

Neufert, Ernst. [1936] 1980. *Architects' Data*. 2nd (international) English ed. Granada Publishing.

Online Etymological Dictionary. n.d. "Behind." Accessed September 12, 2024. https://www.etymonline.com/word/behind.

Online Etymological Dictionary. n.d. "Obscene." Accessed September 19, 2024. https://www.etymonline.com/word/obscene.

Perriand, Charlotte, and Marie-Laure Jousset. 2005. *Charlotte Perriand*. Centre Pompidou.

Peyré, Yves, and Évelyne Toussaint. 2014. *Duchamp à la bibliothèque Sainte-Geneviève*. Editions du Regard.

Plasse-Taylor, Michael. 2022. *Unmasking of Our Interiors: A Queer Incubator of Courage, Resilience and Interior Design Leadership*. FriesenPress.

Poe, Edgar Allen. (1844) 1988. "The Purloined Letter." In *The Purloined Poe: Lacan, Derrida and Psychoanalytic Reading*, edited by John P. Muller and William J. Richardson, 6–27. Johns Hopkins University Press.

Preciado, Paul B. 2014. *Pornotopia: An Essay on Playboy's Architecture and Biopolitics*. Zone Books.

Preciado, Paul B. 2015. "Restif de la Bretonne's State Brothel: Sperm, Sovereignty, and Debt in the Eighteenth-Century Utopian Construction of Europe." *Documenta* 14 (1). https://www.documenta14.de/en/south/45_restif_de_la_bretonne_s_state_brothel_sperm_sovereignty_and_debt_in_the_eighteenth_century_utopian_construction_of_europe.

Preciado, Paul B. 2017. *Testo Junkie: Sex, Drugs, and Biopolitics in the Pharmacopornographic Era*. Translated by Bruce Benderson. Feminist Press at CUNY.

Preciado, Paul B. 2018. *Countersexual Manifesto*. Translated by Kevin Gary Dunn. Foreword by Jack Halberstam. Columbia University Press.

Preciado, Paul B. 2019. "Mi(E)S Conception: The Farnsworth House and the Mystery of the Transparent Closet." Translated by Keith

Harris. *Society + Space*, November 4. https://www.societyandspace.org/articles/mies-conception-the-farnsworth-house-and-the-mystery-of-the-transparent-closet.

Prigent, Daniel. 2017. "Fontevraud, une maison de force et de correction (1804–1963) dans une abbaye." *Les nouvelles de l'archaeology*, no. 149, 24–30. https://doi.org/10.4000/nda.3779.

Proudhon, P.-J., 1876. *The Works of P.J. Proudhon*. Vol. 1, *What Is Property?* Translated by Benjamin Ricketson Tucker. Benj. R. Tucker.

Ragland-Sullivan, Ellie. 2004. *The Logic of Sexuation: From Aristotle to Lacan*. SUNY Press.

Ramos, Regner, and Sharif Mowlabocus, eds. 2021. *Queer Sites in Global Contexts: Technologies, Spaces, and Otherness*. Routledge.

Riach, James. 2014. "Zaha Hadid Defends Qatar World Cup Role Following Migrant Worker Deaths." *The Guardian*, February 25. https://www.theguardian.com/world/2014/feb/25/zaha-hadid-qatar-world-cup-migrant-worker-deaths.

Ricco, John Paul. 1993. "Jacking-off a Minor Architecture." *Steam: A Quarterly Journal for Men* 1 (4): 236–43.

Ricco, John Paul. 1994. "Coming Together: Jack-off Rooms as Minor Architecture." *A/R/C, architecture, research, criticism* 1 (5): 26–31.

Ricco, John Paul. 2016. Preface to the Republication of "Jacking-off a Minor Architecture." *Keep It Dirty*, vol. a, "Filth," i–vi.

Ripley, Colin. 1993. "Safe as Houses." Unpublished manuscript.

Ripley, Colin. 1994. "On Waking: The Interruption in Benjamin and Brecht (and Other Assorted Interruptions)." Unpublished manuscript.

Ripley, Colin. 2018. "Strategies for Living in Houses." In "Trans-Bodies/Queering Spaces," edited by Robert Gorny and Dirk van den Heuvel, special issue of *Footprint: Delft Architecture Theory Journal*, no. 21, 95–108. https://doi.org/10.7480/footprint.11.2.1903.

Robbins, Mark. 1992. *Angles of Incidence*. Princeton Architectural Press.

Rowe, Colin. 2009. *The Mathematics of the Ideal Villa and Other Essays*. MIT Press.

Said, Edward. 1990. "On Jean Genet's Late Works." *Grand Street*, no. 36, 26–42.

Sanders, Joel. 2018. "Stalled! Transforming Public Restrooms." In "Trans-Bodies/Queering Spaces," edited by Robert Gorny and Dirk van den Heuvel, special issue of *Footprint: Delft Architecture Theory Journal*, no. 21, 109–18. https://doi.org/10.7480/footprint.11.2.1904.

Sanders, Joel, ed. 1999. *Stud: Architectures of Masculinity*. Princeton Architectural Press.

Sartre, Jean-Paul. (1952) 1963. *Saint Genet: Actor and Martyr*. Translated by Bernard Frechtman. Pantheon Books.

Sauvestre, Charles. 1864. *Une visite à Mettray*. Paris: Librairie Hachette.

Sbriglio, Jacques. 2008. *Le Corbusier: The Villa Savoye*. Birkhäuser.

Schuster, Aaron. 2020. "Beyond Satire: The Political Comedy of the Present and the Paradoxes of Authority." In *Sovereignty, Inc: Three Inquiries in Politics and Enjoyment*, by William Mazzarella, Eric Santner, and Aaron Schuster, 161–250. University of Chicago Press.

Sedgwick, Eve Kosofsky. 1990. *Epistemology of the Closet*. University of California Press.

Serlio, Sebastiano. 1982. *The Five Books of Architecture : An Unabridged Reprint of the English Edition of 1611*. Dover ed. Dover Publications.

Serres, Michel. 1975. "It Was Before the (World-) Exhibition." In *The Bachelor Machines*, edited by Harald Szeemann, 64–74. Alfieri.

Simons, G.L. 1975. *A Place for Pleasure: The History of the Brothel*. Harwood-Smart Publishing.

Singley, Paulette. 1993. "The Anamorphic Phallus Within Ledoux's Dismembered Plan of Chaux."*Journal of Architectural Education* 46 (3): 176–88. https://doi.org/10.2307/1425159.

Spivak, Gayatri Chakravorty. 2017. "Creative Time Summit Toronto, Keynote." Creative Time Summit, October 18. YouTube. https://www.youtube.com/watch?v=mMxah7jivho.

Steadman, Philip. 2007. "The Contradictions of Jeremy Bentham's Panopticon Penitentiary." *Journal of Bentham Studies*, no. 9, 1–31. https://discovery.ucl.ac.uk/id/eprint/1324519.

Teyssot, Georges. 2013. *A Topology of Everyday Constellations*. MIT Press.

Thomson, John Cockburn. 1856. "Mettray and Red-Hill: French and British Reformatory Schools. An Account." *North British Review*, no. 24, 417–46.

TIME. 1935. "Art: Corbusierismus." November 4. https://time.com/archive/6754520/art-corbusierismus/.

Toth, Stephen A. 2019. *Mettray: A History of France's Most Venerated Carceral Institution*. Cornell University Press.

Tschumi, Bernard. 2001. *Architecture and Disjunction*. MIT Press.

Urbach, Henry. 1993. "Spatial Rubbing: The Zone." *Sites*, no. 25, 90–95.

Urbach, Henry. 1996. "Closets, Clothes, Disclosure." *Assemblage*, no. 30 (August), 63–73. https://doi.org/10.2307/3171458.

Vallerand, Olivier. 2020. *Unplanned Visitors: Queering the Ethics and Aesthetics of Domestic Space*. McGill-Queen's University Press.

Van Sant, Gus, dir. 1991. *My Own Private Idaho*. The Criterion Collection.

Vidler, Anthony. 1987. *The Writing of the Walls: Architectural Theory in the Late Enlightenment*. Princeton Architectural Press.

Viney, William. 2014. *Waste: A Philosophy of Things*. Bloomsbury Academic.

Walker, Lawrence. 2013. "#5. Villa Savoye." *Pure History*, November 11. https://purehistory.org/5-villa-savoye/.

White, Edmund. 1993. *Genet: A Biography*. Knopf.

Žižek, Slavoj. 2004. "What Rumsfeld Doesn't Know That He Knows About Abu Ghraib." https://www.lacan.com/zizekrumsfeld.htm.

Žižek, Slavoj. 2009. *Violence: Six Sideways Reflections*. Profile Books.

Žižek, Slavoj. 2015. *Organs Without Bodies: On Deleuze and Consequences*. Routledge.

Žižek, Slavoj. 2016. "Why Does a Letter Always Arrive at Its Destination?" *The Symptom*, no. 16. https://www.lacan.com/symptom16/why.html.

Zupančič, Alenka. 2016. "Power in the Closet (And Its Coming Out)." In *Lacan, Psychoanalysis, and Comedy*, edited by Patricia Gherovici and Manya Steinkoler, 219–34. Cambridge University Press.

Index